DATE			

IN MY LIFE

IN MY LIFE

Encounters with

THE BEATLES

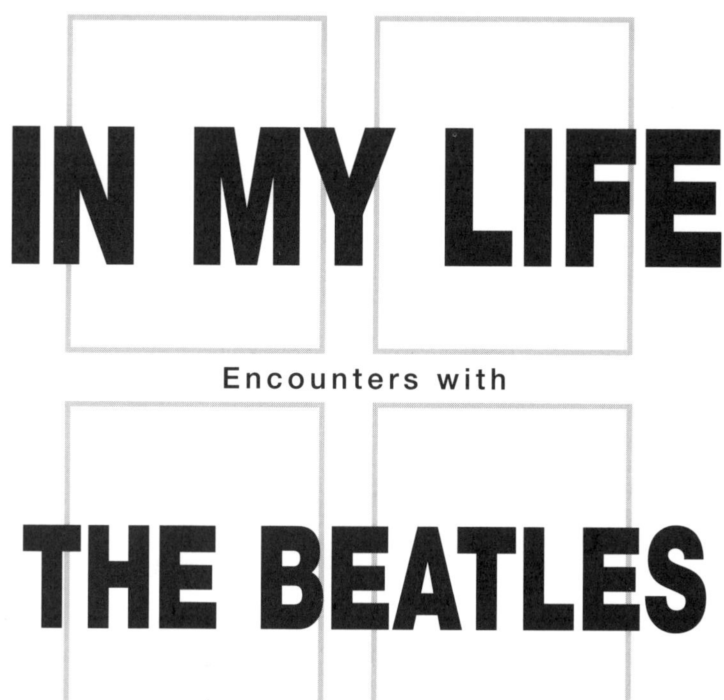

Edited by

Robert Cording

Shelli Jankowski-Smith

E. J. Miller Laino

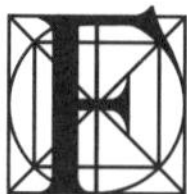

FROMM INTERNATIONAL PUBLISHING CORPORATION
NEW YORK

First Fromm International Edition, 1998

 Published in the United States by Fromm International Publishing Corporation, New York.

LIBRARY IN CONGRESS CATALOGING-IN-PUBLICATION DATA

In my life : encounters with the Beatles / edited
by Robert Cording, Shelli Jankowski-Smith,
E.J. Miller Laino. — 1st Fromm
International ed.
p. cm..
ISBN 0-88064-192-4
1. Beatles—Literary collections. 2. Rock musicians—England—Literary collections. 3. Rock music—England—Literary collections. 4. American literature—20th century. 5. English literarture—20th century. 6. Beatles. I. Cording, Robert. II. Jankowski-Smith, Shelli. III. Laino, E.J. Miller, 1948–.
PS509.B39I6 1998
810.8'0351—dc21 98-17672
CIP

10 9 8 7 6 5 4 3 2 1
Manufactured in the United States of America

Contents

and in the end

introduction

There is no doubt that history will remember the phenomenon of the Beatles: the tossing hair and boyish grins, the playful sexuality, the screaming girls. As the time-out-of-joint sixties catapulted forward, so did the Fab Four. John, Paul, George, and Ringo added an air of genial, irreverent freshness to everything they touched, and seemed to open our eyes to life and joy. Even as traditional values foundered and many of us began looking for a better world through drugs or meditation, the Beatles were charting the course. Their lyrics caught the tension between old and young. They interpreted the headlines for us in that ironic voice of the day: "I read the news today, oh boy." Still, what we will remember best is the music, its excitement and giddy sense of danger. For it is through the music, drawing together hundreds of millions of people as it did, that the Beatles have come to represent the possibility for a sort of all-embracing community, and even for universal (dare we say it in these jaded times?) love, love, and again love.

The Beatles indisputably showed us their greatness in the sixties; but they also proved, once again, that the best art of any age is ageless. In the mid-1990s the *Anthology* releases—three double CDs worth of previously unreleased material and outtakes coupled with a six-hour television special—helped restore to the group the title of World's Number One Band. Now the Baby Boomers' nostalgic question "Where were you when the Beatles appeared on the *Ed Sullivan Show*?" had its sequel, one for their offspring: "Where were you when you first heard the Beatles 'reunited' on 'Free as a Bird'?"

These are the feelings and events that drew the three of us, as fans and writers, to the Beatles. We too experienced that pure joy their music has been inspiring for decades. And we were not alone. *In My Life* brings together the work of writers who, for one reason or another, have found themselves writing about the group. Our intention was quite simple: to gather a cross section of fiction, recollections, and poetry about the Beatles and let the writers spin out a story that, while more fragmentary than a historian's, might still give a full and accurate telling.

As we approach the millennium, there is sure to be an extraordinary number of books published that will attempt to assess the major cultural forces of the century. Surely, the Beatles belong to both the conscience and the consciousness of our times. Their music circumscribes a small but important evolutionary history of the changing politics, spirituality, and mores of the second half of the twentieth century. In this anthology we hope to offer a sense of their part in our personal histories. And so, as you read *In My Life,* know that it is not only a book about the Beatles, it is a book about each one of us. It is a book about you. And, in the words of a great song lyric, "There is no one compares with you."

Robert Cording
Shelli Jankowski-Smith
E. J. Miller Laino
January 1998

one, two, three, four!

Fab Four Tour Deutschland: Hamburg, 1961

David Wojahn

"Und now Ladies und Gentlemun, *Der Peedles!*"
The emcee oozes pomade, affecting the hip American,

But the accent twists the name to sound like *needles,*
Or some Teutonic baby's body function.

The bassist begins, nodding to the drummer,
Who flaunts his movie-star good looks: Pete Best,

Grinning as the drums count four. "Roll Over
Beethoven"'s the opener. McCartney's Elvis

Posturing's too shrill, the playing sloppy,
But Lennon, stoned on Romilar, doesn't care.

Mild applause, segue into "Long Tall Sally . . ."
One will become a baby-faced billionaire,

One a film producer, one a skewed sort of martyr,
And this one, the drummer, a Liverpool butcher.

from a letter to Ken Horton

Stuart Sutcliffe

. . . washed out with talk, sick of faces, fed up of cathedrals and squares, tired of sitting all day, tired of black and white furniture, tired of seeing so many people jabbering away about nothing. Liverpool! Meaning the Cracke, the Jacaranda, the college, the flat, NDD, tired of "egg on toast and a tea, please."

In that Liverpool I know not one thing stands out in my memory. The city sprouts like a huge organism, diseased in every part, the beautiful thoroughfares only a little less repulsive because they have been drained of their pus. Liverpool. When I have something to give, I will give it. When I have something to say, I will say it in paint, in stone or anything my soul touches . . .

Introduction from *The Beatles with Lacan*

Henry W. Sullivan

I still remember the day I first heard the Beatles. The winter of 1962–63 was Britain's coldest in nearly a century. From December to mid-March, snow covered the quadrangles at Oxford University, and a damp-laden chill from the Thames Valley seeped into the colleges' poorly heated rooms. One morning, in Hilary Term, I had wrapped myself in a long white and dark-blue scarf and sat hunched over an electric fire, trying to turn the pages of a book and scribble notes, with gloves on my hands. A knock came at the door. It was our resident "con man," a neighbor from a couple of floors above on the same Back Quad staircase: the usual black bow tie with mother-of-pearl stud and droopy mustache. He had a conspiratorial air.

"I'd like you to come up to my room."

"Why?"

"I have something I'd like you to hear."

I hesitated.

"Come on."

My neighbor claimed to me to have had mystic experiences. This inspired a certain mistrust in me. Perhaps it was justified a year later when he was almost sent down for prodigious theft of Queens' College Buttery tickets—a kind of internal scrip. But now his "no fooling" air broke down my resistance. He sat me in an armchair on the third floor and put a new single on the record player.

"What is it?" I asked.

"Just listen." So I did.

It was quite unlike anything I had heard before. The harmonica, the descending verse melody against a reiteration of the tonic pitch, the heavy percussion and bass sounds; and, then, the unexpected falsetto leap on the words "Please please me, whoa yeah. . . ." I looked up at him with an incredulous gape. He had already been staring at the spot where my eyes would eventually meet his, and wore a complacent, see-what-I-mean? expression. After the breathless two minutes were up, I asked him again:

"What's it called? Who are they?"

More smug omniscience. "It's called 'Please Please Me' by the Beatles."

"How's that?"

"The Beatles. B-e-*A*-t-l-e-s. Get it?"

This pun interested me less than the music.

"Would you play it again?"

He did. I marveled at the antiphonal effects on the words "come on" in the chorus; the unconventional shifts of chord; the sheer energy and forward drive. This time I was even blunter:

"Play it again."

I left his room reeling into the chill. It was perhaps the second or third week of February. By March 2, 1963, "Please Please Me" had gone to number one on the *Melody Maker* charts, and the rest, as they say . . .

Hello, Goodbye

Stefany Reich-Silber

It was London, December 1963. I was thirteen and went to my first Beatles concert at the Finsbury Park Astoria.

My friend Helen and I sat in the second-to-last row and stood up and screamed through every song. All around us girls were screaming and crying. The only people who were not sat directly in front of us and turned round, laughably demanding that we be quiet.

"We're trying to listen," they glared.

"John, John," I screamed, tears flowing down my cheeks. And then a little less loudly, "Paul, Paul." (John was my favorite.) Helen screamed, "George, George," and we both screamed "Ringo" now and again so that he would not feel left out. I wasn't sure why I was weeping, but all around me in the dark, anonymous theater was a turmoil of sobbing and clutching girls tearing out their hair in desperation. It seemed the natural thing to do.

My parents picked us up outside as they had insisted, much to my embarrassment. "She's all flushed. Look at her eyes," they murmured to each other. "Look how wild she looks."

Helen and I went to many Beatles concerts after that. We always rushed the stage, surging down the aisles with all the other uncontainable fans, stopped only by the chasm of the orchestra pit and the few security guards. We would lean over the railing that held us back and lean on each other as we wept, arms and hands outstretched imploringly into the gulf between us and our heroes. From there we hurled gifts at our heartthrobs. Gifts that we hoped would make the contact that we could not. Like the long johns that we embroidered for Helen's George in the school yard at lunchtimes, savoring the thought of the garment's intimacy as we did so. And now there they were on the other side of that unbreachable gap, barely out of reach, absolutely real, right in front of us in their sharkskin suits. I couldn't help noticing John Lennon's bulging thighs in the thin, shiny material, so manly that he had to stand differently from the others.

I always hoped that I would be noticed. That John would look across and see me. That my face would leap out at him from the mass of girls in the front and his eyes would lock onto me and he would see that I was different. That I was not one of the immature, adolescent throng. That I was worldly and sophisticated. That I was girlfriend material.

Looking worldly and sophisticated was a constant struggle back then. We were only schoolgirls, after all. Daily we were forced into gym slips, shirts, ties and navy-blue velour hats trimmed with Petersham ribbon in the school colors, the enameled school crest on the front. But as soon as we were off the grounds, while we waited loudly for the #7 bus, we hiked up our skirts, took off our ties, and jammed our hats into our satchels. And then, sitting together on the long ride home, one of us would carry on with the story.

"And John pins you against the wall so you can't leave and starts to kiss you and tell you that he wants you to be his girlfriend."

"Ooh, he does?"

"Yes, he does. And then he moves closer to you and takes you in his arms and holds you very, very close."

"Ooh, and then?"

We would continue during the many hours we spent in my room, in which every wall and the ceiling had been covered with posters of the Fab Four. We would go into my attic bedroom and eat oranges and smoke cigarettes while we fantasized about our favorites.

From *Beatles Monthly* we knew their favorite colors (Paul's, black), their favorite foods (George's, lamb chops and peas), and the lengths of their inside leg, a more titillating statistic that had been included in the otherwise mundane list. According to the magazine, Paul's girlfriend would have to have "a fine facial structure." This sent me to the mirror to examine my face, even if it was for Paul. He was my second best, but John was married. One had to be realistic. So was my face fine? I practiced a look meant to accentuate my bones. This consisted of sucking in my cheeks without any contortion of the mouth while at the same time flaring my nostrils to make my nose appear thinner. Very hard to maintain.

"Do you think my hair is long, Helen?"

My painstakingly contrived bone structure instantly resumed its natural, bland planes.

"It's below your shoulders."

"Yes, but does it look long? Jane Asher's hair is long. Did you hear how they nearly strangled her by pulling on her scarf when she was leaving a concert with Paul? Is her hair longer than mine?"

One day, on a whim, we decided to find where they lived. Just for a lark. We didn't take our mission really seriously and felt philosophical about our probable failure. Nevertheless, selecting from the vast store of facts we had accumulated as avid readers of Beatles lore, we decided to take the Tube to Knightsbridge, an exclusive area in southwest London where, we had read, they had a house. We arrived and stood around outside Harrods for a while, wondering what to do next.

It seemed like such a stupid question.

"Oh, go on, you ask him. Go on."

"Excuse me. Do you know if the Beatles live around here?" Helen asked a postman we passed as we walked along one of the quiet streets off Old Brompton Road. It did seem like a fantastical question. But we asked it anyway, because now that we were here we didn't know what to do and actually it seemed like quite a smart idea.

"Okay. You go next. I did it last time."

"Excuse me. Do you know where the Beatles live?"

This was shouted to a window cleaner found high up his ladder further on. Surprisingly, neither of the two men found our question ludicrous, and with their help we found ourselves outside the cream fronted, late Victorian house in no time. Rather, it *used* to be cream fronted. It had recently been transformed into a manifesto of teenage love, and in fact it was the graffiti distinguishing this house that let us know we had arrived. Two blank-faced girls were already silently waiting outside the lipstick-covered facade when we got there. But apart from them, we were alone.

We did not have time to revel in that fact before an Austin Princess pulled up, double-parked, and John Lennon got out. We stood frozen on the pavement, transfixed by this apparition. We had been prepared for failure, but we had no plan in the event of our success. Ignoring us, John walked toward the door. We watched his progress toward the house, riveted like animals caught in the headlight's beam. He continued inexorably onward, squinting myopically as he did so. And as he came level with me and then passed me, he banged into my arm.

I was ecstatic. John Lennon had touched me. And I had touched John Lennon. For that moment we were almost holding hands. I was in an internal transport of delight, although I remained absolutely cool and expressionless behind my dark glasses lest I seemed childish or fawning in any way (and not girlfriend material). What should I do? Now that he was right in front of me I was at a loss. Act like you just happen to be passing by, as if you could not care less that it was John Lennon (Oh, my God!) who just crashed into your arm (and who didn't even notice you to say sorry). I could feel the moment, the opportunity, slipping away from us. John was moving toward his house unchecked, as I hung back, paralyzed by my efforts not to seem overly moved by anything. Then Helen seized the moment. Springing into action, she threw herself between him and his front door. Gazing up at him, she spoke.

"Hello," she said, beaming and expectant.

There was a slight pause while he looked down at her, down his long nose.

"Hello." And then, after a moment, "Goodbye," he sneered in his flat, Liverpool voice as he pushed by her into the house.

Oh, the humiliation. The public humiliation. I cringed inside a million times. He had snubbed her. He had cut her dead. Poor, brave Helen. (I am so glad it wasn't me.) How embarrassing. (I had escaped intact. I breathed a sigh of relief.) I looked on in shock in my dark glasses and my cool, black, shiny coat. I saw Paul smiling in the Austin. He was looking at me. Had we shared an intimate moment, I hoped? Or, an awful thought: Maybe he just reckoned I was blind with my sunglasses on and was smiling out of compassion.

We were stunned. We watched as they sped away in their fancy black car. The moment was over.

We did not dwell on our shock and disappointment. We did not dwell on the fact that John had been so shatteringly rude. We rejected the memory of his hostility and crushing dismissal. We refused to let John's coldness depress us or diminish our pleasure. Instead, we made excuses for him. I thought fondly of John's bad eyesight. I found his clumsiness and brusqueness charming. Soon we stopped talking about the incident. It was as if it had never happened.

It was some months later that the Beatles released their next single. The title was "Hello, Goodbye." Ha, ha! Helen and I laughed euphorically. We took it as a sign, as a hidden message from them to us. It was almost like personal contact. How perfect. How well it had all turned out. We knew the title's secret. We knew that we had inspired it. And we knew because we were there.

Another Version of the Chair

Greil Marcus

We were driving through Colorado [and] we had the radio on and eight of the Top Ten songs were Beatles songs. In Colorado! "I Want to Hold Your Hand," all those early ones.

They were doing things nobody was doing. Their chords were outrageous, and their harmonies made it all valid. . . . But I kept it to myself that I really dug them. Everybody else thought they were for the teenyboppers, that they were gonna pass right away. But it was obvious to me that they had staying power. I knew they were pointing the direction where music had to go . . . in my head, the Beatles were *it*. In Colorado, I started thinking but it was so far-out I couldn't deal with it—eight in the Top Ten.

It seemed to me a definite line was being drawn. This was something that never happened before.

—Bob Dylan, 1971

On February 9th, 1964, I was in college in California, a rock & roll fan with creeping amnesia. I remembered Chuck Berry but not the guitar solo in "Johnny B. Goode." The excitement, the sense of being caught up in something much bigger than one's own private taste, had disappeared from rock years before. There was still good stuff on the radio—there had been "Heat Wave" by a group called Martha and the Vandellas the summer before, "Be True to Your School" by the Beach Boys a few months after that, and even "On Broadway" by the Drifters—but in 1963 all of it seemed drowned out by Jimmy Gilmer's "Sugar Shack," the number one song of the year and perhaps the worst excuse for itself rock & roll had yet produced. Rock & roll—the radio—felt dull and stupid, a dead end.

There had been an item in the paper that day about a British rock & roll group that was to appear on *The Ed Sullivan Show* that night: The Beatles (a photo too—were those wigs, or what?). I was curious—I didn't know they had rock & roll in England—so I went down to a commons rooms where there was a TV set, expecting an argument from whoever was there about which channel to watch.

Four hundred people sat transfixed as the Beatles sang "I Want to Hold Your Hand," and when the song was over the crowd exploded. People looked at the faces (and the hair) of John, Paul, George, and Ringo and said Yes (and who could have predicted that a few extra inches of hair would suddenly seem so right, so necessary? Brian Epstein?); they heard the Beatles' sound and said Yes to that too. What was going on? And where had all those people come from?

Back at the radio I caught "I Saw Her Standing There" and was instantly convinced it was the most exciting rock & roll I'd ever heard (with Paul's one-two-three-*fuck!* opening—how in the world did they expect to get away with that?). Someone from down the hall appeared with a copy of the actual record—you could just go out and *buy* this stuff?—and announced with great fake solemnity that it was the first 45 he'd purchased since "All Shook Up." Someone else—who played a twelve-string guitar and as far as I knew listened to nothing but Odetta—began to muse that "even as a generation had been brought together by the Five Satins' 'In the Still of the Nite,' it could be that it would be brought together again—by the Beatles." He really talked like that; what was more amazing, he talked like that when a few hours before he had never heard of the Beatles.

The next weeks went by in a blur. People began to grow their hair (one acquaintance argued with great vehemence that it was physically impossible for male hair—at least, *normal* male hair—to grow to Beatle length); some affected British (or, when they could pull it off, Liverpool) accents. A friend got his hands on a British Beatles album unavailable in the United States and made a considerable amount of money charging people for the chance to hear John

Lennon sing "Money (That's What I Want)" at two bucks a shot. Excitement wasn't in the air; it *was* the air.

A few days after that first performance on the Sullivan show, I spent the evening with some friends in a cafe in my hometown. It was, or anyway had been, a folk club. This night one heard only *Meet the Beatles*. The music, snaking through the dark, suddenly spooky room, was instantly recognizable and like nothing we had ever heard. It was joyous, threatening, absurd, arrogant, determined, innocent, and tough, and it drew the line of which Dylan was to speak. "This was something that never happened before."

It was, as Lester Bangs says in his survey of the British Invasion, not simply a matter of music, but of event. Dylan had heard the Beatles in New York before his Colorado revelation; I had first heard them on the radio in early 1963, when "Please Please Me" was released in the United States. Liked the record, disliked the follow-up, then forgot the group altogether. It was only in the context of the Beatles' event that their music was perceived for what it was.

The event was a pop explosion; the second, and thus far the last, that rock & roll has produced.

A pop explosion is an irresistible cultural upheaval that cuts across lines of class and race (in terms of sources, if not allegiance), and, most crucially, divides society itself by age. The surface of daily life (walk, talk, dress, symbolism, heroes, family affairs) is affected with such force that deep and substantive changes in the way large numbers of people think and act take place. Pop explosions must link up with, and accelerate, broad shifts in sexual behavior, economic aspirations, and political beliefs; a pervasive sense of chaos, such as that which hit England in 1963 with the Profumo scandal, and the United States in the mid-sixties with the civil rights movement, the Kennedy assassination, and later the Vietnam War, doesn't hurt.

Now, it has been argued, by British critic George Melly, that a pop explosion merely "turns revolt into a style" (poet Thom Gunn's line on Elvis, originally), but in fact pop explosions can provide the enthusiasm, the optimism, and the group identity that make mass political participation possible. A pop explosion is more than a change in style even if it is far less than a revolution, though it can look like either one—depending on who is looking, and when. (Not that "changing the world" in the political sense of the term is never a "goal" of a pop explosion, if such an event can be said to have a goal beyond good times; still, a pop explosion changes the world by affecting the moment, which means that the world retains the capacity to change back, momentarily.)

Enormous energy—the energy of frustration, desire, repression, adolescence, sex, ambition—finds an object in a pop explosion, and that energy is focused on, organized by, and released by a single, holistic cultural entity. This entity must itself be capable of easy, instantaneous, and varied imitation and extension, in a thousand ways at once; it must embody, suggest, affirm, and legitimize new possibilities on all fronts even as it outstrips them. This is a fancy way of saying that the capacity for fad must be utterly profound.

And, at its heart, a pop explosion attaches the individual to a group—the fan to an audience, the solitary to a generation—in essence *forms* a group and creates new loyalties—while at the same time it increases one's ability to respond to a particular pop artifact, or a thousand of them, with an intensity that verges on lunacy. Ringo's shout of "All right, George!" just before the guitar break in "Boys" becomes a matter of indefinable and indefensible significance; styles on Carnaby Street outdo the pace of the pop charts and change literally by the hour. Yet within it all is some principle of shape, of continuity, of value.

This principle was the Beatles. As was so often pointed out in the mid-sixties, the sum of the Beatles was greater than the parts, but the parts were so distinctive and attractive that the group itself could be all things to all people, more or less. You did not have to love them all to love the group, but you could not love one without loving the group, and this was why the Beatles became bigger than Elvis; this was what had never happened before. And so it began. The past was felt to dissolve, the future was conceivable only as an expansion of the present, and the present was defined absolutely by its expansive novelty. Towering above Bob Dylan, the Rolling Stones, a score of British groups, American groups, Mary Quant, the Who, whatever and whoever sprung up day by day, the Beatles seemed not only to symbolize but to contain it all—to make history by anticipating it.

Portland Coliseum

Allen Ginsberg

A brown piano in diamond
white spotlight
Leviathan auditorium
iron rib wired
hanging organs, vox
black battery
A single whistling sound of
ten thousand children's
larynxes asinging
pierce the ears
and flowing up the belly
bliss the moment arrived

Apparition, four brown English
jacket christhair boys
Goofed Ringo battling bright
white drums
Silent George hair patient
Soul horse
Short black-skulled Paul
with thin guitar
Lennon the Captain, his mouth
a triangular smile,
all jump together to End
some tearful memory song
ancient two years,
The million children
the thousand worlds
bounce in their seats, bash

each other's sides, press
legs together nervous
Scream again & claphand
become one Animal
in the New World Auditorium
—hands waving myriad
snakes of thought
screetch beyond hearing

while a line of police with
folded arms stands
Sentry to contain the red
sweatered ecstasy
that rises upward to the
wired roof.

August 27, 1965

Waiting on the Beatles

Norman Paul Hyett

At Shumsky's, I had served brisket to the Union's Meany and Dubinsky, made sure that Arthur Godfrey's steak was burned on the outside and raw in the center, assured Ramsey Lewis a long quiet dinner before his concert, helped pick up Eddie Arcaro after he collapsed to the floor while eating our famous cheesecake on the day he won eight races in a row, and fed Sonny Liston four lamb chops twice on the same night.

Every day, two cops would drive their motorcycles into the kitchen and sit at the table next to the bar with their helmets on so they could listen to the police band while they drank coffee and ate. Periodically, their leisure was interrupted by a murder, fight, or some other emergency, and they would zoom out the back door. These two were assigned to look after the Beatles, and it was they who arranged for the truck to help them escape the sea of Philadelphia girls, each hoping to tear the fantasy foursome to shreds.

The dark blue laundry truck backed up quickly to the delivery entrance of Shumsky's, closed to the public by eleven but open this evening to my indifference. It was 1964, and the Beatles were little more than a mop-headed English rock group to me. Their concert across the street in Atlantic City's Convention Hall, the largest convention center in the world, drew my attention about as much as dust on a windowsill. I was an Elvis fan, a Jerry Lee Lewis aficionado, a hard rocker in a 1950s way. I was also a good summer waiter, the best man for the celebs.

Window curtains drawn, lights low, four Beatles, one girl, and a small host of adults entered the main dining room through the same door where Sheriff, a longtime waiter, had dropped dead only two nights before. He was just coming out of the kitchen with his loaded tray of main-course plates when he dropped like Buddy Holly. The noise was shocking, as was the silent aftershock broken only by Johnny Shumsky screaming from the kitchen, "Drag him in the back, he looks like hell!" I didn't know whether to laugh or cry, just as I didn't know how to react to this famous group.

I stood there hardly impressed with the appearance of the Beatles, their rowdiness and lack of manners. They wore dark versions of my old busboy jacket, the one that buttoned all the way up to the neck. They were my age, demanding beer and food and hurry-up service. They hadn't been in the place for two minutes, hadn't even been seated yet, and they were calling orders to me as if I found them as important as my pending tip.

The tall man in charge played host, making the introductions to the four Shumskys. He introduced himself as Brian Epstein, the boys as Ringo, Paul, John, and George, and the girl as Patty somebody; I never did catch her name or the names of the Americans who were with them. Of course, no one bothered to introduce me; after all, I was only the waiter. Three of the Shumskys stumbled over each other to pour champagne. Bill, who was always drunk, was doing his standard "How are you my friend" routine—he repeated the greeting without an attempt of sincerity to each of our late-night guests. Jimmy was in charge, and he seemed torn between making money and watching Johnny pour the best champagne in the house freely. I was glad the doors were locked because five of them were underage drinkers.

The Shumsky brothers were a product of first generation Jewish-Rumanian-American descent, and descent is the operative word. Their father died soon after World War II. He was the one who started and ran the restaurant before it became a free-for-all. Jimmy, the oldest, assumed his role as head of the clan, but that assumption was not accepted by the others. Bill, the next oldest, was the family drunk. He had an eloquence about him which made him a natural people greeter. His role in life was never to get dirty, never to cook, and never to give up his "front man" status. Johnny, the third son, looked like he was spawned from an entirely different family. Unlike the others, who were built like the peasant stock from which they came, Johnny was red-headed and lean. There wasn't a kind bone in his body. He ran the kitchen, and knew how many pickles there were in the pickle barrel, how many matzo balls were in the large soup pot, and how many beers each of the cooks drank each night while he worked. The only balance to him was Sherman, the baby and biggest of the bunch, a good-natured reasonable man. Once I came to work and found Johnny and Sherman on the ground punching each other senseless as the cooks, waiters, and kitchen help stood around. It was Jim who came in and grabbed each by the throat until they turned blue and stopped. Such was the life the Beatles walked into.

The group was seated, and I was beckoned to take their orders. They all seemed anxious to eat. It was hard understanding the guys. Not only did they speak quickly, but the flow of words was almost indecipherable: "Wha du ya ca it?" or "Hav ya gota bear?" kind of speech, as if they had their mouths stuffed with saltwater taffy.

"Wat's its?" Paul asked while pointing to the word *kishka*. "It's stuffed intestine," I replied. "Wat's sit stuffed wit?" John asked in his best taffy mouthed English. "House secret," I said, but then Sherman came over and told them. He would never tell anyone the ingredients of the house specialties, and here he was spilling the beans to these kids. I guess he thought that they wouldn't remember it anyway.

I ended up bringing kishka, chopped liver, herring filets, our famous pickles, sour tomatoes, and challah to the table. They ate as if manners were not important. I had never seen someone pick up a whole piece of herring and bite off half the way George did, nor had I witnessed anyone spit out chopped liver with the lack of pretense displayed by Ringo. Forks became shovels, knives were left unused and, in the end spoons became the instrument of choice.

I knew from the start that serving them matzo ball soup would be a snap but getting their main course order would be tough. I was right. "Boiled beef flanken is beef on the ribs boiled in a pot for several hours," I answered to Ringo's inquiry. "Short ribs of beef is the same meat as flanken, only it's cooked in the oven with a sauce," I answered to his second question. "What's an oven?" he asked. Now I was really dumbfounded. Where had these guys come from, anyway? "An oven is an appliance in the kitchen." I held myself back from asking them if they knew what a kitchen was. "Oh, you mean a cooker," Patty chimed in. I glared in response.

I went through tongue, brisket, and Salisbury steak okay, and was saved from sweetbreads only because Mr. Epstein decided that everyone should eat steaks. Quite grateful, I wished that he had spared me an onslaught of questions. Steaks it would be, and that meant a large tab; hopefully these people had heard of tipping.

They talked endlessly of stuff I couldn't understand. George, who seemed quite slow to me because he responded to things long after the conversation had moved on, said the least. Ringo talked the most, but nobody seemed to be listening to him. The girl just sat quietly next to Paul, who seemed to be her date, and the other two, who were both Americans, didn't seem to understand anything. It was Mr. Epstein, John, and Paul who held center stage. Waiters notice such things. I'd learned to pass the check to the people with the power.

The restaurant was known for its "world famous" cheesecake, the most cherished of the secret recipes. All of the Beatles ate it, some with cherries and some plain. The energy never let up. They had just performed a concert, drank too much champagne and beer, ate a meal as if they hadn't had one in a week, and talked incessantly, and yet they didn't seem the least bit tired. It was 12:30 A.M. and these guys wanted to stay and have the cigars that Bill just offered.

Now, with disgusting smoke filling the room, I watched the four brothers hustle off to the kitchen and followed them as if I had a reason to. Bill and Sherman wanted to give all eight their meals on the house. Jim and Johnny were beside themselves even considering such a thought. I was beside myself too with the notion of no check, because I knew that my tip would then come from Jimmy Shumsky, who made Jack Benny seem like a big spender. It was scotch that saved the day. Bill, who stood a chance of winning an argument against Jimmy, passed out drunk before he had the opportunity.

Minutes later, I handed a check to Mr. Epstein, who proved to be most generous. Finally, as the Fab Four jumped back into their truck and their fame, I cleared their dirty dishes and thought, "No way will they ever be as famous as Elvis!"

Dunraven School, South London, 1964

Rosalind Brackenbury

Miss! Which do you like best?
John, Paul, George, Ringo.
Carved in desk lids
with compasses, penknives,
darkened with ink or blood,
their holy names.

The lids bang, the air is stale.
Legs in white kneesocks
twine under too-small
chairs. It's winter, short
blue skirts and cardigans, and
all they want for Christmas is—
guess.

I'm the new young teacher
with the engagement ring.
Guess, Miss! Which one I like!
Is that your fiancé?
Have you got a photo?
When you getting married?
What you gonna wear?
Miss, is he handsome?
Can I see? Miss, have you—
you know—yet?

Oh, he's fab, almost
as good as Paul.

Miss, can I come
to your wedding? Do we
have to have homework?

Miss, it's John I love.
Last week I thought it was Paul
but Jeannette says he's hers.
Miss, I like your boots,
bet they cost a lot,
are those real, did he
buy them for you?
Can I see your ring?

Miss, I'm leaving next year.
I'm getting married.
I'm going to marry Paul.

Miss, can we go now?
Will anybody love me?
Miss, will it all happen
the way it's s'posed to?
Miss, it's Ringo I like best.
I've decided. All the others
are taken. Ringo's mine.

The bell shrills.
We herd out to freezing tarmac
under low London skies;
that one winter, and then
I married, left them there.

You Say You Want a Revolution

Kay Sloan

"Who's winning?" called Paul McCartney, smiling out at the "game" played as policemen and a few fans swarmed onto the football field in New Orleans' City Park Stadium. We were darting this way and that, trying to avoid the inevitable hand that would drag us back to the stands, back to the anonymity of the screaming masses. But, for a second at least, we hoped Paul had seen us, that we had separated ourselves from the hordes of other Beatlemaniacs.

For months my sister and I had campaigned with our parents to get to that magical place, to the football arena where Paul McCartney may have eyed me, ever so briefly. Throughout the hot summer of 1964 we had begged our parents to make the three-hour trip from our home in Jackson, Mississippi, to New Orleans for the Beatles concert—and to write notes to excuse us from junior high school for two days.

Even now, more than thirty years later, I'm still not sure what convinced our conservative parents to allow that big adventure. Maybe they'd finally been worn down by the constant barrage of music and life-sized Beatles posters. Perhaps it was because most of the family attention that summer had gone to our oldest sister's wedding. Or perhaps our parents, too, had recognized that something unfathomable and fascinating was happening, something that helped you forget everything that was wrong in Mississippi, made you feel that the world might not be as horrible as it seemed on the front page of the local newspaper every morning.

Late at night in the dark house, my sister and I sat in the windows of the bedroom we shared, adjusting the dials on our transistor radios to pick up faraway stations: KAAY in Little Rock or, if we were lucky, even WLS in Chicago. Through the static we listened to "All My Loving" or "I Want to Hold Your Hand," and we could imagine that we were part of a big community, friends with girls everywhere who loved the Beatles as much as we did.

In those dark Mississippi nights when the train that ran from New Orleans to Memphis would whistle an invitation that reminded us of how isolated we felt, we would pretend that we could walk down the crowded avenues of a city like Chicago or New York—places that seemed almost as foreign as Liverpool, almost as exotic and wonderful as the Beatles' accents.

George was the one I loved the most, and, after him, John. My sister and I would get into heated arguments over who was cuter, Ringo or George. She loved the way Ringo tossed his head and made his hair shake in the air as he drummed. She could hug him, she said, without even having to stand on tiptoe. Even though my sister and I loved to tease each other, I'd never say anything bad about any of the Beatles. It would've been a sacrilege, and we both knew it.

My best friend loved Paul. One afternoon after school we were dancing to "Till There Was You," and she stopped suddenly when Paul sang the words "they tell me." "*Me,*" she whispered, with both surprise and awe in her voice. I stopped too, realizing along with her that they were people, these four gods we worshipped.

We watched them on *The Ed Sullivan Show* on both Sunday nights in February, staying home from Baptist Training Union to scream and jump while the camera traveled from one close-up to the next. "Sorry, girls—he's married," read the caption beneath John's close-up. But any self-respecting Beatlemaniac already knew that, knew that Cynthia and baby Julian were waiting back in Liverpool for John to return. So, if I couldn't have John, then it would be George instead, with his intelligent, serious face and his thin legs, one booted foot always keeping the beat of his lead guitar.

In the pages of *Sixteen* magazine, we learned how to iron our hair to make it as straight as Patti Boyd's or Jane Asher's. Even though we professed to despise them, we wanted to look just like them. We bought every fan magazine that appeared at the local drugstore, collected Beatles' bubblegum cards, wore sweatshirts adorned with their faces—and canceled our Elvis fan club memberships. Elvis, after all, was just a Mississippi boy who'd made it big. He even had a polite Southern accent. It was impossible to imagine the Beatles joining the army, like Elvis. They were too full of irrepressible joy, too full of taunting jibes aimed at authority to salute anyone. Listening to the Beatles' voices was enough to know how exotic, how magically foreign they were. They were a force that could shatter the world as we knew it, so things would never again be the same.

In the Mississippi of 1964, I wanted everything to change. I'd just finished seventh grade at a junior high school where some students had cheered at the news of Kennedy's assassination. I had sat in my science class, wondering how the teacher could go on talking about dissecting frogs after the president had been killed. Nothing would be the same, I thought. After class, someone had stepped on a live frog, brought to school to scare the girls. The remains left a bloody trail on the linoleum near my locker, where later I would keep George's picture taped inside. It was a grisly sight, and I had nearly vomited.

Only a few months before, in the summer of 1963, three civil rights workers had been found dead, after weeks of local rumors that the Northern press was simply trying to make the state look bad. "They're just back up North, hiding," my Sunday school teacher explained, during the long weeks when the three young men were missing. Letters to the Jackson *Daily News* encouraged secession. "Just look at all the local talent we have on *Teen Tempos*, wrote one woman, about a Jackson television show. "We don't need the North to tell us what to do. We don't even need their entertainers."

There was one truth in the woman's letter: she understood the power of entertainment. The Beatles' first album filled an entire bin of the record stand at the five-and-ten store just down the street. John, Paul, George, and Ringo were unlike anyone I'd ever seen, their faces seemingly rising from the shadows on the record cover, half in darkness, half in light. Like the moon, I thought, when my sister first pointed out their faces. They were unsmiling, the hair framing four pairs of mysterious eyes.

When I heard "I Want to Hold Your Hand," the mystery behind the faces came surging forward in the music, exploding upward with an energy that made my heart race. The music made me want more than the world I saw around me, more than I thought the world could possibly give. It wasn't the lyrics, it was the raw, pounding energy and the community that shared it.

When my sister and I heard that the Beatles were coming to New Orleans, we taped banners of Beatles lyrics across the kitchen, plastered the den with pictures of George and Ringo, and played their music constantly. Finally, our parents relented. On July 29, 1964, we bought two money orders for five dollars and fifty cents each from the post office, and sent off to Metairie, Louisiana. for our tickets.

My father pulled our blue-and-white Chevrolet station wagon into one of the single remaining spaces outside the stadium in New Orleans, and my sister and I ran inside. "We'll be waiting right here," our mother called, but the words hung in the air behind us. Too much excitement lay ahead to pay attention to such reassurance.

We never did settle into seats. Instead, we ran up the bleachers and back down, screaming, then raced around the bend in the horseshoe-shaped stadium, trying to get closer, to get a better look at those small figures on stage. But we could tell who was who: John bending his knees slightly, keeping the beat; Paul with his left-handed guitar; George in the middle; and, of course, there was Ringo shaking his hair so that a chorus of screams would rise up from the crowds, my sister's above all.

For me it was an exercise in frustration. I wanted to touch the magic, grab some light or dust to carry back to Mississippi with me like an amulet. Without warning my sister, I suddenly climbed over the railing and dropped the five feet to the ground. I nearly lost my balance and fell down on one knee. John was singing, "Well shake it, shake it, shake it, ba-a-by." Then I was up and running, hearing my sister call "Go, Kay!" while I raced as fast as I could toward the gleaming spotlights on the stage. I saw a policeman coming at me from the right, the dark blue of his uniform as threatening as the Baptist sermons about hellfire I'd heard, a reminder of all those firehose-wielding sheriffs downing civil rights workers on the sidewalks of Birmingham.

I made a quick left, and that's when I heard Paul lean into the microphone and ask, "Who's winning?" My heart leaped. Maybe he'd seen me, at least for a second. But a hand grabbed my arm from behind, a policeman I hadn't seen coming. For a second I thought about going limp, the way I'd seen civil rights workers do on television. I imagined him dragging me back to the stands, my new loafers carving two trails into the muddy grass—leaving my mark behind.

"See that wagon?" the policeman said. He pointed to a paddy wagon just beyond the stage. "We're not going there *this* time." A few bedraggled-looking girls were being led inside, crying. It was hard to tell if the tears were for the Beatles or for being arrested.

So I let him take me back to the stands and deposit me at the chained-off steps that led up to the seats. But something would never be the same. I was thirteen years old, on the verge, and I'd glimpsed something beyond the tired words and dull boredom and violent hatred of Mississippi in 1964. I was tired of how hateful and hypocritical adults could be—and even kids. The Beatles, though, weren't exactly kids or adults. They were a new breed of cocky, cool guys, a sign that you didn't have to automatically step into adulthood. Instead, the Beatles made fun of authority, made it all seem absurd, even laughable. It was a new kind of power.

That night I was too excited to sleep. My parents had driven as far as Hattiesburg, Mississippi, and we stayed in a motel. Even after my sister had fallen asleep, I lay awake, still feeling the beat of the music in my blood and the iron grip of the policeman's clutch on my arm.

It was a memory that came back to me a few years later, when I'd fled Mississippi to be a student at Berkeley one summer. With thousands of others I was marching to an antiwar rally in Golden Gate Park just as the policemen began to rush into our midst. At Berkeley half the students, it seemed, were humming "Let It Be," and the rest, "Revolution."

But on that August night in New Orleans in 1964, my entire world was shaken by the roots. Letting things be would never again be possible.

you've got to hide
your love away

Not a Second Time

Nancy Fox

It's an odd and offhand role that the Beatles played in changing my life so violently.

I see the filmstrips now of adoring girls and realize I was one of them, bigtime. Not that I ever bought a concert ticket or thought to ask for such unthinkable freedom. In my neighborhood, you found the LP in the rack near the checkout at the Acme, you promised your mother weeks of making the bed right if she would buy it, and not too soon you got a reluctant okay.

Then you played that LP until you could feel exactly where Paul's voice wavered in the last stanza of "I Want to Hold Your Hand," until you discovered that the flaw in his record made the guy himself more perfect, and you thought you might survive this new puberty if all its vast territories proved as sweet to probe as this one.

Oh, love me do.

I thought the screamers were Not Cool. I lived in the 'Burg, the Italian town in Trenton. In my neighborhood the bigger and harder the hair, the smaller the mouthpower, the more dateworthy the girl. Entire courtships were conducted in human silence. The shiny Chevy double-parked, the guy got out to show off the black sheen of his ankle-lengths and to slick back his hair with both hands, the steady got in, she rolled up the window, he revved the engine, and to points mysterious and marvelous they drove. This was the height of Cool.

I thought the Beatles, especially Paul, must be like the Raymond and Al and Tinky I knew—fastidious about the behavior of girls around them. The men—and I knew, even at twelve, that this was a man I was in love with, not a giddy boy who giggled in gaggles of boys—would be mucho annoyed by the noise and the . . . something else . . . that I didn't have the vocabulary to describe but which I felt to be graceless and improper. These girls were not ladies, as we of the macho neighborhoods defined them.

Now I think I was jealous as hell.

I myself stayed apart from the roiling crowd—or would if I were actually in New York at the time, and if New York conformed to my fantasy of it: one roped-off sidewalk for the unruly shrillers, a parallel sidewalk, aloof, free of the chaos, for me. Perhaps one well-meaning cop would try to shepherd me toward the wild shrieks and I would shimmy away from him, and Paul would look down—elegant, lonely, *I'm so sad and lonely*—from his hotel window and see: me.

Introducing Miss Enigmatic. I didn't know that word then either, but I'd seen plenty of *Saturday Night at the Movies* and Debra Paget. So I knew the general gorgeousness of look to achieve here—innocent, waiting, I had no idea for what. Something like *Baby, take a chance with me.*

"You are a lady," my friend Carol Ann responded at once to this picture when I confessed it. "Like my brother Louis's old girlfriend. You are more intelligent than the typical bimbo model." The fantasy seemed so natural, so easy, like pictures you sing to yourself in lullaby before sleep. "In fact you are only a model until you make enough money to buy your country estate. Then you will quit the rat race forever."

"What will I do?"

"Well you're such a good speller. And you're way ahead of me in the SRA's. I know. You will write books."

I should mention right here that my mother and I lived in a tan one-bedroom apartment and I was expected to someday be a stenographer, with slimmer ankles and larger obedience skills than I had exhibited so far.

This writer career was thrilling. At school I was known among the nuns, and thus among girls, who cared what the boygaggle thought, as *the one who is good with words.* And I couldn't wait until we furnished the country estate.

"What kind of books?" I asked Carol Ann.

"Oh, very big books." Carol Ann had the first Barbie on the block, but the girl was no reader. "Now, I like modeling. I like clothes, black leather I think, it goes with my long blond hair, which I keep just so, wild but neat, you know? Not bleached. And I own a black T-bird convertible that I drive everywhere. I'd rather drive than sleep. I drive very fast, but expertly."

Carol Ann was one of a series of middle children, all nutlike and plain, in an ever-expanding Italian family that had more rules for its daughters than the Vatican. I knew: her family took care of me until my mother came home from work. You passed through the thicket of that family in relative safety if you remembered this one rule: Boys did anything, girls did not.

But we were allowed to wander certain streets after school. Sometimes we'd tease the dating couples who strolled the neighborhood—Carol Ann, since she had older dating brothers, was more daring than I in the wicked words department. Sometimes we'd toddle off to the drugstore and read *Archie* and *True Romance* and *Movie Life* together.

We weren't best friends. We weren't school friends. But we were the same age—and lately, with periods and complexions and garter belts and so on to fret about, Carol Ann didn't call me fatso anymore and run off to cartwheel with more gymnastic and less scholastic friends.

Then two things happened.

First, I heard in Carol Ann's basement, on Carol Ann's brother Louis's radio, the most endearing and heart-searing words that anyone had ever said to me: *I wanna hold your hand.*

(Mom consulted the family watchdogs—a scolding older sister, a bigmouth brother-in-law, and a chilly aunt or two—and the okay came from on high about the LP.)

Then came the night we convinced our families to give over the TV sets. Amused, they conferred and agreed. And if our generational Beatles obsession began on that Ed Sullivan Sunday, my own particular Beatles tragedy started on narrow Liberty Street outside the 'Burg in Trenton a day or so later, when our little story sparkled to life.

"What do I look like?"

"You are quiet. So you don't wear black leather like I do. Which is what Ringo likes. Do you think I look like Ringo?"

Actually she did a little. "But you're blond?" I said, staying safely inside the story.

"Yes, I am. Not as tall as you are—when you cross your legs both feet touch the floor, like my brother Louis's old girlfriend, and I need high heels to get that tall, which is good because Ringo is short. Or maybe I'm dating George. Both, I think, at the beginning, I can choose later. You wear blue, like they say, true blue, and you will always date only one person, and that person is Paul."

The story as we constructed it that winter and spring went something like this: Our chosen Beatles (and we Catholic children respected the Holy Sacrament of Matrimony so completely that I doubt we knew what Beatle John looked like) saw us standing there outside the hotel and embarked on a quest to find us. The plot, as it turned out, was a lot of running, as in *A Hard Day's Night*—which by the way decided Carol Ann on the Ringo question definitely, given the appeal of the big sulky raincoat and the mean, sullen lady who yelled at him—but the grail was not the Boys' freedom from confinement: it was the lovely and elusive two of us.

Carol Ann was Sandy and I was Donna.

We began to accumulate Beatles things, and Carol Ann's mother gave us a basement closet to keep them in:

- wonderful magazines, wherein we first encountered Jane Asher the actor and Maureen Cox the hairdresser and had to tack them—curtly—onto our story ("You, Donna, are intelligent, and so you talk Jane Asher right back home, but I fight Maureen. " "Carol Ann, look at her nails," which were curved talons the likes of which I'd never seen and thought extraordinarily *ugh*. "I wear cleats on my heels," said Carol, which satisfied both of us on that score: we were, after all, Trenton girls);

- Beatles cards, which came in bubblegum packages for . . .

maybe a quarter: the price was steep enough that we weren't allowed to buy more than one a week, and we of course had to collect a double set, a shoebox of cards for each of us, filed and categorized, so that we knew in a true love's way of knowing (I think the clothes were the clues here) which photos were Beatle and which were Beatlemania—two entirely different periods, in our informed and scholarly view;

- various Beatle accouterments like charms and coloring books and a newspaper clipping of a girl in Trenton who touched one of the Fab Four and wrapped her hand in a plastic bag;

- a bootleg copy of "Love Me Do," before the new one wherein Ringo hit the cymbals on the drumbeat solo was released in its stead.

Carol Ann had the black corduroy hat; I had the signature sneakers; and we both had the albums, but only Carol Ann was allowed to play hers in the house without a mother walking by and saying it gave her a headache, please turn it off and go to bed right now, followed by whispered sessions on the phone with the family watchdogs.

Lucky Carol Ann had the brothers who listened to "Bristol Stomp" and such, and a father who built them a music room in the basement.

"Get the heck downstairs if you're gonna sing that twaddle," he'd say when we, as Sandy and Donna, drove that black T-bird around New York with Paul and Ringo in tuneful pursuit.

All my loving, I will give to you. All my loving, darling I'll be true.

So we kept our *Meet the Beatles* and *With the Beatles* and *Introducing . . . The Beatles* and 45 collection there. And soon I wanted to hear my records and work on our story on weekends, too, instead of almost hearing whatever whispers I heard at home and working on making dusting good enough or scrubbing my school uniform blouses and socks on the washboard since my mother got mad at me for wanting to be at Carol Ann's and refused to put them in her Maytag.

"Tell me again about my mansion, and Paul almost finding it that rainy night. . . ."

But I could always, and I did—always—go to my Paul story in my head, and sometimes I pushed a bit further than Carol Ann did in our conversations. Maybe, who knows, alone, she pushed her story too.

No, Paul and I never were less than virginal. No one did That in my neighborhood (I believed) but the bleached bimbs with runny mascara and bruised looks, and I didn't know what That was anyway. The news I'd heard from Carol Ann's cartwheeling circles was pretty *ugh*, and I discounted It. My scholastic friends at school did not discuss It. To me, two people en route to marriage—and the message of Beatle songs was marriage, what else could *mine all mine take a chance with me* mean to a twelve-year-old in 1964?—were speechless as trading cards. The only sign of life was that thing Debra Paget did to her eyes so they seemed to turn into big wool blankets that covered up the Jeffrey Hunter hero so completely only she could see him.

But I did, in my weekend workday story, travel to Liverpool and meet the brother and dad. I drank a cuppa and walked, indifferent to all the watchingly envious world, on the banks of the Mersey.

And I guess the first sign that we were gathering trouble here was the day that the sixth grade nun, Sister William Ann, called me away from Carol Ann in the schoolyard and said, "What do you two talk about?"

I offered the predictable nothing of the blindsided preteen: "We talk." That was a giveaway right there. The pre-Paul me would have been more eager to please Sister—not as eager as some, but friendly enough ("We want to be like the Blessed Virgin Mary"), the sort of thing we were all good at gushing to nuns by now. But someone else in my life had asked *Please please me.*

"You used to talk to me in the school yard," she said—and that was true. My scholastic friends and I showed off for Sister's favor. I remember wondering why it wasn't okay for me not to want to do that anymore.

"And what happened when he saw me at the party?"

I remember watching the hundreds of kids playing in the school yard around us, some in rope-jumping groups, some in chatting pairs. I saw boys trading cards the size of the cards we traded. Why were they free to pursue *their* stories?

I sensed that the family watchdogs had their hands in this.

"Now you walk around and talk to Carol Ann. You never were friends with her before. What do you two talk about?"

"Things."

"I think you talk about things you shouldn't talk about."

I had no idea what she meant, but a statement like that from a nun, to anyone who knows nuns, was a threat.

"We talk about music," I said. Which was true, if not accurate.

Sister shook her head. "That's not what your mother and I think."

The thing about nuns in those days was that little of their persons showed to enable expression—not forehead, nor neck, nor anything really but eyes, mouth, and hands—and so they had learned to press their features together and scare you to death. Because they didn't stop there. I'd seen them crack two heads together like coconuts and break a wooden pointer on a boy's backside, and I'd been whacked a time or two myself. And so you did what they asked. And here it was: "We don't want you to walk with Carol Ann."

"Why?"

"You talk about things you shouldn't talk about."

"Beatles?"

She waved the word away. But I had nothing else to give her. I remember asking what it was she wanted me to say, and I remember her staring at me as if she thought she were staring through me, and I felt for the first time that peculiar delight that tells you, in spite of everything, that you are free, that people who think they've got you don't, and as soon as you physically can you will go. "I want you to stay with me in the school yard from now on," she said.

"Yes, Sister."

"You can walk home from school with Carol Ann"—which was not giving much, since it was to her house that we both walked—"but nowhere else."

"Yes, Sister."

"You are to stop these talks."

"Yes, Sister."

Carol Ann's mother shrugged and pressed her lips together when we asked about all this. Why can't we walk? Why can't we talk? She had seven children by then, five of them boys: that says it all in terms of her daily priorities. But I learned years later that she didn't buy a word of It.

And what was It?

Well, some brightlight in the family watchdogs had decided that Carol Ann and I were gay. I was twelve. She was eleven. We talked, their fantasy said, too much.

"Tell me about Paul and the lost notebook."

"What he didn't know was that you had the notebook, and he got that worried look on his face, the one in card twenty-seven."

"So cute! And Ringo said . . ."

The words I read describing Beatlemania later in my life—*necessary*, *innocent*, *harmless*—tapped a part of me I thought I'd buried, or resolved. The part that always felt there was something wrong with me because my family acted decisively but didn't tell me why. Their friends stopped talking kindly to me or started to act as if they knew something unseemly about me, and I was sent permanently to live with scolding noisy watchdogs. Beatle Paul was okay with them, but I never saw Carol Ann again.

I began at this point to watch all sorts of passionate movies that I was forbidden to see—*Diamond Head, The Haunting, The Cardinal*—and although I didn't understand or even care about the plot, I did connect with and dream about the intensity of emotion in the characters' faces.

Most especially: longing.

Barbershop

Larry Schug

It wasn't only the Beatles,
It was the bottles—
Whiskey behind the Wildroot,
Bourbon behind the Brylcreem,
That shut the doors on my old man's shop.
But my old man's face went white
That Sunday night in sixty-four
When the mop-tops shook their shaggy manes,
Looking cool as hell, and a generation
Sang "yeah, yeah, yeah."
He closed his eyes in disbelief
And shook his balding head, "No, No, No."
That night, before we went to bed,
My brother and I and a million other kids
Washed the Butch Wax from our heads.
Forever.

Beatle Wig

Joyce E. Peseroff

Why did my father buy a Beatle wig,
and why did he provoke my rage
at dinner one night, howling with a fake

pelt on his head? He was asking
to be laughed at—more Three Stooges than Fab Four—
but something in the gesture's mockery

he flung straight at me, fat as a fist.
My metamorphosis of hair, my minidress
and long *L*'s of leather boots, the boom-

a-lacka radio, an after-school job in the library,
he knew would loose me from his table. He put on
his wig (and judged my affections: foolish,

common)—acrylic thing he shook against
my new world, my America—and struck.

A Hard Night's Day

Janna Bialek

It is the force of our memories that carries us through childhood; sometimes the facts alone are not enough.

On a warm winter morning when I was seven, we came home from church and found my father in the living room, reading the newspaper as if he belonged there. I ran to get a hug, and as I sat on his knee, trying to believe he was really there, as I rubbed against the smooth coolness of his starched shirt and tried to smell and breathe and take him in, he started talking excitedly to my mother.

"You're going to watch, aren't you?" he mildly scolded her. "It's the biggest thing ever. History. Tonight. I can't wait." It was enough that my dad had even *appeared* in our living room, but now he was sharing his excitement with us, with my mother, letting us become part of his life. Something was going to happen, maybe something we could all share. I could hardly breathe.

My mother listened, trying to take it in. She looked worried instead of happy. I could barely contain my anger at her. Why couldn't she just be glad he was there, that he was talking to us, including us?

This is what I remember of my father, maybe fifteen minutes of a conversation. After that he was gone.

Thirty-some years ago it was normal for seven-year-olds to be kept pretty much in the dark about the things that were important in the world. Teachers did not teach current events, did not believe that kids needed to know about war and bad things, except in some abstract way where it all worked out in the end. And parents didn't talk in front of you about anything that was not directly related to cleaning up your room or eating your peas. Anything.

So maybe it wasn't unusual that my dad's excitement about the

Beatles' premier on Ed Sullivan made such an impression. Maybe kids all across the country were being introduced to the world of rock and roll in mysterious, astounding ways. Somehow, though, out of all the memories that I must have had about those few years before my father disappeared from our lives, the morning he came home to tell us of the Beatles' premier is the memory I have kept, the only one that has stuck.

My dad, of course, didn't hang around to watch the Beatles with us. Most likely he was at a party, in a crowded room with lots of friends and noise and people who were sophisticated and fun and more like him. Or maybe he was with the woman he would eventually run off with, so that the warm night in February when the Beatles went on television became part of their history together. Maybe he doesn't even remember stopping to see us that day.

Rock and roll did not exactly invade our sad house, it just sort of came in like something we invited but knew didn't belong. Music like this was for other people, for families who put records on the stereo and danced in the living room. As 8:00 finally came and we turned on the TV, we watched, my mother, my grandmother, and I, and felt the full force of being alone. On the screen, women screamed in happiness, some of them fainted, even Ed Sullivan seemed excited. Something was going on, but clearly the three generations sitting in our living room were not part of it.

They came to our town once, the Beatles, to an airport not far from our house. My mother said "No, you can't go, it's too dangerous." There was a catch in her voice, something different that made me back off instead of nagging her like I usually would. I know now what it was—my mother, a young bride left alone with three children to raise, *she* should have been the one to meet the Beatles at the airport. She should have stood there screaming, laughing with the excitement of being young and in the middle of something big and historic, hoping herself to get a glimpse, to catch a word. My mother must have realized how separated she had become from the generation that should have been hers. My father, who could have shared those things with her, instead took them away from us all.

After the Beatles sang that night, I was sent upstairs to brush my teeth and get ready for bed. I took a long time getting dressed, stalling until the end of the show, when I knew they would come back again. I waited outside the door of my grandmother's bedroom till Ed Sullivan said the magic words, till the screaming started. My grandmother let me sit on the foot of her bed as she crocheted, whispering, "Don't tell your mother." Paul played the guitar, and as the women in the audience screamed and cried, a little smile crept into the corner of his mouth. I tried hard not to wonder or to think about anything, just to listen to the music, just to watch him. How could he have felt, having this much power?

Annus Mirabilis

Philip Larkin

Sexual intercourse began
In nineteen sixty-three
(Which was rather late for me)—
Between the end of the *Chatterley* ban
And the Beatles' first LP.

Up till then there'd only been
A sort of bargaining,
A wrangle for a ring,
A shame that started at sixteen
And spread to everything.

Then all at once the quarrel sank:
Everyone felt the same,
And every life became
A brilliant breaking of the bank,
A quite unlosable game.

So life was never better than
In nineteen sixty-three
(Though just too late for me)—
Between the end of the *Chatterley* ban
And the Beatles' first LP.

Sod Manila!

Eric Gamalinda

At half past three in the afternoon of July 5, 1966, a mob hired by President Ferdinand Marcos chased the Beatles out of Manila International Airport. I remember the jittery footage of the scene being replayed over and over on the News Tonite on Channel 5, and a grim-looking commentator saying the Fab but Discourteous Four had openly humiliated the First Lady and her children by refusing to pay a courtesy call at Malacañang Palace. Imelda Marcos herself hastily issued a statement saying the Beatles were to be treated humanely despite the snub, but this was said after the fact—after the Beatles had been kicked, spat at, cursed, and chased into a waiting jet.

Julian Hidalgo, known by the nickname Jun, took me and my sister Delphi to the Beatles' concert at Rizal Memorial Stadium. At that time he was courting my sister and was hoping to win me over by playing the older brother. They were both twenty, and the rituals of this older generation meant nothing to me beyond a few free passes to the movies, where I had to chaperone Delphi. But the three of us would witness, not by accident, the Beatles being beaten up at the airport, and we would become, after this experience, bonded in a way conspirators are mystically united by their stealth. Jun explained to me a few things about this incident eighteen years later, when, in the ironic twists of fate that coursed through our lives during the dictatorship, we found ourselves colleagues once again in the censorship office in Malacañang. But in 1966 we were young, brash, and bold with hope, and, like the entire country, we seemed on the verge of a privileged destiny.

Three days before the concert, Jun rushed to our house with three front-row tickets. Delphi's eye widened like 45s. "Where did you get the money this time, ha?" she asked, incredulous.

"The First Lady gave them to me," Jun said proudly. And, in response to our howls of disbelief, "Well, actually, this reporter from the *Manila Times* gave them to me. The First Lady was giving away sacks of rice and tickets last week. This reporter owed me for a tip I gave him years ago. The one that got him the Press Club award. He wanted the rice, I asked for the tickets. He was one of those Perry Como types."

Imelda Marcos had flown in friends and media to celebrate her birthday in her native island of Leyte. There was roast suckling pig and a rondalla playing all day, and she herself obliged requests for a song with a tearful ballad in the dialect, "Ang Irog Nga Tuna," My Motherland. To commemorate the sentimental reunion, each guest went home with the rice and tickets.

"Now that's style," Delphi said. Then, upon reflection: "They won't let Alfonso in."

"Of course they would," I protested. I was just thirteen but I was already as tall as she was back then.

"That's not the point," Jun said impatiently. "I'm going to get myself assigned to cover the Beatles and we can talk to them ourselves."

"All the other reporters will beat you to it," I said. Jun was stringing for the *Manila Times* and was convinced that getting an exclusive interview would land him a job as a staff reporter.

"All the other reporters listen to nothing but Ray Conniff," he said. "Besides, nobody knows where they're staying. But I do."

Jun's modus operandi wasn't going to be that easy. He managed to get stage passes for the three of us, which turned out to be inutile; it was the official pass, printed and distributed in London, that we had to wangle if we were to get near the Beatles.

"Go ahead and do your job," Delphi told him icily. "We'll see you at the stadium."

"I can still get you the pass," Jun said. "Somehow." He was beginning to realize that concert security would directly affect his personal relationships. But not even his religious coverage of preconcert press briefings seemed to help. Local promoters announced that the Beatles' only press conference was going to be held at the War Room of the Philippine Navy headquarters, and that the concert was being staged, not by coincidence, on the fourth of July as a birthday gift to the Republic (July 4th) and the First Lady (July 2nd). Other questions were left unanswered. Had the Beatles secretly arrived by submarine? "That's confidential." Were they actually going to stay at the Palace? "That's confidential." In the end somebody asked if the Beatles actually existed, and the joke was that *that*, too, was confidential.

The excitement was further fueled by a series of wire stories the dailies ran on page one, including coverage of the Beatles' world tour, warnings of possible riots all over the world, and a rare discordant moment in Tokyo, where a reporter asked the group, "What are you going to be when you grow up?" The reply: "If you grow up yourself you'd know better than to ask that question."

Radio stations kept playing Beatles hits (most requested: "Yesterday" and "Help!"), and DZUW, Rainy Day Radio, preempted everyone and began playing the new single, "Paperback Writer." The Philippine Security Corporation created the biggest stir when it insured the Beatles for a million pesos. Two hundred Philippine Constabulary troopers, seven hundred policemen, detachments from the Pasay City and Parañaque police, the Civil Aeronautics Administration, the Bureau of Customs, and the Marines were on red alert. The First Lady bought fifteen hundred tickets and distributed them to volunteer recruits to Vietnam, who were going to be the show's guests of honor. Pro-Beatle fan clubs were staging rallies, counterpointed by anti-Beatle demonstrations where placards said, "No one is more popular than Jesus!" Government bureaucrats had to drive away contractors who were bribing them with concert tickets. And on the eve of the Beatles' arrival, a young *colegiala* threatened to jump off the roof of the Bank of the Philippine Islands building unless she was granted a private audience with the band.

Backstage at the Rizal Memorial Stadium, an air-conditioned dressing room was hastily installed a day before the concert, complete with state-of-the-art TV monitors and audio equipment. Quarter-page ads appeared in the dailies for a week, announcing concert schedules and sponsors. Finally, on the day of the Beatles' arrival, July 3, a full-page splash appeared in all the dailies:

LIVE! THE BEST IN THE WORLD!
THE BEATLES IN MANILA
With Asia's Queen of Songs, Pilita Corales, Carding Cruz and his Orchestra, The Wing Duo, The Lemons Three, Dale Adriatico, The Reycard Duet, and Eddie Reyes and The Downbeats!

Early that morning, Jun called us up. "Get dressed, both of you," he said. "We're meeting the Beatles at the airport."

"What do you mean, we?" Delphi asked.

"I told you we'd talk to them, didn't I?" Jun said. "Did I ever break a promise?"

On many occasions, yes, but this was one promise for which Delphi was willing to risk her life—and mine, if need be. She drove our parents' '64 Ford to the airport as though she wanted to mow down everything in our way, laughing as irate motorists yelled obscenities at us.

When we finally met Jun at the parking lot, he handed us a pile of obviously used porter uniforms. "I paid the guy twenty pesos to rent them," he said proudly.

"Does this guy know what you're renting them for?" Delphi asked, crinkling her nose as she daintily held her uniform away.

Jun held up a bootleg 45, the kind they pressed in Hong Kong, in red vinyl. "If I get an autograph, we get a refund."

The Cathay Pacific jet swooped in at half past four. The airport was jam-packed with the biggest crowd I had ever seen in my life: girls in bobby socks and leatherette miniskirts and boys in seersucker shirts, all perspiring and scrunched against a chain-link fence. This was definitely the wrong place to be. As the jet taxied in, we tore ourselves away from the crowd and wormed our way to one of the departure exits, just in time to catch a baggage trolley rattling toward the plane. Jun hopped on, and Delphi and I awkwardly clambered after him. I was afraid Delphi's bobbed hair would spill out of the cap she was wearing and blow our cover. But, having regained her composure, she stood handsomely in the last car, gripping the rail; it was no wonder Jun risked life, limb, and career for her.

The trolley rattled past armored cars, fire trucks, riot squads, and troops of motorcycle police who were wearing special cowboy hats for this occasion. As soon as the trolley cranked to a stop under the jet, Jun hopped off. He was about to head toward the stairs when a limousine careened and cut him off. Three official-looking men dressed in the formal *barong Tagalog* got off the limousine and rushed up to the plane, and what followed was an interminable, bated-breath pause. Jun walked up the stairs and saw the officials arguing with passengers near the plane's exit. Somebody was saying, "Is there a war going on?"

Finally, one official tentatively walked out of the plane. This was enough of a presence to excite the increasingly impatient crowd, and immediately a cacophony of screams burst from the viewing deck. The screams grew louder as other officials and soldiers walked out of the plane. By the time Brian Epstein groggily stepped out, the screaming had reached earsplitting level—no matter that the soldiers surrounded the Beatles from jet to limousine and we caught glimpses of them only through spaces in the cordon sanitaire: George Harrison, his hair tousled by the humid wind, his red blazer flashing like a signal of distress, Ringo Starr in peppermint stripes and flapping foulard, Paul McCartney, round-eyed and baby-faced, and John Lennon, hiding behind dark glasses.

Jun hurried down the stairs and motioned for us to follow him.

"What happened in there?" Delphi asked him.

"I don't know," Jun said. "All I heard was a lot of words your folks wouldn't want you to hear."

"What does that mean?" Delphi asked.

"Nothing we can't find out," said Jun.

The *Manila Times* ran a story about the press conference at the War Room. Jun fumed over his colleague's story, saying, "This idiot did little more than transcribe from a tape." It turned out, however, that the Beatles' replies would be uncannily prophetic.

THE BEATLES! YEAH!
By Bobby Tan

When did you last get a haircut?
In 1933.
Would you be as popular without your long hair?
We can always wear wigs.
How much taxes do you pay?
Too much.
What attracted you to your wives?
Sex.
Do you feel you deserve the Order of the British Empire?
Yeah. But when you're between 20 and 23, there are bound to be some criticisms.
How will you solve the Vietnam War?
Give it back to whoever deserves it.
What's your latest song?
"Philippine Blues."
Mr. Lennon, what did you mean by *Spaniard* in your latest book?
Have you read it?
No.
Then read it.
If there should come a time when you have to choose between the Beatles and your family, whom would you choose?
We never let our families come between us.
What is your favorite song?

"God Save the King."
But it's the Queen now.
"God Save the Queen" then.
What will you be doing ten years from now?
Why bother about ten years from now? We don't even know if we'll be around tomorrow.

On the eve of July 4, Philippine-American Friendship Day, President Ferdinand Marcos urged Filipinos to "recall the lasting and valuable friendship between America and the Philippines" and issued a statement saying a revamp of the government bureaucracy was imminent. "Heads Will Roll!" the dailies shrilled, their bold prediction thrust audaciously by street children against car windows along Highway 54.

At the Quirino Grandstand the next day, the President sat in the sweltering heat as troops paraded before him. Three stations covered the Friendship Day rites, but Channel 5 ignored it completely and ran a twenty-four-hour update on the Beatles. Marcos seethed in the grandstand, and cameras caught the expression on his face that might have said: Damned Trillos, they really get my goat. The Trillos owned the *Manila Times* and many broadcast stations and refused to accommodate First Family whims. But Marcos had the last laugh. On this very afternoon, back at the Palace, Imelda and the children would be having lunch with the Beatles. All television stations and papers had been invited for a five-minute photo opportunity—all, that is, except the Trillo network. Marcos tried to stifle a smirk as he saluted the troops. Proud and dignified in his white suit, he stood out like some sartorial titan: people said you could tell he was going in for a second term.

The calla lilies were brought in at nine by Emma Fernandez, one of the Blue Ladies in Imelda Marcos' retinue. They adorned the corridors of the palace all the way to the formal dining hall, where about a hundred youngsters, ages three to fifteen, listlessly waited for the Beatles. Imee, the eldest of the Marcos children, sporting a new bob-cut hairdo, sat at the head of the table. Irene sat beside her, reticent and uncomfortable in Sunday clothes. Ferdinand Junior, master Bongbong to one and all, was wearing a bowtie and a starched cotton shirt, and his attire apparently made him restless, as he kept sliding off his seat to pace the floor. Around them were children of ministers, generals, business tycoons, and friends of the family, sitting under buntings of red, white, and blue and paper flags of the United States and the Philippines.

Imelda Marcos walked in at exactly eleven. Emma Fernandez approached her, wringing her hands, and whispered in her ear: "They're late!" Imelda brushed her off, an imperceptible smile parting her lips. She kissed the children one by one, Imee dodging and receiving instead a red smear on the ear. She inspected the cutlery, the lilies, the nameplates: two *r*'s for Harrison, yes; two *n*'s for Lennon; and no *a* in Mc. She scanned the room proudly, deflecting the grateful, expectant faces, the small fingers clutching cardboard tickets to the concert.

At half past eleven the children began complaining, so breadsticks and some juice were served. Imelda walked around the hall, stopping to strike a pose for the palace photographers. "Good shot, Madame!" The photographers were the best in the field, plucked out of the newsrooms to accompany her on all her itineraries. They had been sufficiently instructed on which angle to shoot from and which side to take, and anyone who took the wrong shot was dismissed posthaste, his camera and negatives confiscated. The children were more difficult to shoot: bratty and impatient, they always came out pouting, with their chins stuck out. It was always best to avoid them.

Unknown to this gathering, a commotion was going on at the lobby of the Manila Hotel. On hand were Brian Epstein and members of the concert crew; Colonel Justin Flores and Captain Nilo Cunanan of the Philippine Constabulary; Sonny Balatbat, the teenage son of Secretary of State Roberto Balatbat; Captain Fred

Santos of the Presidential Guard; Major Tommy Young and Colonel Efren Morales of the Manila Police District; and local promoter Rene Amos.

"We had an agreement," Colonel Flores was saying. "We sent a telegram to Tokyo."

"I don't know about any fucking telegram," Epstein replied.

"The First Lady and the children have been waiting all morning."

"Nobody told them to wait."

"The First Lady will be very, very disappointed."

Epstein looked the colonel in the eye and said, "If they want to see the Beatles, let them come here."

At the stroke of noon, Imelda Marcos rose from her chair and walked out of the dining hall. "The children can wait," she said, "but I have more important things to do."

As soon as she was gone, Imee pushed back her chair, fished out her ticket, and tore it in two. The other children followed, and for a few seconds there was no sound in the hall but the sound of tickets being torn. Bongbong hovered near the plate that had been reserved for John Lennon. "I really much prefer the Rolling Stones," he said. Photographers caught the young master at that moment, his eyes wide and blank. Imee looked at him and remarked, "The only Beatles song I liked was 'Run for Your Life.'" She looked around the hall defiantly. She had never been so embarrassed in her life. People always said she was an emotional child. That morning she seemed she was about to cry.

The Beatles: Mass Hysteria!
By Jun Hidalgo

Eighty thousand hysterical fans cramped into Rizal Memorial Stadium to watch the Beatles, the largest crowd Manila has seen since the Elorde-Ortiz boxing match in the same stadium.

While traffic snarled to a standstill along Dakota Street, 720 policemen, 35 special detectives and the entire contingent of the Manila Fire Department stood guard as the Liverpool quartet

> performed their hits before thousands of cheering and screaming fans, many of whom had waited to get inside the stadium since early morning.

When the gates finally opened, pandemonium broke loose. I held on to Delphi, who held on to Jun, and the three of us braved the onslaught as we squeezed past security and found ourselves, miraculously intact, on the front row beside the Vox speakers.

"I don't want to sit here," Delphi protested. "We're going to blast our ears off!"

"Relax," Jun said. "Everybody'll be screaming anyway. We have the best seats in the house."

Everyone in the stadium was a mop-head, except the Vietnam volunteers sitting in our row, whose heads had been cleanly shaved; they were young men plucked from the provinces, and many of them were never coming home again. I was so relieved I had grown my hair longer that summer. My hair was a clear sign that, despite my young age, I had gained honorary membership in the exclusive cabal of this generation. You could tell who the pigs were: they were the ones who roamed around, their ears pink and their heads shaved clean like the Vietnam volunteers. Some of them had guns tucked into their belts; they had been warned that a riot could break out.

> Soaked in sweat, Beatles fans impatiently heckled the opening acts, and emcees had to threaten the crowd that the Beatles would not perform until the audience simmered down.

And when the Beatles finally opened with "I Wanna Be Your Man," you could feel the excitement ripping through you, a detonation of such magnitude your entire being seemed to explode. I couldn't hear anything except a long, extended shrill—the whole stadium screaming its lungs out. I looked at Delphi. She was holding her head between her hands and her eyes were bulging out and her mouth was stretched to an *O*, and all I could hear was this long, high-pitched scream coming out of her mouth. I had never seen Delphi like that before, and I would never, for the rest of her life, see her as remorselessly young as she was that afternoon.

The morning after the concert, Jun asked Delphi if we could take the Ford to Manila Hotel.

"Why do you have to take us along?" Delphi asked him. It was clear that for her the concert had been the high point of our adventure.

"We still have to get that interview, don't we?" Jun reminded her. "Besides," he added, "I need you to cover for me," Jun said.

"Cover?" asked Delphi. "As in war?"

"Looks like war it's going to be," said Jun.

I was going to pose as a bellhop. Delphi was going to be a chambermaid. Jun had bribed someone from room service to let him take a snack to the Beatles. Apparently our plan was to swoop down on them in the name of impeccable service, with Jun secretly recording this invasion with the help of a pocket-sized tape recorder. As usual, he had the uniforms ready, rented for the day for half his month's wages. "The hotel laundry boy's a childhood friend of mine."

"You're the company you keep," Delphi teased him, because she knew it tortured him whenever she did that.

I wore the monkey suit perfectly, but somehow it still didn't feel right. I looked at myself in the men's room mirror and knew I was too young for the role. And Delphi looked incongruous as the chambermaid: her bob cut was too *in*. As it turned out, all my misgivings would be proven true. We crossed the lobby to the service elevator. Jun walked several paces ahead of us, nonchalantly jiggling the car keys, but I kept glancing nervously around.

"*Hoy,* where you going?"

Jun didn't seem to hear the house detective call us, or maybe the detective didn't notice him walking past. I felt a hand grab my collar and pull me aside. Immediately, Delphi was all over the detective, hitting him with her fists: "You take your hands off my brother or I'll kick your teeth in!" Struggling out of the detective's arm hold, I could see Jun hesitating by the elevator. I motioned for him to go. The detective dragged Delphi and me out to a backroom where several other detectives were playing poker. "*Oy*, got two more right here!"

As he recalled later, Jun wheeled the tray into Suite 402 expecting to find telltale debris of a postconcert party (and hence an excuse for us to mop up). What he came upon was something less festive.

"Compliments of the house, sir," he announced cheerfully as he came in.

George Harrison and Brian Epstein were sitting on the sofa, and Paul McCartney was precariously perched on the TV set, brooding. The three of them apparently had been having an argument and they all looked up, surprised, at the intruder.

"All right," Epstein said, curtly. "Bring it in."

"I'll have to mix the dip here, sir," Jun said, to prolong the intrusion. "House specialty."

Nobody seemed to hear him. George Harrison continued the conversation, "We came here to sing. We didn't come here to drink tea and shake hands."

"That's precisely the reason we've got to pay customs the bond for the equipment," said Epstein.

"Let them keep the money then," Paul said. "Everyone says here come those rich mop-heads to make more money. We don't care about the money."

"We didn't even want to come here," George reminded them.

"The only reason we came here," added Paul, "was because these people were always saying why don't you come over here? We didn't want to offend anyone, did we? We just came here to sing. You there," indicating Jun, who jumped with surprise. "Do you speak English?"

"Fairly well," replied Jun.

"Does the government control the press here, as they do the customs people, the airport managers, and the police?"

"Not yet," said Jun.

Paul then observed that everything was "so American in this country, it's eerie, man!" He also remarked that many people were exploited by a wealthy and powerful few. Epstein wanted to know how he knew that, as the others had simply not heard of the country before, and Paul replied that he had read one of the local papers.

"What are we supposed to do?" he asked. "Show up and say, 'Well, here we are, we're sorry we're late!' We weren't supposed to be here in the first place. Why should we apologize for something that's not our fault?"

At that point John Lennon and Ringo Starr, who had been booked in the adjacent suite, walked in. Ringo, sweating and tousled, plopped into the sofa between Epstein and George Harrison. John Lennon, wearing his dark glasses, walked straight to the window and looked out. "We've got a few things to learn about the Philippines," he said. "First of all is how to get out."

The Manila Hotel detectives deftly disposed of Delphi and me with a push via the back door, where a sign said THROUGH THIS DOOR PASS THE MOST COURTEOUS EMPLOYEES OF MANILA. We walked back to the Ford in the parking lot and waited for less than an hour when Jun, struggling out of the hotel uniform and back to mufti, sprinted toward us and hopped into the driver's seat. "Get in!" he shouted. "We're going to the airport!"

"Did you get the interview?" Delphi asked.

"Better," Jun said. "The Beatles are going to try to leave this afternoon. They're paying something like forty-five thousand dollars as a bond or something. Customs is charging them so much money in taxes for the concert."

"Wait a minute," Delphi protested. "Is that legal?"

"Who cares?" Jun said. "All I know is they're paying the bond and now all they want to do is to get out. But they think something's going to happen at the airport. There's been talk of arrest and detention."

"Who said that?" Delphi asked.

"John Lennon, I think. I don't know. I was mixing that stupid dip."

We were driving toward the south highway now, past the mammoth hulls of ships docked at Manila Bay. "You know all those people who've been trying to get the Beatles to go to the palace? You know why they were so keen on bringing the band over to Madame's luncheon?"

"Can't waste all that food, right?" Delphi said.

"Bright girl, but no. There's going to be a major revamp soon. It's all over the papers, if you've been reading. All these guys are going to get the top posts. Well, most of them were, until the Beatles screwed everything up. "

"What guys? Who?"

"That Colonel Fred Santos, the one who led the group to talk to Epstein, he's being groomed to head the Presidential Guard. Real heavy-duty position, accompanying the First Family all over the world, luxury apartment at the Palace, the works. There's one Colonel Flores, Justin Flores I think, who's bound to be chief of the constabulary. Then there's Colonel Efren Morales, most likely head of the Manila Police."

"But these are junior officers," Delphi said. "Marcos can't just promote them to top posts."

"That's the point. Marcos is going to bypass everybody and build up an army of his own. All these new guys will be licking his boots and there's nothing the generals can do about it. That young mophead, the son of Balatbat, he was there for his father, who's going to be reappointed secretary of state. And if I'm not mistaken, Salvador Roda, the airport manager, wants to take over customs. The man's going to be a millionaire, kickbacks and all."

"How do you know all that?" Delphi demanded.

"Homework," Jun said, swerving the car toward the airport, his reply drowned out by the droning of jets. "I'm the best damned reporter in the city, and everybody's going to find out why."

Salvador Roda was briefing the press agitatedly at the VIP lounge of the airport that afternoon, explaining why the republic was withdrawing security for the Beatles and why customs had slapped a hundred-thousand-peso tax on Liverpudlian income. "Too much Filipino money wasted on such a paltry entourage, gentlemen of the press, and not one centavo of the profits going to the nation. *Puta,* where's the sense in that?"

We walked up the escalators to the second floor to change into our porter uniforms, which we had lugged in backpacks.

"This airport gets worse everytime I come here," Delphi complained. "Nothing's working."

"And there's nobody around," observed Jun. The entire second floor was deserted. "Lucky for us," he said, pushing Delphi into the ladies' room and then pulling me into the adjoining gents'. We changed into the uniforms and stuffed our clothes above the water tanks.

"You think there's going to be trouble?" I asked Jun.

"Will you guys back out if I told you there might?"

I had to give that some thought. In the past Jun had taken Delphi and me on some insane adventures, mostly juvenile pranks that left us breathlessly exhilarated, but with no real sense of danger. For the first time I was afraid we were up against something, well, real.

"We'll stick around," I said, tentatively.

He put his arm around me and said, "*Kapatid!* That's my brother!"

July 5, 2 P.M. The Beatles arrived at the airport in a Manila Hotel taxi. They weren't wasting any time. They ran straight up the escalators, their crew lugging whatever equipment they could carry. At the foot of the escalators a group of women—society matrons and young college girls—had managed to slip past the deserted security posts and, seeing the Beatles arrive, they lunged for the group, screaming and tearing at the band's clothes. Flashbulbs blinded the band as photographers crowded at the top of the stairs. It would have taken a miracle for the band to tear themselves away from the mob and to reach, as they did in a bedraggled way, the only booth open for passport clearance, where Roda had been waiting with the manifest for Flight CX 196.

"Beatles here!" he hollered imperiously, and the band followed his voice meekly, almost contritely. Behind the booth a crowd that had checked in earlier restlessly ogled.

"Those aren't passengers," Jun observed as we stole past a booth. "They look like the people we saw earlier with Roda."

"Beatles out!" Roda boomed.

And then something happened. As the Beatles and their crew filed past the booth, the crowd that had been waiting there seemed to swell like a wave and engulfed the band, pulling them into an undertow of fists and knee jabs. There was a thud—Epstein falling groggily, then being dragged to his feet by security police. Someone was cursing in Tagalog: *Heto'ng sa 'yo bwakang inang putang inang tarantado ka!* Paul McCartney surfaced for air, his chubby face crunched in unmistakable terror. He pulled away from the crowd, and the other three staggered behind him. Somebody gave Ringo Starr a loud whack on the shoulder and pulled at John Lennon, who yanked his arm away, tearing his coat sleeve.

That was when we started running after them—the three of us, and the whole mob.

The crowd overtook Delphi, who was shoved aside brusquely. They were inching in on me when the exit doors flew out into the searing afternoon. From the viewdeck hundreds of fans who had been waiting for hours started screaming. The band clambered up the plane. I kept my eye on the plane, where Jun was already catching up with John Lennon.

"Please, Mr. Lennon," he pleaded. "Let me help you with your bags!"

At the foot of the stairs a panting John Lennon turned to him and said, "A friendly soul, for a change. Thanks, but we're leaving."

"I'm sorry," Jun said, trembling.

John Lennon made to bolt up the stairs. At the top he stopped and took off his coat and threw it down to Jun. "Here," he said. "Tell your friends the Beatles gave it to you."

• • •

A few weeks after the Beatles' frantic egress from Manila, Taal Volcano erupted, perhaps by way of divine castigation, as happens often in that inscrutable, illogical archipelago. The eruption buried three towns and shrouded Manila in sulfuric ash for days. A month later a lake emerged from what had been the volcano's crater—a boiling, putrefied, honey-yellow liquefaction.

The Beatles flew to New Delhi, where they were to encounter two figures that would change their lives and music: the corpulent, swaying Maharishi, and the droning, mesmerizing sitar. Back in London later, they were greeted by a swarm of fans carrying placards with mostly one message:

SOD MANILA!

Manila's columnists took umbrage, and the side of the offended First Lady. Said Teodoro Valencia, who would later become the spokesman of the Marcos press: "Those Beatles are knights of the Crown of England. Now we have a more realistic understanding of what knights are. They're snobs. But we are probably more to blame than the Beatles. We gave them too much importance." And columnist Joe Guevarra added: "What if 80,000 people saw the Beatles? They're too young to vote against Marcos anyway!"

Imelda Marcos later announced to the lavishly sympathetic press that the incident "was regrettable. This has been a breach of Filipino hospitality." She added that when she heard of a plot to maul the Beatles, she herself asked her brother and her tourism secretary to make sure the Beatles got out of the airport safely.

But the virulence of anti-Beatles sentiment would not be assuaged by her magnanimity. The *Manila Bulletin* declared that Malacañang Palace had received no less than two hundred letters denouncing the Beatles by that weekend. Manila councilor Gerino Tolentino proposed that the Beatles "should be banned from the city in perpetuity." Caloocan City passed an ordinance prohibiting the sale, display, and playing of Beatles records. And Quezon City passed a law declaring Beatles music satanic and the mop-head hairstyle illegal.

Jun Hidalgo wrote his story about the Beatles' departure, with insider quotes taped, as an editor's introduction to the story revealed, "while undercover as a hotel employee." A few weeks later he was accepted into the *Manila Times,* where he played rookie, as was the custom then, in the snakepit of the local press: the police beat. He gave John Lennon's coat to Delphi, who dutifully mended the sleeve, and they went steady for a while. But like most youthful relationships, the series of melodramatic misunderstandings, periodic separations, and tearful reunions finally ended in tears and many unprintable words. My sister, older and more healthily cynical, later immigrated to the United States, from where she sent me postcards and books—and once, a note replying to one of my continuous requests for records, saying she had lost interest in the Beatles when they went psychedelic. I myself, being the obligatory late bloomer, only then began to appreciate the magical, mysterious orchestrations and raga-like trances of the band.

Delphi left John Lennon's coat with me and I became known in school as the keeper of a holy relic, and, like the martyrs, I was the object of much admiration and also much envy. One afternoon, armed with a copy of an ordinance recently passed in Manila, directors of the school rounded up several mop-head boys, including myself. In one vacant classroom we were made to sit on hardboard chairs as the directors snipped our hair. I sat stolidly under the scissors, watching my hair fall in clutchfuls on the bare cement floor. Back in my room that evening I stared at myself in the mirror for a long time. Then I folded John Lennon's jacket tightly, stuffed it in a box, and tucked it under my books and clothes. I felt no bitterness at all. I knew that something irrevocable in my life had ended.

Playland

Richard Foerster

The 8-track clicked through tunes as we two
cruised from heady Bronxville down to Rye
in my '66 eggshell blue
Volkswagen. Jesuit-schooled, I tried

to be all a Catholic girl would want:
left hand suavely at the wheel; right hand
on her knee; plus bon-vivant
banter and *The Lonely Hearts Club Band.*

We joined the paired and wholesome troops
beneath the razzled night
and shrieked through Cyclone loop-the-loops,
then braved the hokey House of Frights,

but when my student's budget failed
we walked the dark along the shore.
There the steady obligato of the male
swelled above the fun park's roar.

We sat by rocks and listened to the Sound's
clouded water lap, then clamber
and withdraw. I cupped her breast, wound
a finger through her hair. My tongue remembered

silent speech, but soon she pushed
my lips away and pointed with surprise:
Everywhere were phosphorescent fish,
a thousand up-turned saintly eyes.

489 East 11th, Apt. 3C

for Emily

Pam Bernard

Cabbies dropped us at 14th and Avenue A,
refusing to drive into the neighborhood.
Roaches crawled on our toothbrushes.
How we loved that apartment.

We'd mimic the whiney voice
of our landlord in his bad black toupee,
the neighborhood men's dreamy rage—
stalking, on the hottest summer evenings,

some potent idea of themselves—the cats'
lewd and pitiable cries. We walked
thirty-five blocks to the Chelsea Theater
for the Beatles double feature,

returning night after night until
we'd been there nineteen times—the man
in the ticket booth never once looked up—
memorized every word of both films

and clowned the parts on the subway home.
Sunk into our busted velvet sofa,
like the fleshy pulp of some great red fruit,
we'd spread the map of the world between us,

calculate the distance to everywhere else.
And when you touched my breasts
something in me let go—
the sad work of my childhood over.

relax and float downstream

Thank God for the Beatles

Timothy Leary

Obeisances to the Four Divine Gurus.

Believe me, beloved Psalmists, this essay is no attempt to dissect, analyze, explain that unfolding, mysterious power that the middle-aged mind cannot understand. I will not patronize the God that laughs out of the eyes of the young.

This essay is a logical exercise designed to prove that the Beatles are Divine Messiahs. The wisest, holiest, most effective avatars (Divine Incarnate, God Agents) that the human race has yet produced.

My thesis is a simple one. I declare that John Lennon, George Harrison, Paul McCartney, and Ringo Starr are mutants. Prototypes of a new young race of laughing freemen. Evolutionary agents sent by God, endowed with mysterious power to create a new human species.

"You" are surprised by this effulgence? (Footnote: The term "you" as used in this essay refers to the editor, the publisher, and anyone else who reads this essay from the standpoint of secular perspective. I am usually "you.")

Why should you be surprised? What in God's name do you expect from the Beatles? What do you want me to expect from them? Shall I see them as pitiful wretches less wise than me? Robot figures to be pushed around the chessboard of my self-enhancement? Should I, can I use the Beatles for my own purposes?

Let me admit, straight off, that I do not limit my celestial expectations to the Beatles. I continually hope that *everyone* I meet will turn out to be a Divine Agent, will turn me on to a deeper revelation. With, perhaps, one penetrating glance.

People continually disappoint me. Each new person I meet sets about immediately and ruthlessly to hide his divinity behind frowns and narrowed looks. I look in his eyes and silently beg him to lay off. Are you testing me? Is this some code? Are you putting me on, God?

Don't get me wrong. I'm not complaining. No, sir. I'm going to stick by my system. It's like long-shot gambling, I'm going to hold out for the big winning ticket. The system is bound to work. Later, or perhaps, now, sooner, the Divine Messenger is gonna appear. It's that terrible, awful truth that you catch on to after a while. Everyone gets what he desires. The relentless fact of karma. You get what you desire.

I desire only that this planet earth be taken over by laughing young messiahs who will dispel fear and hook us back into the dance of harmony. Is that a long-shot gamble? Is it any wilder than the ambition of an uneducated Texas schoolteacher to become President? Perseverance furthers. Keep betting and you'll hit your lucky number. But, for God's sake, be careful what you desire.

I have watched the Beatles now for five years hoping that their divinity would continue to prosper. They have never disappointed me. So far they have given me no reason to doubt their revelation. Can you point to any major action on their part that could not be divine?

Now if you were born before 1940 you might think that this is foolish talk. Too bad. If you were born before 1940 you might find it very difficult to understand the Beatles. The genetic gulf, the generation gap, cannot be exaggerated. The abyss between the pre-forties and the post-forties is inconceivably great. The possibility of communication, of dialogue, grows daily more interspecies. Is it possible that we who are writing these essays about the Beatles will produce a book that the Beatles can only laugh at kindly, the way Christ would laugh at the sermons of Billy Graham or the preachings of Cardinal Spellman?

The key to the generation gap is this: old dependable stasis versus young flowing change.

The virtues of the old mechanical, Newtonian age were dependability, uniformity, practicality, consistency. Efficient work. You were frozen into nationality, class, race, profession. Know your place. Limits. Limits. You are locked into one space-time, lifelong-tailored suit. Hey, keep still! Don't rock the boat! You can't do that! The machine don't like that changing around.

What you were at 15 you are at 65.

The Taoist virtue of the post-forties is cool centeredness. Can you keep your head while all about you has exploded into a space-shattering, time-fissioning, multichannel, Day-Glo, multimedia, multiphonic, kaleidoscopic dance of vibrations? And then, as the pace hurtles faster, can you let go, lose your head smiling, serene, confident in the ever-changing, all-moving, basically, essentially good? No limits. No boundaries. The affluence of internal power. You literally *can* do anything you want. With the help of your friends.

Here is my vision about the Beatles.

It starts in God's mind. Continually in touch with the planet earth. Sees the suffering and rigor mortis of mechanization. The metallurgic cancer. Decides it's time to reincarnate as a Divine Agent.

Wait a moment. We run into semantic problems here. You don't believe in God, reincarnation, and Divine Agents?

Good. Here we have stumbled on a basic difference that divides the generations. The young revolution today is a religious renaissance. Turned-on kids believe in a living, down-to-earth God because it's more fun than being an atheist or a humanist. God? Superior intelligence that designs and operates the whole business. The DNA code is its agent. The fact of the matter is that it's a twenty-four-carat stone gas to believe in a celestial conspiracy. A simple trick of faith that immediately charges everything you see and do with multiple meaning. Believing in God is a mind-blower, baby. The cosmic mystery thriller. Do you prefer to believe that the ultimate power you can conceive of resides in Washington, or Moscow, or in the secret English tobacco cartel, or in a bunch of Swiss bankers? We are limited only by the poverty of our paranoias. Think very big, baby.

And reincarnation. The turned-on kids today tend to accept the theory of endless rebirth. Again, it's more fun, it's more graceful, it's more modest, it's more aesthetic to believe in the Cosmic Theater to which we repeatedly return to play our parts. Do you really prefer to believe in one divine person 2000 years ago or a clockwork, Darwinian, one-shot struggle for survival? Or maybe you'd rather not think about the whole thing. But the turned-on kids are thinking about it because there's nothing better to think about. Is there?

Okay. Put yourself, if you will, in God's place. Christ! What a mess down there! Time for another avatar. Another Divine intervention to loosen things up and restore the beauty and laughter and harmony of the natural order. You gotta come back down and cool out the feverish planet. How to do it this time?

First of all, to whom do you appear? That's obvious. To the Romans or the Americans or whatever the rulers of the machine-empire call themselves today.

And in what form do you appear? Do you drop, full-grown, from a spaceship? Incarnate, incandescent in a pool of blinding light? Careful, now. You are God coming back in human form. Remember the rules. You made them yourself. You gotta manage to fuse the single DNA strands of a healthy male and female within the maternal body. Choose a womb and then the genetic-coded instructions begin to unfold like a cellular teletype machine chattering out the amino-acid instructions.

Choose a congenial womb in a country related to but not part of the dying empire. Canada? England! Excellent!

Of course you have to wait for twelve years. Patiently learn the rudiments of the primitive language and culture. Study the customs. Learn all you can from Mary and Joseph. Locate the holy underground. Prepare to act when the time is right.

Whom do you address? Do you walk right up to the White House, the Vatican, the UN building on First Avenue, you, the teenage visionary ready to confound the elders by the announcement of your mission? Never! Your genetic-coded instructions warn you that a direct, open announcement to the power holders will burn down your scene right in front. Tell the bosses of the establishment that you're a Divine Messenger come to cool things out and they'll wipe you out with one reflex swipe.

So whom do you address? Who are the key people who will listen to the revelation, open up to it, eager for it? Who won't kill you or imprison you for declaring the joyful news that this is the Garden of Eden right here and now? Obvious. The adolescents. The arising suns. The teenyboppers. Zap them with the word before their minds are frozen, while they are still fresh, trembling, alive. Then, once you've contacted them, grow with them, tenderly nurture their blossoming wisdom. In ten years the planetary mutation will have been accomplished.

And how do you announce the revelation to the fresh flower heads? Proclamations? Nope. Pass laws and resolutions? Nope. Books? Nope.

You use music. The mythic voice of the epic minstrel. Sing it. The old refrain. In tune.

And what about the mathematics of it? If you come down to run a number, what is the number?

Four thousand years ago it was the duality. Krishna-Rhadha. Yin-Yang. Siva-Sakti. The Blessed Union of the Divine Couple. Two. The twin serpents. The Seal of Solomon. The maha-mudra.

Then came the single-messiah trip. The model for the last 2000 years has been the lonely lightbulb. The single candle. Odd man out. One. Three. Five. Seven. Nine. Eleven. Thirteen. The only Son. Jesus, Mary, and Joseph. The Holy Trinity. The thirteen reduced by the cops to eleven.

This time let's do it in even numbers. Let's bring back the balance.

You see, the odd-number trip is unbalanced. The equilibrium thrown off into bizarre, exciting thrusts of eccentricity. The father-son trip. The power trip. God the celibate machine. Machines don't mate. There are no happily married Christian saints. It's not Jesus and Mary Magdalene. It's not St. Patrick and St. Bridget arm in arm, loin to loin.

The Life Mantra of this next time has got to be DNA. Watson and his girl, *au pair*, and Crick and his wife, *au pair.* The magic number is four. The Sacred Quartet. Guanine. Cytosine. Thymine. Adenine.

(Footnote: Rosemary says that I should explain this reference. Watson and Crick cracked the secret of life by deciphering the language of the DNA code. In their long, frustrating struggle to figure it all out they perfectly recapitulated in their own personal lives the structural evolution of the DNA code itself. At first there were the three of them: Dr. Crick, Mrs. Crick, and Dr. Watson. Their theory that the DNA code was a triple strand just didn't pay off. Watson, a bachelor, sat night after night shivering in an ill-heated room thinking about the structure of the DNA code and wishing that he had a nice warm girl. Thus it had to be that it was the frustrated, lonely, twenty-three-year-old Watson [and not the calm, wise, kindly, sexagenarian grandfather Linus Pauling] who caught on to the obvious fact [any Hindu or Buddhist Tantric could have told him] that the life game is played in even numbers. A double-intertwined serpent coil—itself based on four essence-paired units: guanine, cytosine, thymine, and adenine—otherwise known in human form as Dr. and Mrs. Crick and Dr. and Mrs. [newly married] Watson. May the four of them be blessed with many children. And the four Beatles two. Two-four-six-eight . . . this is the way we mutate.) Upon these Holy Four we shall build our multifoliate double-helix church.

Then with a clap of electronic lightning the Beatles are born. The Liverpool quartet. The living pool four. The four-sided mandala, the four-petaled lotus. Each with His mate. Laughing octet. Ready to multiply.

Over the electric noosphere of the global village comes the first message. They want to hold our hand. Yay. Yay. Yay. They love us. Yay. Yay. It's all young, and good and fun. And they love us.

Are they really Divine Agents? How can anyone know? What's the criterion?

Miracles, of course.

And so it came to pass that in one year the Four Evangelists, brash, uneducated carpenters' sons from Liverpool, became the most powerful VOICES the world has ever listened to.

Holy minstrels. Electronic instruments of the divine current.

The first message. Yes. Yes. Yay. Yay. Love. Dispel fear. Yes. Laugh. Yay. Yay.

Then comes the first public ordeal. The test. What do they do with this power? Do they become successful, career-oriented, ambitious showbiz stars? Culture heroes—living out the material dreams of the rest of us? Cadillacs and swimming pools and yachts? Pop stars or messiahs?

Did the Beatles use their power like the minstrels of last year? Bing Crosby, genial owner of a chain of corporations? Elvis Presley, leather upholstered? Frank Sinatra smashing golf carts through plate glass windows of gambling casinos at Las Vegas? Nelson Eddy singing the National Anthem at the World Series?

No. The Beatles flow with the evolutionary current and it's flowing fast.

There came that time when every promoter and hustler in the world wanted to get the Beatles to endorse their product. Man, it's worth a few million dollars to get the Beatles to endorse your beer or your soap. Sign 'em up, offer them anything. What do they want?

Then comes the first endorsement. The first message to the millions of followers. Do as we do. We don't drive Cadillacs or have golf tournaments named after us. We turn on!

Hey! Stop the presses. The Beatles have come out for, wait a minute, oh no! Psychedelic drugs! LSD! They want to legalize marijuana! They want to turn us on!

Please notice the incredible neurological power that the psychedelic rock group has available. Electronic equipment does to the hand musical instrument what the machine did to the horse-drawn buggy. The electronic recording studio makes it possible to take any sound that man has ever produced by hand and complicate it infinitely in volume and quality. What was a simple vibration of air becomes the center of a network of electrical pulsation. The listening eardrum trembles to, and becomes one with, an interstellar harmony of new tonics.

The *Sgt. Pepper* album, for example, compresses the evolutionary development of musicology and much of the history of Eastern and Western sound in a new tympanic complexity.

Then add psychedelic drugs. Millions of kids turned on pharmacologically, listening to stoned-out electronic music designed specifically for the suggestible, psychedelicized nervous system by stoned-out, long-haired minstrels.

This combination of electrical-pharmacological expansion is the most powerful brainwashing device our planet has ever known. Indeed, if you were an observer from a more highly evolved planet wondering how to change human psychology and human cultural development (in other words, if you were a Divine Messenger), would you not inevitably combine electrical energies from outside with biochemical catalysts inside to accomplish your mutation?

The stereophonic machine plus psychedelics (and throw in an acid-light show for good measure) provides an instrument for evangelic education, propaganda that few people over the age of thirty comprehend. And the message of the Beatles, the Rolling Stones, Country Joe, the Grateful Dead, and the Moody Blues is revolutionary.

Do you get the picture? The Beatles and the Stones goofing around all night in a London studio, high on attar and arranging rhythms and psychedelic lyrics to be picked up by millions of teenagers goofing around, lying down opened up like exultant flowers in their rooms. And Mom and Dad in the parlor drinking martinis and wondering about the smiling serenity of the kids. The quiet conspiracy of the turned-on young.

They get high with the help of their friends. They found God in acid. They're on the religious trip and there's no Madison Avenue mileage from acid and no advertising budget for the grass industry. They are telling us to relax. Turn off our minds. Float downstream. This is not dying. They'd love to turn us on. No golf carts and no Academy Awards. It's beyond all that. They must be mad. They'll never sell an album. It's the old reincarnation merry-go-round of Mr. K. and Mr. H. The act we've known for all these years. And they're selling more albums than ever. They've been in and out of style for a long, long while. The Beatles receiving intimations of immortality. We're more popular than Jesus, said John. And most priests and ministers had to agree. They'd like to take us home with them. They hope that we will dig their song. It's the one and only message with a new rock beat. Turn on. Tune in and . . .

Drop out! Wait a minute! First the Beatles dropped out of cute mop-top pop stardom and now they're dropping out of drugs. They're laying down a new revelation. The journey to the East.

George is humbling stumbling at the feet of Ravi Shankar. Ringo's wearing Hindu beads. They're all meditating with the Maharishi. They're off drugs and into mantras. A hundred million youngsters are suddenly asking, What's meditation? and What's satori? and What's reincarnation? and Where can you find a guru? and How do you get a mantra? and Can you really get high from praying?

The Beatles have endorsed disciplined yoga. Oh, no, baby, it's not just pop-a-pill and find God. It's the ancient, mysterious process of the spiritual search, perplexing, paradoxical, demanding. There are dozens of complex yogas developed by God-seekers over the centuries and the Heavenly Quartet has cut out on the pilgrimage, started the yoga of diet, of mantra, of obedience to the guru, of humble renunciation.

Far out! In 1966 the Beatles at the pinnacle of fame and influence threw it all over to sit at the feet of a little, bearded, brown man who might be able to teach them something about God. The Search for the Miraculous. It's the unmistakable mark of a turned-on Divine Messenger that he continually humbles himself in search of a more Direct Connection. (Footnote: The difficult position of the turned-on Divine Agent on this planet has rarely been appreciated. He's like a spaceship traveler from another galaxy dropped here millennia ago, the return ship centuries overdue, separated from the other members of the crew, the original mission instructions half forgotten. The hipper you are, the wiser you are, the more eager you are to contact anyone who might be from your ship, someone who might have a fresher memory of the original plan. Hello, Maharishi. We want to believe in you. Take us to your leader.) Do you want to find God's Agent? Don't look on the episcopal throne or even around the church. Search for the fellow who is sitting looking up into the faces of children, studying the clouds, or little

Hindu holy men. Or wandering up the dusty trail to Rishikesh.

The Beatles and the Maharishi. Cosmic confrontation. But who is the guru? Who is sent to teach whom? What?

The first rule of the God-seeker game is that all the secular game rules are reversed. In the interaction between guru and disciple it is the guru who learns the most. The Beatles were sent to the Maharishi *to teach him* and all other Indian mystics and saddhus and Western seekers after the wisdom of the East that if you keep traveling east you'll end up back home where you started from. The planet is round.

There comes a time in the spiritual growth of the seeker when the direction points east. Walk to the sun. When you go east you are really going past. *Orient* means ancient. A voyage to India is a trip down the time tunnel. Take it, by all means. But don't get caught in the history tube. There comes a time to . . . drop out again.

You realize that the past teaches us how to face the future and, indeed, create the future. Thanks for the trip, Maharishi. Thanks for showing us your way. Thanks, old friend. Are you going to come along with us to the future?

So the Beatles return to the twentieth century.

Where are they going next?

In July 1968, Rosemary and I went to a Hollywood party in the enormous, rambling motel-mansion that the Beatles one time rented. We wandered around the plastic chambers—thick-carpeted, rarewood rooms. The house was built by a contractor. Get it? A television singing star was the host. He came over to talk. Looked nervous. I looked him in the eye and said, I'm glad to meet you. I'm prepared to accept you as one of the wisest, most influential men in the world. He turned me down. Flat. He became irritable. Started to explain that you have to keep in with the establishment or you'll lose your effectiveness. Timothy, you've blown it. Sorry about that. You should have stayed at Harvard and become the scientific authority. I become depressed. I know that TV star is from the spaceship. How could he have forgotten?

Later, in the acre-wide motel kitchen I meet Benny Shapiro. Twinkling, wise Levantine philosopher. Benny knows the Beatles.

"Benny. Where are the Beatles at?"

Benny nodded sagely and pulled at his GI Gurdjieff mustache. Meetings with remarkable men. "The Beatles are right there."

"Right where?"

"They are the most powerful force in the world. And they know it. They know they can determine how things go."

"But where are they?"

By this point Benny is sitting cross-legged in his Sufi rug shop, a multicolored tent in the Casbah. Candlelight flickering across his face. "The Beatles are together. Together as a group and together in their heads."

YOUNG JESSE KRISHNA IS DRIVING ROSEMARY AND ME DOWN FROM THE MOUNTAIN PARADISE TO THE DESERT TO VISIT A NAVAHO HOGAN. BY THE TIME WE COME DOWN TO THE DESERT WE ARE HIGH, HIGH, HIGH. WE END UP DRIVING AIMLESSLY FOR HOURS THROUGH THE SACRED DESERT. HOPILAND. SKY. STARS. SPACE. SAND. CACTI. SPACESHIPS SIGNALLING. A WEIRD DANTE TRIP. LOST. WE STOP THE CAR AND GET OUT AND LIE SPREAD-EAGLED ON THE MACADAM ROAD. DRIVING HOME I CONFESS TO JESSE MY DILEMMA. MY NAME IS LINKED TO LSD. LSD IS THE FIRST PROTOTYPE PSYCHEDELIC TEACHER. A DIVINE GIFT. THE FIRST CRUDE BOOK IN THE LIBRARY OF THE FUTURE. THERE HAS NEVER BEEN ANY DOUBT IN MY MIND THAT PSYCHEDELIC DRUGS WILL BE THE KEY SPIRITUAL INSTRUMENT OF THE FUTURE. WE ARE ABOUT TO WITNESS IN 1969–70 A POSITIVE BACKLASH FROM THE ANTI-ECSTASY PROGRAM. A CALM ACCEPTANCE OF TURNING ON. THIS MEANS THAT THERE IS A FAIR-TO-GOOD PROBABILITY THAT MY NAME WILL BE ASSOCIATED WITH A SACRAMENT THAT WILL CHANGE HUMAN DESTINY MORE THAN ANY SACRAMENT IN THE PAST. LSD IS THAT EXPONENTIALLY DIFFERENT. THIS MEANS THAT THERE IS A GAMBLING CHANCE THAT WE ARE INVOLVED IN LEGENDARY, MYTHIC, BIBLICAL DRAMAS. THERE HAS PROBABLY NEVER BEEN A GROUP IN HUMAN HISTORY MORE CONSCIOUS, SPECIFICALLY AWARE, OF THE IMPLICATIONS OF WHAT WE ARE DOING FOR THE SPIRITUAL FUTURE OF THE RACE. ANY LITTLE CHANGE WE INTRODUCE COULD

WELL DETERMINE THE RITUAL PRACTICES AND MYTHS OF BILLIONS OF PEOPLE TO COME. WE HAVE A SPORTING CHANCE OF BECOMING GODS THE CREATOR. WHEN THE HUMAN BEING REALIZES WITH A GASP THE PRECARIOUS NATURE OF HIS NEUROLOGICAL EQUIPMENT AND THE EFFECT OF CONDITIONING UPON HIS ONTOLOGY, HE DISCOVERS, READY OR NOT, THAT HE CREATES THE UNIVERSE, CONSTRUCTS REALITY. EVERYTHING HAPPENS BECAUSE WE WANT IT TO HAPPEN. EVERYTHING WE SEE IS A HOLLYWOOD STAGE SET DESIGNED BY AND FOR US. AT THE MOMENT OF THIS REALIZATION ONE DIES AS A MAN AND IS REBORN AS A GOD. AWFUL POWER. I WILL GET WHAT I DESIRE. I DESIRE THAT THE BEATLES BE DIVINE TEACHERS. THAT THEY LEAD THE WORLD INTO THE AQUARIAN AGE. THAT THEY ACCEPT AND USE THEIR POWER. THAT THEY CREATE A NEW REALITY BASED ON HUMOR, HARMONY, BEAUTY. THAT THEY BECOME THE BEAD GAME MASTERS OF A NEW DESIGN FOR LIVING. AND THAT THIS HOLY QUARTET BUILD INTO THE NEW GOD GAME THE ELEMENT OF SURPRISE. THAT THEY CONTINUALLY UP-LEVEL THEMSELVES, AMAZE THEMSELVES, FREAK THEMSELVES OUT, HUMBLE THEMSELVES, AND EVENTUALLY CONSTRUCT THOSE TENDER TENDRILS OF GROWTH THAT WILL ALLOW THEM TO PASS ON THEIR GODHOOD, INVISIBLE, GRACEFUL, TO THE NEXT YOUNG FORCE THAT EMERGES.

The television star party was fading out, but I kept hanging around Benny. It was his birthday and he was high on love and rebirth.

"The situation is like this. The Beatles learned from the Maharishi that the guru is within. They've accepted this fact. They've got a hundred and fifty million dollars at their immediate disposal and another hundred and fifty million available. They know they are the most powerful single force in the world."

"What are they going to do?"

"They have passed out the word through the underground and in press conferences and even in newspaper ads. They are inviting anyone in the world who has a celestial vision, a creative plan, to send it to them and, if it's Apple, they'll back it."

"Apple?"

"Yeah, you know, Apple. 'A' is for Apple. 'B' is for ball."

"You mean the Garden of Eden?"

"Why not?"

Apple. This time we can write it different. How did the old vision read?

> Genesis 3:22 And the Lord God said, Behold, the man is become as one of us, to know good and evil: and now, lest he put forth his hand, and take also of the tree of life, and eat, and live for ever;
>
> 23 Therefore the Lord God sent him forth from the garden of Eden, to till the ground from whence he was taken.
>
> 24 So he drove out the man; and he placed at the east of the garden of Eden Cherubims, and a flaming sword which turned every way, to keep the way of the tree of life.

I had to think for a while about this one. "You mean that the Beatles are offering to help anyone who has a new vision of Eden?"

Benny nodded and grinned in a pleased manner. "Yup."

"Wow. That means they are playing God-on-God."

"I guess that's the point," said Benny.

"Thank God," I said.

First Party at Ken Kesey's with Hell's Angels

Allen Ginsberg

Cool black night thru the redwoods
cars parked outside in shade
behind the gate, stars dim above
the ravine, a fire burning by the side
porch and a few tired souls hunched over
in black leather jackets. In the huge
wooden house, a yellow chandelier
at 3 AM the blast of loudspeakers
hi-fi Rolling Stones Ray Charles Beatles
Jumping Joe Jackson and twenty youths
dancing to the vibration thru the floor,
a little weed in the bathroom, girls in scarlet
tights, one muscular smooth skinned man
sweating dancing for hours, beer cans
bent littering the yard, a hanged man
sculpture dangling from a high creek branch,
children sleeping softly in their bedroom bunks.
And 4 police cars parked outside the painted
gate, red lights revolving in the leaves.

December, 1965

"Cloud," from *The Electric Kool-Aid Acid Test*

Tom Wolfe

A hulking great sign on the gate out front:

THE MERRY PRANKSTERS WELCOME THE BEATLES

The Beatles were going to be at the Cow Palace outside of San Francisco on the evening of September 2. The papers, the radio, the TV could talk of nothing else. Kesey's idea, the current fantasy, is that after the show the Beatles will come to La Honda for a good freaking rout with the Merry Pranksters. Now as to how this is to all come about . . .

But one has to admit the sign creates an effect.

THE MERRY PRANKSTERS WELCOME THE BEATLES

Out on Route 84, Mom&Dad&Buddy&Sis in their Ocelot Rabies 400 hardtop sedans, they slow down and stop and stare. The last sign, the one reading THE MERRY PRANKSTERS WELCOME THE HELL'S ANGELS, for that one they mainly just slowed down. After all, it didn't say *when*. It might be thirty seconds from now—hundreds of the beasts, coming 'round the mountain in a shower of spirochetes and crab lice, spitting out bone marrow from the last cannibal rape job up the road.

Well, it worked with the Hell's Angels. They put up the sign THE MERRY PRANKSTERS WELCOME THE HELL'S ANGELS, and sure enough the Angels came, these unbelievable bogeymen for the middle class, in the flesh, and they became part of the Prankster movie, in the rich ripe cheesy Angel flesh. So they put up the sign THE MERRY PRANKSTERS WELCOME THE BEATLES and maybe the Beatles will come. There is this one small difference of course. Kesey *knew* the Hell's Angels. He invited them, face to face. Ah, but comes a time to put a few professed beliefs to the test. Control, Attention, Imagine the little freaks into the movie . . .

Kesey raps on to Mountain Girl out in the backhouse. They lie there on the mattresses, with Kesey rapping on and on and Mountain Girl trying to absorb it. Ever since Asilomar, Kesey has been deep into the religion thing. Miracles—Control—*Now*—The Movie—on and on he talks to Mountain Girl out in the backhouse and very deep and far-out stuff it is, too. Mountain Girl tries to concentrate, but the words swim like great waves of . . . The words swim by and she hears the sound but it is like her cerebral cortex is tuned out to the content of it. Her mind keeps rolling and spinning over another set of data, always the same. Like—the eternal desperate calculation. In short, Mountain Girl is pregnant.

And yet with all this desperation rolling and spinning going on, something he says will catch hold. They are that bizarre, but that plausible, Kesey's dreams are. It's a matter of imagining them into the movie. The Beatles. It is like an experiment in everything the Pranksters have learned up to now. We can't *make* the Beatles come out here to our place. We can't *cause* them to do it in the usual sense. But we can imagine them into the movie and work them into the great flow of acausal connection and then it will happen of its own accord. This sign starts the movie going, THE MERRY PRANKSTERS WELCOME THE BEATLES, and our movie becomes their movie, Mom's and Dad's and Buddy's and Sis's and all the Berkeley kids' and all the heads' and proto-heads' of the San Francisco peninsula, until our fantasy becomes the Beatles' fantasy. . . . Wonder when they will first feel it. . . . Despite the rolling and spinning and all, Mountain Girl can't hardly help but marvel at the current fantasy because there has already been so much . . . weird shit . . . that worked. Bringing the Angels in, like Kesey did, the most feared demons in America . . . and finding Good People like Buzzard and Sonny and Tiny and Frank and Terry the Tramp, who Done Well, and Beautiful People like Gut . . . And the poor tortured intellectual angels at Asilomar, from Watermelon Henry to freaking Rachel—for a week Kesey had mystified, like *mystified,* and taken over the whole Unitarian Church of

California. They would never be the same again, which was just as well. A true Miracle, in fact, since they had been the same for so goddamn long. Control :::: and it was so plausible, the way it sounded in Kesey's certain Oregon drawl. So few humans have the *hubris* to exert their wills upon the flow, maybe not more than forty on the whole planet at any given time. The world *is* flat, it *is* supported by forty, or maybe four, men, one at each corner, like the cosmic turtles and elephants in the mythology books, because no one else dares. Mountain Girl is 18 and she is pregnant, but this is Kesey . . .

And *Miracles?* You haven't seen miracles yet, Job, until you see the Pranksters draw the Beatles into their movie.

September 2. Faye's sewing machine is the first thing everyone hears as they wake up. Faye and Gretch pull out the big costume chest, full of all sorts of ungainly theatrical shit, swashbuckle swords and plumed hats and Errol Flynn dueling shirts and Robin Hood boots and quivers and quail masks and Day-Glo roadworker vests and sashes and medals and saris and sarongs and shades and beaks and bells and steelworker hard hats and World War I aviator helmets and Dr. Strange capes and cutlasses and codpieces and jumpsuits and football jerseys and aprons and ascots and wigs and warlock rattles and Jungle Jim jodhpurs and Captain Easy epaulets and Fearless Four tights—and Merry Prankster Page Browning special face paints. The Merry Pranksters are getting ready to head bombed out into the mightiest crazed throng in San Francisco history, come to see the Beatles at the Cow Palace.

One of the Pranksters' outer circle, so to speak, a fellow called C——, from Palo Alto—C—— had worked out some kind of a deal and gotten thirty tickets to the Beatles concert for the Pranksters, even though tickets were supposed to be impossible to get. C—— was one of the Pranksters' acid sources. Another was an old guy known as the Mad Chemist, an amateur chemistry genius who was also a gun freak. Anyway, this C—— worked out some kind of a deal and he also got enough acid for everybody for the trip. Just before the Pranksters, inner and outer circle, and kids climbed on the bus, Kesey grinned and passed out the acid. It was in capsules, but it was such a high concentration it just coated part of the inside of the capsules, so it looked like there was nothing in there. The Pranksters called it acid gas. So they all took acid gas and got on the bus. Cassady was off somewhere, so Babbs drove. Kesey was up on top of the bus, directing the movie. Well, it was colorful enough, this movie. The bus was super-rigged, all the sound equipment, two big speakers up top, records and tapes, plus the whole Prankster band up top of the bus, George Walker's drums, and basses and guitars and trombones and plumes spilling out the windows and flashes of Day-Glo and flapping epaulets, freaking flashing epaulets, and the Beatles album from the movie *Help!* screaming out the speakers, and up on top, Kesey and Sandy, Mountain Girl, Walker, Zonker, and a new Prankster, a little girl called Mary Microgram, and guitars and drums—*He-e-e-elp I ne-e-e-e-ed somebody*—the whole flapping yahooing carnival of a bus bouncing and jouncing and grinding up over Skylonda, Cahill Ridge, and down through Palo Alto and out onto the Harbor Freeway heading toward San Francisco, a goddamn rolling circus once again. Everybody was getting kind of high on acid, *wasted,* in fact, and starting, one by one, Mountain Girl and Sandy and Norman, who was inside the bus, to have that thing where the motion and the roar of the bus and the beat of the music and the sound of it are all one thing rolling together, and like Babbs is driving to the exact tempo and speed of the Beatles music, since they are all one thing together, growing high as baboons down through the freaking motels and electric signs and gull lights in Burlingame, near the airport, the Hyatt House super-America motel spires aloft—pitching and rolling and gunning along in *exact* time to the Beatle music, that being the soundtrack of this movie, you understand—and then off the expressway at the Cow Palace exit and down the swerving—*ne-e-e-ed some-body*—ramp, down an incline, down a hill, toward dusk, with the fever millions of cars streaming south on the freeway and the sun a low bomb over the hills, zonked, in fact. And grinding down to the stoplight, thunk, and the brakes sound like a cast-iron flute A below high C—and at that very moment, that very moment of bus stop—the Beatles song "Help!" ends, in that very moment, and weird music starts, from the part of the movie *Help!* where the Arab is sneaking up behind Ringo, and in the weird moment the wind rises over the freeway and to the right there is an abandoned factory, all brick and glass, mostly glass, great 1920s factory glass panes and all of them bending weird in the wind and flashing sheets of that huge afternoon sun like a huge thousand-eyed thing pulsing explosions of sunlight in *exact* time to the weird Arab music—and in that very moment Kesey, Mountain Girl, Sandy, Zonker, all of them—no one even has to look at another because they not only *know* that everyone else is seeing it at once, they *feel*, they feel it flowing through one brain, Atman and Brahman, all one on the bus and all one with the writhing mass sun reflector ripple sun bomb prisms, the bricks, the glass, the whole hulk of it, Pranksters and Beatles and sun bombs flashing Arab music—and then in *that* very moment, they all, the all in one, the one brain flow, see the mouldering sign silhouetted against the sky above the building:

CLOUD

Suddenly it seemed like the Pranksters could draw the whole universe into . . . the movie. . . .

And then, curiously, being as it is so freaking high out here—Mountain Girl thinks what the fuck is this. It looks like a slaughterhouse. In fact, it is the Cow Palace. She can't even focus on the big hulking building itself for the miles and endless rings of slaughterhouse fences around it, fences and barbed wire and a million cars jamming in and being jammed in in the cold fag end of the dusk. Curiously, it isn't terrifying to Mountain Girl, however. It is just a slaughterhouse, that's all.

But to other Pranksters—a concentration camp. We're going to jail, for the rest of our lives only. Everybody scrambling down off the bus, all still in motion with the ground and the concentration-camp fences flailing in the gruesome gloaming while billions of teeny freaks rush by them, screaming and freaking. They have their tickets in their hand like it is the last corner of salvation extant but they can't even read the mothers. They are wasted. The letters on the ticket curdle and freak off into the teeny freak flow. Thirty Pranksters in full flapping epaulets and plumes desperately staring at the minute disappearing tickets in their hands in the barby antepens of the concentration camp. They are going to arrest us and lock us away for the rest of our lives. That seems very certain, almost like well, that's why we came. Thirty acid heads, with innocent children in tow, in full Prankster regalia, bombed out of their gourds on the dread LSD, veering, careening in delirium sun pulse. In public, stoned out of their skulls on LSD, not only in public but in this momentous heaving Beatles throng amid two thousand red dog forensic cops, in full go-to-hell costume—*exterminate the monsters*—

. . . but . . . no one lays a hand on them or says the first word, thousands of cops and not even one hassle . . . because we're *too* obvious. Suddenly it couldn't be clearer to Norman. We're too obvious and we've blown their brains. They can't focus on us—or—we've sucked them into the movie and *dissolved* the bastids—

Inside the Cow Palace it is very roaring hell. Somehow Kesey and Babbs lead the Day-Glo crazies up to their seats. The Pranksters are sitting in a great clump, a wacky perch up high in precipitous pitch high up pitching down to the stage and millions of the screaming teeny freaks. The teeny freaks, tens of thousands of little girls, have gone raving mad already, even though the Beatles have not come on. Other groups, preliminaries, keep trooping on, *And now—Martha and the Vandellas,* and the electrified throb and brang vibrates up your aorta and picks your bones like a sonic cleaner, and the teeny freaks scream—great sheets of scream like sheets of rain in a squall—and *kheew, kheew, pow, pow, pow*—how very marvelous, how very clever, figures Norman. From up out of the Cow Palace horde of sheet scream teeny freaks comes this very marvelous clever light display, hundreds of exploding lights throughout the high intensity lights, ricocheting off everything, what a marvelous clever thing they've rigged up here for our . . .

—Mountain Girl smiles . . . the incredible exploding lights explode out in front of her, a great sea of them, and then they explode on her retina in great sunburst retinal sulphur rockets, images and afterimages that she will never forget as long as she lives, in truth—

. . . for our entertainment, and it is twenty or thirty minutes before Norman, stoned, realizes that they are flashbulbs, hundreds, thousands of teeny freaks with flashbulb cameras, aimed at the stage or just shot off in optic orgasm. Sheets of screams, rock 'n' roll, *blam blam,* a sea of flashbulbs—perfect madness, of course.

—Mountain Girl grins and takes it all in—

Other Pranksters, stoned, are slowly getting uptight, however, including Kesey and Babbs. The vibrations are very bad, a poison madness in the air—

Each group of musicians that goes off the stage—the horde thinks *now* the Beatles, but the Beatles don't come, some other group appears, and the sea of girls gets more and more intense and impatient and the screaming gets higher, and the thought slips into Norman's flailing flash-frayed brain stem ::: the human lung cannot go beyond this :::: and yet when the voice says *And now—the Beatles*—what else could he say?—and out they come on stage—*them*—John and George and Ringo and uh the other one—it might as well have been four imported vinyl dolls for all it was going to matter—that sound he thinks cannot get higher, it doubles, his eardrums ring like stamped metal with it and suddenly *Ghhhhhhwoooooooooowwwwww,* it is like the whole thing has snapped, and the whole front section of the arena becomes a writhing, seething mass of little girls waving their arms in the air, this mass of pink arms, it is all you can see, it is like a single colonial animal with a thousand waving pink tentacles—it *is* a single colonial animal with a thousand waving pink tentacles,

—vibrating poison madness and filling the universe with the teeny agony torn out of them. It dawns on Kesey: it is *one being.* They have all been transformed into one being.

—Mountain Girl grins and urges them on—its scream does not subside for a moment, during after or between numbers, the Beatles could be miming it for all it matters. But something else . . . does . . . matter . . . and Kesey sees it. One of the Beatles, John, George, Paul, dips his long electric guitar handle in one direction and the whole teeny horde ripples precisely along the line of energy he set off—and then in the other direction, precisely along that line. It causes them to grin, John and Paul and George and Ringo, rippling the poor huge freaked teeny beast this way and that—

Control—it is perfectly obvious—they have brought this whole mass of human beings to the point where they are one, out of their skulls, one psyche, and they have utter control over them—but they don't know what in the hell to do with it, they haven't the first idea, and they will lose it. In Kesey the vibration is an awful anticipation of the snap—

Ghhhhhwooooooooooowwwww, thousands of teeny bodies hurtling toward the stage and a fence there and a solid line of cops, fighting to hurl the assault back, while the Beatles keep moving their chops and switching their hips around sunk like a dumb show under the universal scream. In that surge, just when you would have thought not another sound in the universe could break through, it starts—*thwaaaack—thwaaaack*—the sound of the folding chairs on the arena floor collapsing and smashing down on the floor, and the remains are down there amid the pink tentacles, crushed to a pulp, little bits and splinters that used to be folding chairs, debris being passed out from hand to hand traveling over the pink tentacles from one to the other like some hideously diseased lurching monster cockroaches. And then the girls start fainting, like suffocation, and getting tromped on, and they start handing out their bodies, cockroach chair debris and the bodies of little teeny freaks being shuttled out over the pitched sea like squashed lice picked off the beast, screaming and fainting and *Ghhhhhwoooooowwwwww* again up against the cop fence while the Beatles cheese and mince at them in the dumb show, utterly helpless to ripple them or anything else now, with no control left—

CANCER. Kesey has only to look and it is perfectly obvious—all of them, the teeny freaks and the Beatles, are one creature, caught in a state of sheer poison mad cancer. The Beatles are the creature's head. The teeny freaks are the body. But the head has lost control of the body and the body rebels and goes amok and that is what cancer is. The vibrations of it hit the Pranksters, in a clump, stoned out of their gourds, in sickening waves. Kesey—Babbs—they all feel it at once, and Norman.

—Mountain Girl looks very surprised. She wants to see the rest of it. But Kesey and Babbs have decided they should all leave—before the Monster Snap occurs, the big cancer wrap-up of the whole process.

—Wait a minute, says Mountain Girl.

But the Pranksters get up in a clump and rustle of plumes and epaulets and Day-Glo, zonked out of their heads on acid, and all sorts of people start getting up—but like, *concrete*. The more headway they make toward the exits, the more it becomes a claustrophobia of pens, an endless series of pens. They head down long corridors, all concrete, and already hundreds are jammed in the corridors, all looking kind of raggy—because— They get the total vibration from them—everybody has the one same feeling: suppose this thing snaps *now* and there is panic and everybody makes a rush for it, the exit, but there is no exit, only concrete walls and concrete ceilings weighing down like a thousand tons and ramps—toward nothing—leading down—then up in a great clump of hump—and then down, outside, there is the sky, but it is black, it is nighttime by now and sick ochre floodlights, but they have merely made it to another pen, more Cyclone fences and barbed wire and frantic raggy people—all *fleeing*—milling around in it like rats, trying to get to the exit, which is a turnstile, an upright turnstile with bars, like an iron maiden, and you have to get inside of it, totally, one person at a time, with a frantic crush on both sides, and even then you have only made it to another pen, a parking lot, with more Cyclone fence and barbed wire and now teeny freaks and cars crushed in here, all trying to get out, seven and eight cars at a whack trying to nose through an opening big enough for one.

Cages, cages, cages and no end to it. Even out there, beyond, where cars have escaped and they are in a line with their lights on—trapped by the hills, which are another great pen trapping the whole place in . . . in . . . The Pranksters all silent and numb with the apprehension of the Great Cancer Snap to come—

—Except that Mountain Girl says, Wait a minute—

—and Zonker, with his huge euphoric Zonker grin on, fraternizing madly with all teeny freaks as they stream out, saying to all who listen: "The Beatles are going to Kesey's when they leave here. . . . The Beatles are going to Kesey's . . ." and the word spreads among the crowd in the most delirious way—

Kesey plunges back in for survivors. See if there are any Pranksters trapped inside. He tells the rest to go to the bus and stay there, and he plunges in. The Pranksters touch the bus and their morale revives a bit. They rev up the amplifiers and the speakers and climb up on top in their crazy costumes and start idling over the drums and electric guitars. The thousands of little raggy girls keep pouring out into the parking lot, still wound up like a motorcycle and no release and of course they see the bus and these strange Day-Glo people. One group of kids is protesting that the music business is rigged and they're carrying placards and screaming and they figure the Pranksters support them—the Pranksters grin and wave back—everybody figures the strange Day-Glo people are for whatever they're for. They start piling around the bus, these little teeny freaks, and start pelting it with jelly beans, the hard kind, the kind they brought to throw at the Beatles. The Pranksters sit on top of the bus with the jelly beans clattering off the side and the flaming little teeny freaks pressed around screaming— So *this* is what the Beatles feel, this mindless amok energy surging at them for—what?

At last Kesey returns with the last to be rescued, Mary Microgram, looking like a countryside after a long and fierce war, and Kesey says let's haul ass out of here. Babbs starts the bus up and they pull out, bulling their way slowly out toward freedom.

Cancer! We saw it. It was there. Bad vibrations, say all. Endless cages. They all rock and sway, stoned on acid.

"Hell," thinks Mountain Girl. "I have to come here with a bunch of old men who never saw a rock 'n' roll show before."

On the way back they put the Beatles' tape on again, from *Help!*—but it was no use. They were all too dispirited. Except for Mountain Girl and Zonker. Mountain Girl said she'd wanted to stay and see the rest of the show. Well—what the hell. Zonker was smiling about the Beatles coming. Well—that was what he had told the whole world, anyway. And where the hell *else* would they go from there? In fact, the current fantasy—the imminent arrival of the Beatles—had hardly crossed anybody's mind for the last hour, not even Kesey's. Get the hell out of there, that was the main thing. Where were the Beatles? Who the hell knew. The little vinyl dolls had probably cheesed and minced off into a time warp. . . . In any case, it wasn't very hulking likely they were coming to La Honda.

Finally the bus comes grinding around the last curve round the mountain, up to Kesey's place, and the bus noses across the bridge and the headlights hit the yard—and the sight is gruesome and comical at the same time. It is like a super version of the nightmare of the man who just wants to go home and go to bed. The Pranksters have guests. In fact they have three or four hundred guests. They are all jammed into the big yard between the main house and the backhouse, with big bitter lollipop eyes. It's like every head, freak, boho, and weirdo in the West has assembled in one spot, the first freak-out, with a couple of hundred teeny freaks thrown in for good measure. Half of them are hunkered down with their big lollipop eyes turned up like somebody spit them up against the house and they slid down to the ground like slugs. Naturally they all came for the big beano with the Beatles. The party. Zonker did his work in the highest Prankster tradition. The sign still hangs on the gate:

THE MERRY PRANKSTERS WELCOME THE BEATLES

Kesey is not in the mood for a goddamned thing and heads into the house. The whole head-freak-boho-slug mob stares at him, all these lollipop eyes, as if he is going to produce the Beatles from out of a sleeve. Then they start grumbling, like a bunch of prisoners who haven't been fed but don't know whether this is the time for the slave revolt or not. It is a debacle, except that is so damned comical. The look on their faces.

That, and the appearance of Owsley.

A cocky little guy, short, with dark hair, dressed like an acid head, the usual boho gear, but with a strange wound-up nasal voice, like a head with the instincts of a roller-skating rink promoter—this little character materializes in front of Kesey from out of the boho-slug multitudes and announces:

"I'm Owsley."

Kesey doesn't say Hi, I'm Kesey. He just looks at him, as if to say, all right, you're Owsley and you're here—and then what?

Owsley looks stunned—*I'm Owsley.* In fact, Kesey never heard of him. It was like, if Owsley suddenly found himself in a place where nobody ever heard of him, he didn't know what to do. He and Kesey are just standing there trading eyeballs until finally Owsley produces a little bag he has and opens it and it is full of capsules of acid. He's Owsley, the greatest LSD manufacturer in the world, which turns out to be just about right, the Sandoz Chemical Corporation included.

Mountain Girl looks and just smiles. Everything gets funnier and funnier on the Beatle patrol! He's got his little bag of acid. Mountain Girl figures him for a wiseacre right away. Kesey looks at the bagful of acid. One thing the little wiseacre's got is acid.

The world's greatest acid manufacturer, bar none, standing out in the dark in the middle of nowhere amid the boho-slug multitudes under the shadowy redwoods.

By and by they had most of the boho-slugs off the place and sliding up the highway in the dark looking for christ knows what, seeing as how the Beatles never made it. Kesey and Owsley and the Pranksters sit down around a fire out by the big stump. And who the hell shows up but the Mad Chemist. He and Owsley start sniffing and eyeing each other. It's like the slick sharp young neurological doctor genius from out of the Mayo Clinic face to face with the old blowsy homey country doctor—on the most puzzling and difficult case in the history of medicine. Owsley and the Mad Chemist start arguing over drugs. It's like a debate. All of the Pranksters, even Kesey, keep out of it and the two of them start hammering away. Let the little wiseacre have it, Mad Chemist, Mountain Girl keeps thinking, and most of the Pranksters feel the same way. But Owsley, the little wiseacre, is tearing him up. Owsley is young and sharp and quick, and the Mad Chemist—the Mad Chemist is an old man and he has taken too much dope. He's loose in the head. He tries to argue and his brains all run together like goo. Owsley, the Pranksters figure—well, maybe he never even took acid himself. Or maybe he took it once. It is just something they sense. And the poor old Mad Chemist, he has taken so much dope—caressing his guns and hooking down dope—he is loose in the head, and Owsley just tears him up. The Mad Chemist is getting crushed. The Mad Chemist never came around again but once or twice, it was all so humiliating. So the Pranksters had this little wiseacre Owsley on their hands whether they liked it or not. But he did make righteous acid and he had money. Between the two of them, Owsley and the Pranksters, they were about to put LSD all over the face of the globe.

Little by little, Owsley's history seeped out. He was thirty years old, although he looked younger, and he had a huge sonorous name: Augustus Owsley Stanley III. His grandfather was a United States senator from Kentucky. Owsley apparently had had a somewhat hung-up time as a boy, going from prep school to prep school and then to a public high school, dropping out of that but getting into the University of Virginia School of Engineering, apparently because of his flair for sciences, then dropping out of that. He finally wound up enrolling in the University of California, in Berkeley, where he hooked up with a hip, good-looking chemistry major named Melissa. They dropped out of the university and Owsley set up his first acid factory at 1647 Virginia Street, Berkeley. He was doing a huge business when he got raided on February 21, 1965. He got off, however, because there was no law against making, taking, or having LSD in California until October 1966. He moved his operation to Los Angeles, 2205 Lafler Road, called himself the Baer Research Group, and paid out $20,000 in $100 bills to the Cycle Chemical Corporation for 500 grams of lysergic acid monohydrate, the basic material in LSD, which he could convert into 1.5 million doses of LSD at from $1 to $2 apiece wholesale. He bought another 300 grams from International Chemical and Nuclear Corporation. His first big shipment arrived March 30, 1965.

He had a flair, this Owsley. By and by he had turned out several million doses of LSD, in capsules and tablets. They had various whimsical emblems on them, to indicate the strength. The most famous, among the heads, were the "Owsley blues"—with a picture of Batman on them, 500 micrograms worth of superhero inside your skull. The heads rapped over Owsley blues like old juice heads drawling over that famous onetime brand from Owsley's Virginia home territory, Fairfax County Bourbon, bottled in bond. Owsley makes righteous acid, said the heads. Personally he wasn't winning any popularity contests with the heads or the cops, either. He is, like, arrogant; he is a wiseacre; but the arrogant little wiseacre makes righteous acid.

In fact, Owsley's acid was famous internationally. When the acid scene spread to England in late 1966 and 1967, the hippest intelligence one could pass around was that one was in possession of "Owsley acid." In the acid world this *was* bottled-in-bond; certified; guaranteed; and high status. It was in this head world that the . . . Beatles first took LSD. Now, just to get ahead of the story a bit—after Owsley hooked up with Kesey and the Pranksters, he began a musical group called the Grateful Dead. Through the Dead's experience with the Pranksters was born the sound known as "acid rock." And it was that sound that the Beatles picked up on, after they started taking acid, to do a famous series of acid-rock record albums, *Revolver*, *Rubber Soul*, and *Sgt. Pepper's Lonely Hearts Club Band*. Early in 1967 the Beatles got a fabulous idea. They got hold of a huge school bus and piled into it with thirty-nine friends and drove and wove across the British countryside, zonked out of their gourds.

They were going to . . . make a movie. Not an ordinary movie, but a totally spontaneous movie, using handheld cameras, shooting the experience as it happened—off the top of the head!—cavorting, rapping on, soaring in the moment, visionary chaos—a daydream! a black art! a chaos! They finished up with miles and miles of film, a monster, a veritable morass of it, all shaky and out of focus—blissful Zonk!—which they saw as a total breakthrough in terms of expression but also as a commercial display—shown on British TV it was—that might be appreciated even outside the esoteric world of the heads—

THE MOVIE

—called *Magical Mystery Tour.* And . . . the great banner rippled on the Prankster gate in the nighttime in ripples and intergalactic billows of great howling Owsley electro-mad-chemical synchronicity . . .

THE MERRY PRANKSTERS WELCOME THE BEATLES

The Yellow Sub

Joseph Wollenweber

Skinny and I were cruising around the hills in his Jeep when the song "Yellow Submarine" by the Beatles first came on. We were driving Skyline not far from school, but everything suddenly turned red, yellow, and orange; then shifts to blue and green started to occur off near the horizon. It was closing down on sunset.

"Do you know what this means?" Skinny said as he cranked up the stereo as loud as it would go, making the speakers crackle and hiss, before backing off.

"Sounds incomprehensible to me," I said, thinking this a lame excuse for not offering a more tangible answer.

"Incomprehensible? Dude, this tune is plain as the lines on my palm." He turned his hand over and shoved it under my face.

"What do they say?" I asked, running my finger quickly along their main roads.

"I've a long life line but expect plenty of misery along the way. But the submarine, man, that's about going under the surface of things. Getting to the depths. I mean, who in their right mind would choose to live in a sub, unless they were explorers who had enough of up above and wanted to get down." Skinny went on to explain how diving down beneath the sea was a high thing to do.

Skinny had it all sewed up in his own fashion, but he never alluded to actually knowing anything. I think a good philosophy is to find solace with those who're searching for truth and run like hell from those who suggest they've found it. Back then we knew that we did not know and never fooled ourselves into believing we'd find out.

"Yellow Submarine" infiltrated our consciousness; then the movie hit, with its Blue Meanies and cartoon Beatles, and I soon forgot the whole thing until a few months later when Skinny and I were cruising around again like before.

"So how's your subbing?" Skinny asked with a lit joint hanging from his lips and the stereo blasting the Stones.

"You mean have I been going down?"

We were driving Ashby into Berkeley, headed toward Telegraph Avenue to find John the Red, our carrottopped connection.

"Yeah, have you been taking that sub under?"

You could never be sure what Skinny was after; sometimes he made sense, and sometimes it was like talking to a drunk poet who circles the point (if there is one), then leaves you vacant and drifting along a random circumference.

"I get down sometimes," I said, "but I like soaring better. Let's get high, man. Let's get high!" I shouted.

Skinny snuffed out the joint in response to my exuberance. "Listen, dude, if you keep going like that you'll end up hooked on the high instead of the intensity and you'll lose yourself, man."

We turned on Telegraph and passed by the confluence of hitchhikers, tooling up the street, our eyes cocked for big John's orange crop.

"You're spending too much time in the ambulance," I told Skinny, as if to explain his passion for the bottom side of things. He drove three nights a week.

"Sure, that's right," he agreed, "seeing people in pain, and seeing them die, it changes things. I used to think just like you. Get high. Fly. Don't look down. But the Yellow Sub opened me to a truth which I'd been suspecting all along. You'll find out."

And I did find out, years later, just what Skinny was trying to tell me, though we lost touch and I spent far too long getting high, going from one drug to another, up to and including meditation.

But that's where it stops—when you finally face yourself and sit alone, cold sober, and watch what actually transpires inside your soul.

Just like Skinny suggested, there's a high-flying bird and a submerged submarine, and the bird is red and the sub is yellow and they alternate like hard and soft, and you never get high enough to lose the depths that only the yellow submarine can take you to, and there's no end to this diving and soaring.

The Beatles in Tonypandy

Euron Griffith

1.

In 1967, a mere twelve weeks before they flew out to Rishikesh with the Maharishi, the Beatles came to Tonypandy, South Wales, and spent six days with Tom Morris of 23 Upper Chemical Terrace. Up until now the details of what occurred during these six days have remained something of a magical mystery for Beatles scholars, but, following Tom's death last year, important papers, letters, and tapes were recently put up for auction at Sotheby's by Tom's widow, Eileen, and as a result of their purchase by Professor Remi Carne of UCLA we are now, with Professor Carne's kind permission, able at last to throw some light on what went on in that tiny terraced house.

2.

It has not yet been possible to establish with any certainty how the Beatles came to be aware of Tom Morris and his pigeons, although Gannon and McCall have suggested that it could have been through an article in *The Sunday Times* from August 28, 1966, entitled "Tom Morris—A Man and His Birds." However, Mark Sammon's conviction that the Beatles were made aware of Tom Morris through one of his talks, "Pigeons and Their Ways," delivered at the London-Welsh Pigeon Fanciers Society, was confirmed this year with the historic publication of the Tom Morris diaries. According to an entry, Morris first met the Beatles at a talk he gave to the Kent Pigeon Society at Maidstone's Memorial Community Hall on September 23, 1967. The Beatles at this time were filming additional scenes for *Magical Mystery Tour* at nearby West Malling, and it was through a suggestion made by one of the extras that Paul McCartney and

Ringo Starr decided to attend Morris's lecture. The entry for that night makes it obvious that he had no idea who these two young men were.

> Saturday, 23rd.
>
> Caught 9.05 from Cardiff to Paddington. Got lost on tube but eventually got connection. Arrived at Maidstone. Nice spread laid out by Society, chicken sandwiches and hot sausage rolls. Met Ken, the chairman—lovely fellow. Said he'd done some of his National Service in Wales. Met Lynne, his lovely lady wife. Complemented her on the sausage rolls. At their house was impressed with micromesh netting system. The pigeons love it apparently. Must make enquiries at Jepson's on reaching Ton. Gave talk. Halfway through two young men came in. Both long-haired. One had v. big nose. Expected the worst but both sat down and listened intently. At end they asked lots of questions about pigeons. Invited me to their hotel but politely declined. Gave them my address. Said if they needed more information they were welcome to correspond. They thanked me and left. Ken seemed v. excited. "Fancy that," he kept saying, "who'd have believed it?" "Yes," I said, "nice to know that not <u>every</u> young man these days is obsessed with pop music and drugs." Got paid 10 shillings and caught last train to London. Sore throat. Might have developed a summer chill. Made a note to ring Dr Meredith on return.

It is obvious that Tom Morris's talk had an immediate affect on McCartney and Starr. Three days later, according to receipts which have recently been acquired by the Beatle Museum of Japan in Kyoto, they bought six pigeons from champion breeder Alf Baker of Wood Green at five pounds each. Problems began to arise, however, when it came to the subject of feeding. "We knew nothing, really," said McCartney in a BBC Radio One interview from last year. "At first we tried All-Bran and Ready Brek mixed with water, but it was clear that the birds weren't happy. I phoned Ringo and both of us agreed that something had to be done, otherwise we'd lose them." Ringo, in fact, had even bigger problems. After a late-night session for "I Am the Walrus," he and John Lennon returned to Ringo's flat in Kensington and, on seeing the pigeons, Lennon fed them some sugar cubes laced with LSD. "They just went mad," said Ringo, "they literally cooed themselves to death." Maureen Starr, who was also present, remembered the occasion in her recent autobiography, *My Life with Ringo*. "Very strange," she wrote. "One minute they were sitting on their perch, and the next they just kind of dropped off. I think the acid must have convinced them that they couldn't fly."

It must have been at this time that McCartney wrote his first letter to Tom Morris. Unfortunately, the document has not survived, but Tom Morris's reply has, dated October 8, 1967.

Dear Mr McCartney,

Thank you for your letter. I'm glad that you enjoyed my little talk, and I was glad also to learn of your new interest in pigeons. I was sorry to hear of your friend's mishap with his birds. I've never heard of pigeons being savaged by stray Alsatians before, but I have been told, on many occasions, that keeping prize birds in a big city poses different kinds of problems.

With regard to your enquiries about feeding, may I suggest that you and your friend try Haith's maize or Willsbridge. A twenty-eight pound bag of mixed corn, maize and wheat barley shouldn't cost you more than sixteen shillings. Alternatively, you could purchase a half-hundredweight bag at around one pound and seventeen shillings. Let me know how you get on. Must close now. It's settling-up day at the Co-op.

Yours,

Tom Morris

Ringo replaced his dead pigeons on October 10, and, according to Alf Baker's records, he and McCartney arranged for deliveries of half-hundredweight bags of mixed corn and maize to their respective addresses. These arrived on October 12, although on this day both Starr and McCartney were overdubbing "Blue Jay Way" at De Lane

Lea Recording Studios in London. After a couple of days they were delighted to see that their pigeons were thriving on their new diet, and they were also delighted with their newly arrived membership cards for the Pigeon Fancier's Club of Great Britain (McCartney's number was 012435B and Starr's was 012437B). The other two Beatles, at this time, were skeptical about pigeons. Harrison in particular appeared especially hostile, and McGarry and Locke have indicated that this was probably due to his recent introduction to the Maharishi Yamesh Yogi. "That was George's thing," said McCartney, "and he was dead keen to turn us on to it. Me and John had been to a couple of his lectures in London, but even though he was a cool guy and everything we remained suspicious. Pigeons were straightforward by comparison. It was mind-blowing in a way, but when you released a pigeon from your loft in the back garden you got this real buzz. I got the riff for 'Lady Madonna' whilst flying pigeons."

As a means of introducing Harrison to pigeons, McCartney and Starr took him to the South Bucks Meet on October 21; when Lennon arrived unexpectedly, this must have been the first time that the Beatles, as a collective, interacted with what was to become for them a door to a new universe. From a home-movie shot that day by Ringo (and currently in the possession of Neil Aspinall at Apple), it is remarkable how Paul and Ringo had assimilated this new culture. Their clothes that day are indicative of this. Whilst John and George are wearing kaftans, beads, and bells, Ringo and Paul are already parading the Crombie coats, cloth caps, and scarves which the other Beatles would soon adopt and which would become their "fashion mode signifier" for the next four months. At one point Paul even lights up a pipe.

3.

Marian Payne, in her famous study of Hispanic children of the Tenderloin district of San Francisco, coined the term "Purified Grandfather Syndrome." Here, young children who had been nurtured and culturally defined within a rigidly urban environment were proved to be dislocated from direct parental influence through various factors. The unsettling pace of the children's development made it difficult for them to accept the authority of their parents. Their parents were too close. These children needed someone with distance, someone with a pre-media concept of reality. Their grandparents fitted the bill because their rural cultural instincts forged a valuable sense of balance in the social landscape of their disenfranchised grandchildren.

By September 1967 the Beatles were displaying many symptoms of Purified Grandfather Syndrome. Their gang mentality, forged through many years of touring and performing, had bereaved them of anything resembling a conventional form of social interaction, and their considerable fame ensured that outside influences of any kind were extremely difficult to assimilate. Like those children Payne described, the Beatles distrusted direct parental control. Indeed, the closest thing to a father figure they had, their manager, Brian Epstein, had recently died; as mistrusted as he was toward the end of his life, the Beatles no doubt found his loss alienating and disconcerting. It was natural in these circumstances therefore that the gang, childlike in its collective grieving, should search for a grandfather figure. Someone who could instill the wisdom of a previous era and give them direction in a dark and troubled time. It is in this new light which we should see Tom Morris. In the end it was he who elevated the Beatles to a higher spiritual plane. Cast in the unconscious role of "grandfather," he began a crucial process of self-examination and cosmic awareness in the group which would ultimately lead them to the Maharishi and the challenging ideas of the East. It was Tom Morris who gave the Beatles back their sanity, not his pigeons. In the end his pigeons were nothing more than red herrings.

4.

Whether the Beatles were at all conscious of any symptoms of Purified Grandfather Syndrome, one thing is at least certain: They needed to see Tom Morris and their need was great enough to lure them out of their protected social pattern in London.

Up until the recent publication of the Tom Morris diaries, the exact nature and chronology of the Beatles' visit to Tonypandy has remained shrouded in mystery and somewhat open to speculation. Indeed, many Beatle scholars appeared unaware of any such visit in the first place. There is no mention of it in the mainstream biographies of Hunter Davies and Philip Norman, and Mark Lewishon's otherwise excellent and exhaustive study of 1992 omits any reference to Tom Morris or pigeons in general. Perhaps these shortcomings are pardonable, however, when we take into account the Beatles' unusually tight security during this visit. Unlike their previous trip to Wales (when they'd traveled from Euston Station, London, to Bangor with the Maharishi, on August 25, 1967), this time there were no press releases and no itinerary. As far as the world was concerned the Beatles were in the studio putting the final touches to the music for their film *Magical Mystery Tour.* The visit to Tonypandy (although mentioned obliquely in interviews by the Beatles since the mid-seventies) was only confirmed by the Apple office last year following Tom Morris's death, and it was only six months ago that the Beatles offered any kind of explanation for their military-style secrecy concerning the trip. It was done, they said, "as a mark of respect for Tom. We didn't want him or Eileen to be hassled by the world's press, and we didn't want his world, or his pigeons, to be crushed by the media circus." If the visit came as a surprise to Beatles scholars last year, it was, according to his diary, at least just as much of a surprise for Tom Morris himself at the time. Although he had entertained a healthy correspondence with the Beatles (and with Paul McCartney in particular) since his first meeting with Paul and Ringo in Maidstone, he was nonetheless very surprised to find them standing at the front door of 23 Chemical Terrace on the early evening of Saturday, November 11, 1967. An extract from his diary entry for that date will confirm this.

Had tea and some of Eileen's lovely scones. Tried to take my mind off Brenda's legs. Two weeks now since the injury. Thought of taking her to the vet on Monday but dreading the verdict. She's getting on now. Might have to put her down. Was just about to pick up the *Rhondda Leader* to finish the crossword when the doorbell went. Eileen said it was for me. Most surprised to find young Paul and his friends from London. Surprised also to find them dressed up as miners. John seemed to have boot polish rubbed into his face. They came in and had some tea. Asked if they could stay for a few days. Eileen was delighted. Ever since Ifan left home she's missed the company of youngfolk. She cleared out the spare room and brought the tin bath in from the shed. She filled it up in the front room and bathed them one by one. I could tell it was the hard bristled brush by their screams. She offered to cut their hair but they said no. Later I showed them the loft and John helped me with the crossword. Very bright lad. Paul tuned the old piano for Eileen and then we turned in. All in all a very unusual day.

The miner's hats and Davy lamps which the Beatles had rented two days earlier from Berry's Fancy Dress of Islington were intended as disguises, but the group soon discovered that such precautions proved to be unnecessary on the streets of Tonypandy. Whereas during their touring days the Beatles had been forced to develop a fine instinct for camouflage in order to negotiate the streets of cities like London, New York, and Los Angeles without provocation, Tonypandy was refreshingly different. Here was a town which, in 1967, could boast only two fully-operational television sets. One was in the window of "Jenkins and Sons Radio Hire" and the other was the property of the Reverend Issac Eynon. Until the establishment of a new transmitter for the area in September 1968, television reception in Tonypandy was notoriously poor. The set in the window of Jenkins and Son showed nothing but constant interference, and the Reverend Eynon's reasons for possessing a television were a mystery to the entire town, because he had been blind from birth and, according to medical records, prone also to lengthy bouts of periodic deafness. His obituary in the *Rhondda Leader* of 1971 remarked how he had often been forced to "yell out his sermons by braille."

In this media vacuum, therefore, the Beatles were pleasantly surprised to discover that nobody appeared to recognize them. According to Tom Morris's entry for Sunday, November 12, his suggestion that they "pop down to the Institute for a lunchtime pint" had initially provoked a visible air of apprehension in his guests.

> [T]hey got a bit tense and looked at each other as if I'd said something out of place. After a couple of minutes I threw on my coat and said, "Look, I'm off, you're welcome to help Eileen in the kitchen if you want." With that they decided to come. I think they were scared of her since the bristled brush incident. They reached for their miner's hats and Davy lamps. "Don't be ridiculous," I said, "you'll only get folk staring at you if you wear those silly clothes." For some reason they thought this was hilarious.

At the Tonypandy Miner's Institute the Beatles, for the first time since their pre-fame days in Hamburg during the early sixties, found themselves able to interact with people on a fairly normal everyday basis. "I couldn't believe it," said McCartney. "They'd obviously *heard* of the Beatles, but I don't think anybody in Tonypandy had the vaguest idea what they *looked* like. To them we were just Tom's young friends from London who'd come to see his pigeons. Apparently he had a lot of visitors. He was quite a celebrity in pigeon circles." The Beatles were especially drawn to the Institute, and it's clear from Tom Morris's entry for Tuesday, November 14, that the group found it an easy place in which to relax.

> Tuesday, Nov 14.
>
> Knees-up Night at the Institute. The boys came with me and Eileen. Ianto got up and played "She'll be Coming Round the Mountain" on the piano, and Dilys did the Can-Can (as usual! I wish someone would have a quiet word with her!). To my surprise Paul got up and sang "Yesterday" and, though we all applauded politely, I think we all agreed he was no Matt Monroe. During the bingo John gave me one of his Special Woodbines. Apparently they were very popular in

London. It was very long but I soon got used to it. I couldn't concentrate on my bingo card so I gave it to Eileen. Afterwards, Danny came on and told some jokes. Even though I'd heard them all before, I embarrassed Eileen by laughing like a fool. Had chips on the way home. After Eileen had gone to bed, John gave me another of his special Woodbines. When I woke up in the morning I was surprised to find that my shoes were on top of the coalshed.

From Eileen Morris's recollections of the period it is clear that key elements of Purified Grandfather Syndrome were consistently present in the Beatles' relationship with Tom. "They were very close," she says. "One minute they were cleaning out the loft together and the next they were helping Tom carry big sacks of maize from the Davies Feed Warehouse. It wasn't just pigeons though. One day they went up the hills to collect wild mushrooms. And then there was Dai of course. The boys were fascinated with him."

Dai, or David, Llewelyn was Tom's next-door neighbour. A keen birdwatcher, he was the proud owner of a Bush reel-to-reel tape recorder which he used to record the songs of wild birds in the area. "He carried this tape recorder everywhere," remembered Paul, "and this was very useful for John and me because we were inspired and new songs came out every day." (These tapes were discovered in Llewelyn's attic following his death in 1979. There were three reels in all, all of them labeled YELLOW WARBLER, and they featured rough versions of songs which later appeared on *The White Album*. It remains in the hands of the Llewelyn family, but in the presence of a solicitor, fragments of it were played to me in August 1995. What came over was the obvious joy in John and Paul's singing and writing. A version of "Ob-La-Di, Ob-La-Da" is improvised on Spanish guitar and washboard whilst a chaotic rendition of "Back in the USSR" is broken up when Eileen bangs the wall to tell them that their tea is ready. There follows a cascade of giggles before the tape runs out.)

The Beatles had temporarily escaped from the multifaceted pressures of fame. Like the children in Marian Payne's study, they had returned to the womblike comfort of a predominantly rural generation and, in Tom Morris, they had found their symbolic grandfather.

This idyllic period was shattered, however, on the morning of Friday, November 17, 1967.

5.

The Maharishi arrived in the Tonypandy coach depot on the 45 bus from Cardiff at 11.23 a.m.

How he came to be aware of the Beatles' precise whereabouts remains a mystery, but he later claimed it was a karmic force which drew him to Wales. He took a taxi to Upper Chemical Terrace and knocked on the door of number 23. "When I first opened the door," recalled Eileen, "I thought he was a Jehovah's Witness. I told him to go away, but he had his foot in the door. 'Beetles,' he kept saying, 'you have beetles here.' 'Not anymore,' I said. 'The man from the council came last month—he got rid of them all.' But then Paul came up and they seemed to know each other so I let the man in. I don't think Paul was happy to see him though. I know for a fact that Tom wasn't." Tom's hostility toward the Maharishi is evident from his diary entry for that day.

> Friday, November 17.
>
> That bloody man arrived. He sat in the lounge squeaking like a hamster and spreading welsh cake crumbs everywhere. The boys looked uncomfortable. Poor old Ringo stared at me with those sad eyes and Paul kept running his hand through his hair nervously. John kept telling the man that he should have let them know he was coming. He said some rude things but the man didn't seem to mind. He just sat there laughing. Before John could hit him I suggested we go down the chip shop. I thought it might calm things down a bit. It was a big mistake.

The Chip Shop Incident, as it has since been dubbed, has been outlined and reported by many Beatles scholars. Among the papers of Tom

Morris, however, a tape was discovered which was apparently recorded accidentally by Dai Llewelyn as he accompanied Tom, the Beatles, and the Maharishi to Fat Ifan's Chip Emporium on the corner of Bryn Street and Caradoc Close. This tape (which also includes various recordings of starlings and thrushes) gives an invaluable insight into the events of that day. The full transcript, presented here for the first time, explains why the Beatles were forced to leave Tonypandy, and it also sheds some light on the mysterious story which appeared on the front page of the *Rhondda Leader* the following morning.

The Chip Shop Tape: A Transcript

JOHN: What do you want, then?

PAUL: Eh?

JOHN: What do you fucking want? You deaf or what?

PAUL: No, it's just that I . . .

(answer obscured by passing bus)

MAHARISHI: Well, I'd like a pasty.

FAT IFAN: Pasty and chips, is it mate?

JOHN: Hang on, you can't have a pasty!

MAHARISHI: Why not? I have the money.

FAT IFAN: Three and six it is.

JOHN: What?

FAT IFAN: Pasty and chips. Three and six. It's on the board.

RINGO: I'll have pasty and chips please.

FAT IFAN: Right you are.

(Sound of chips frying)

MAHARISHI: And me please.

JOHN: But you're supposed to be a fucking vegetarian.

MAHARISHI: I eat goats.

JOHN: You what?

MAHARISHI: Goats and rice.

PAUL: Goat curry?

MAHARISHI: Oh yes, with peas pulao and a side dish of mushroom bhaji. Most favourite dish.

FAT IFAN: I've got some curry sauce if you like.

GEORGE: I'll have some.

FAT IFAN: Righto.

MAHARISHI: And a chips with a pasty.

FAT IFAN: Don't worry, I haven't forgotten.

MAHARISHI: With a pickled onion.

JOHN: You're gonna be a fat Maharishi if you're not careful, Maharishi.

(Maharishi laughs.)

FAT IFAN: And what about you, Tom? Usual, is it? And a meat pie for the missus?

(Sound of a scuffle)

UNKNOWN VOICE: Bloody Hell, it's them!

PAUL: Who the hell—

UNKNOWN VOICE: It's the Beatles!

PAUL: Let's get out of here!

(There is considerable distortion and tape disruption.)

FAT IFAN: Hey, come back! Who's going to pay for all this food?

(Tape ends)

The unidentified voice on the tape belonged to Sam Fowler of the *Rhondda Leader.* Stopping by chance for some fish and chips with his photographer Lenny Tudor, he'd stumbled upon one of the major scoops in his paper's history. Unfortunately, in his excitement Lenny Tudor dropped his camera in the middle of the road, and as he tried to retrieve it he was struck unconscious by a Mini. The Beatles (and a totally confused Tom Morris) dashed down Upper Chemical Terrace and Fowler was left standing outside the chip shop.

The following day's *Rhondda Leader* carried a story of how the Beatles had been spotted on the streets of Tonypandy. Without photographs, however, it failed to be taken seriously. Fowler returned to Tonypandy on the afternoon of Saturday, November 18, but by then the Beatles and the Maharishi were on their way to London. They never returned to Wales.

6.

Whether Tom Morris, his pigeons, or his "self-contained social context" had any tangible benefits for the Beatles is almost impossible to calculate, but it is interesting to speculate whether he served as a catalyst for a new maturity in their lives and music. By the spring of 1968 the Beatles were in Rishikesh with the Maharishi, but Tom Morris had not been forgotten. The gratitude they felt was reflected in a postcard which arrived at Upper Chemical Terrace on February 23, 1968.

> Dear Tom,
>
> As you can see, we're in India. It's hot as hell and Ringo's moaning about the food. Hope you and Eileen are well. Sorry we had to leave so suddenly that day—I'll explain it to you sometime. Thanks a lot for what you did. I don't think you know what you did, but thanks anyway.
>
> Best wishes from us all, love, Paul.

The postcard remained on Tom Morris's mantlepiece until the day of his death.

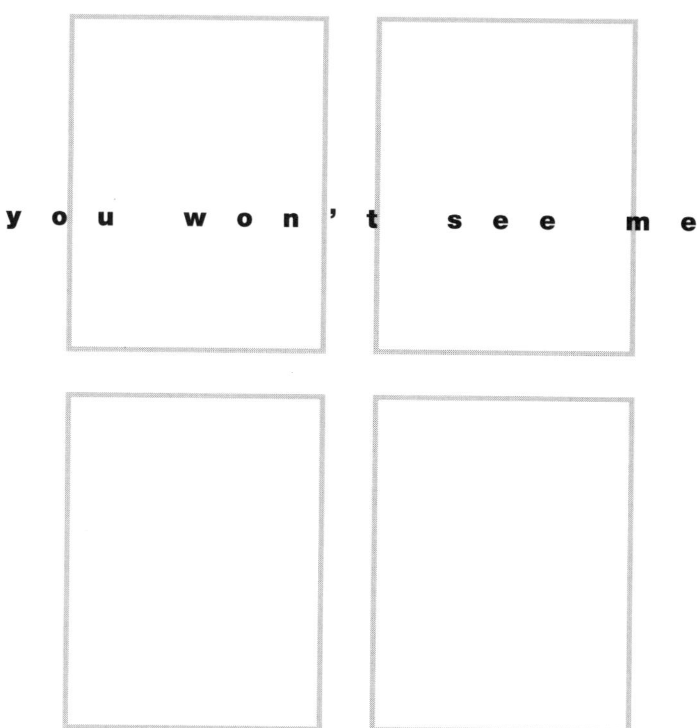
you won't see me

Expatriates

Shelli Jankowski-Smith

Here in Iran we're just
"the Amreekans," "the Brits."
We move conspicuously

through streets sounding
with the clatter of strange words
(it's always the same,

this journey each traveler makes
to become a stranger) yet
still we insist on carrying

a land along with us
on our tongues. Old
hippies, untethered by speech,

hitch on down to Shiraz,
up to Rasht, looking
for hash and poets' graves

and it's they who should be
our prophets in this land,
they who can live on mere

gestures and mute wanderlust.
But the rest of us, trenched
together in this great

bazaar, come to crave
the Hollywood dialogue,
the soft wrinkle of paperbacks

loaned from hand to hand,
the exhilarating rush
of *thump-thump-pahhh*

in rock lyrics. We hide
inside our English, scratch
about for Beatles tapes,

and say without thinking,
OK, it's OK,
insistent in a way

the Persians make fun of,
imitating our strange
and urgent sounds, but

damn it! yes, we're different
and we stake fervent claims
to our sleazy novels,

our Corn Flakes boxes,
our Maltese Falcon,
our Sgt. Pepper's,

to what we groan in bed
together, to *oh yeahhh*
what words make real

even here where
we've got nothing to say
but *it's OK.*

The Moment of Truth

Terry Watada

Twelve-year-old Michael slid back from the ten-inch screen, the seat of his heavy corduroy pants rasping along the linoleum. His mother chortled, her jowls jiggling, her thick thighs vibrating in sympathy.

"*Maaa*, what crazy music!" she exclaimed in Japanese. "I can't believe it." She laughed out loud at the shot of a sobbing girl mouthing her idol's name as the Beatles shook and gyrated through *The Ed Sullivan Show*.

"Mama, you're *kichigai* too!" Michael's father said, startled by the outburst. Lying on the couch, he stroked the stubble on his prominent chin and contemplated the scene with a bemused expression.

"*Hakujin* do funny things, don't they?" Mrs. Akamatsu declared.

Michael looked back and forth from his parents to the television screen. "Boy, they are nuts!" he blurted in agreement. He turned again, his eyes widening to take in as much as he could. He became aware of the bristles of his brush-cut hair. His feet tapped with the rhythm of the music. The refrain swirled in his head.

In his parents' upstairs bedroom later that evening, Michael listened from the big bed to the faint muttering of prayer his mother performed in front of the *hotokesama*. He had left his father slumped in his easy chair in the living room, dozing in front of the television set. Michael never disturbed either of his parents. A great gulf of silence and experience lay between them. Their rudimentary knowledge of English and the imperatives of Japanese culture governing children divided them. He knew what they were saying for the most part, and he did try to connect. But never in Japanese. Every night he gazed at the family altar visible to the left of his mother's soft sloping back, at the black-and-white photographs framed to preserve the memory of dead relatives, strangers to him but loved ones to her.

He did remember standing in front of their graves in Japan about six years ago. His parents had decided to take him on a trip to discover his heritage. His apprehension was fanned by his friends.

"Hey, Mike, you gotta go and give them Japs what for."

"Yeah, show 'em what Canadians are made of!"

Ken Fleming, Frank Wayne, and Mike Akamatsu made up a trio of pals who lived close to one another and were of the same age. Michael spent a great deal of time at his friends' houses, but, oddly, he never invited them into his home even though they often gathered on his front porch. Ken's parents were the rich ones on the street, a half-block down. Mr. Fleming, gray and suffering from premature curvature of the spine, was a bank manager and drove a luxury-model Chevrolet. Mrs. Fleming, a heavyset matron from the British Isles, took it upon herself to set the tone for the neighborhood. Accordingly, she was tolerant of Michael to a point. She once told neighbors he should play with kids of "his own kind down in Chinatown."

"You spend too much time here," she said to him.

Frank's father, a Canadian Army war veteran, always wore his beret and often sat on the veranda steps, working on beer and memory.

"Mike-*san*," he growled, "you stay away from my kids. We didn't finish the job, as far as I'm concerned."

Michael didn't quite know what he meant by that, but he was afraid of the gaunt face with the red, cracked eyes and bone-dry hands and the sour smell of him.

"Sure, Mike, you're a Canadian!" said Frank, surreptitiously winking at Ken. "You gotta make them Nips pay!"

Ken stepped forward. "Mike, make us proud of you."

Michael was surprised by the encouragement of his friends, yet he liked the swell of nationalism in his chest. "Yeah, I'll get them Japs," he said nervously, his eyes darting side to side.

The incense burned steadily and its smoke clung to the ground, the stone grave markers in the rural Japanese cemetery acting like anchors. The summer air was still and heavy with humidity. The *bonsan* chanted a steady stream of Sanskrit verse while the crowd of Akamatsu relatives quietly observed the ritual.

Michael found Japan a completely foreign experience. No Frosted Flakes in the morning—only fish and rice. No running water, no indoor washrooms. The milk tasted funny. And no one spoke English, making him strain to understand every conversation.

At the cemetery he met all his relatives, living and dead, before paying respect to the ancestors. Feeling shy and not wishing to talk to anyone, he stood by his mother solemnly. With the drone of the minister in the background and the sweet, cloying smell of the incense dulling his senses, he turned away and looked to the distance. Above the horizon black smoke emitted from a smokestack atop an anonymous building.

"Mama, what's that?" he asked, pointing to the billowing clouds.

"Mai-ko, shii!"

"Mama . . . mama," he persisted.

She relented and looked up. "Oh, that's where they get rid of dead horses."

"Get rid of horses? How?"

"They burn them up."

They burn them up. The sentence gave Michael pause. He then took notice of all the gravestones around him. Most bore his last name. An aunt who had overheard the conversation teased him about his mother's fate. "Your *okasan* will be burned up too when the time comes." Dread suddenly filled his rapidly mounting thoughts. Michael burst into tears and reached for his mother's arms, crying "No! No!" at the same time.

The crowd glared at him in disdain, but the *bonsan* continued undisturbed.

After the ceremony, Michael was assigned to his young cousins' care. When he met them he knew they weren't exactly thrilled to meet him. The group of three stood on the gravel road outside the slumping homestead of wooden walls and bamboo roof. Tatsuo, the lean and older one, laughed while he spoke to his brother Satomi, chubby and younger. "Look at this *gaijin*! He's like all Americans, stupid looking!" he said in a mocking Japanese.

"You shut up," warned Michael, resorting to English. "I'll show you . . ." He remembered his friends' encouragement as he pulled back a fist and let go.

Tatsuo shifted slightly, caught the fist in the crook of his arm, twisted, and hurled his assailant over his shoulder. Michael hit the ground with arm and knees extended. The thud and scrape shocked him. Cloth tore, skin split. The flush of pain blocked all efforts to understand what had just happened.

The two brother-cousins laughed as they ran down the road toward the village. Michael sat up, his tears stinging the bleeding knee that had popped through his pants. He remained in the road a long time, nursing his wounds and contemplating the merits of being a Canadian.

Back home, Michael eyed his parents with uneasiness. He imagined each of them withering away, falling to the ground in a lifeless heap. Even as his mother laughed with friends over a meal of chow mein takeout, or as his father figured out his strategy for the Japanese Credit Union meeting, his heart would beat faster, his breathing would quicken. He panicked at the thought of death.

"*Mai-ko,* what's wrong with you?"

The scream in his head subsided and he answered with silence. Fear evaporated, leaving an inexplicable residue of guilt.

• • •

"Did you see those guys last night?"

"They were cool."

"Yeah, I love that song. "'I Wanna . . .' 'I Wanna . . .'"

"'I Wanna Hold Your Hand,' dummy."

School was abuzz with the excitement of the new. The girls gushed over the relative cuteness of the band members. The boys indulged in vicarious fantasy. Frank, Ken, and Mike carried their enthusiasm back home to Mike's veranda. They stood together, steaming the cold winter air with their conversation.

"We should form a group," Ken proposed.

Frank curled his lip. "And do what?"

"Play."

"But none of us can play instruments," Michael reminded.

Ken responded quickly. "So we'll fake it."

"What?"

"Listen, I got their album. We'll play it and we'll play along to them." The two seemed skeptical. "I've got two guitars. Frank, you can rig something for drums."

"I guess I could use boxes. My parents save all kinds."

Ken continued, "We'll give a concert in my basement. You know, call all the kids in the neighborhood."

They envisioned the black-and-white hysteria of the night before. Anticipation grew.

"Hey, what'll we call ourselves?"

Ken turned and declared, "The Box Men."

"*Mai-ko*!" A voice from inside the house. "*Gohan!*" The door opened. Mrs. Akamatsu's large form filled the doorway.

"Gotta go, guys."

"Wait, Mike. Can we practice at your place tonight?" asked Ken.

"I don't know," he said, shaking his head. Ken stepped toward Mike's mother.

"Mrs. Akamatsu, can we come over tonight?"

She lowered her eyes, her face flushed as she turned away. "*Mai-ko, hayaku!*"

Mike moved to the door. "I gotta go. It's supper. I can't practice tonight. Maybe tomorrow. Okay?" He followed his mother inside.

Two weeks later, the Box Men made their debut. Word had gotten out quickly and every kid in the neighborhood knew where to be Saturday night.

Ken was enterprising and charged a ten-cent entrance fee. His father approved of his son's initiative, even though Mrs. Fleming worried about the kind of children that filled their newly finished basement.

The rec room was dark with the pungent smell of mothballs and fresh plaster. Candles melting onto plastic skulls flickered in corners. By eight o'clock the room bustled with an audience unsure of what to expect.

An unseen hand switched on red and blue Christmas spotlights to reveal an arrangement of four cardboard boxes of varying sizes in front of the entrance to the furnace room. Two broken hockey sticks with paper cups glued to one end stood in boxes in front. A portable record player sat beside the "drums."

A smatter of applause raced through the crowd and camphor as the three Box Men came out of the furnace room. They were dressed in similar red shirts and white pants. One sat behind the boxes with two well-used drum sticks. The other two stood in front of the "mikes" with worn nylon-string guitars, refugees from the misbegotten guitar lessons of older siblings. Ken was obviously the leader. His height, sandy blond hair, copious freckles, and clear blue eyes placed him high on the cuteness scale for the girls in the audience. Frank, with his dark complexion, thin body, and intense eyes gave off an aura of danger, of juvenile delinquency. Mike seemed the friendliest with his smile and stocky build. He was the perennial sidekick.

The scratchy pop of audio needle to record surface signaled the beginning of the concert. The surge of music set the musicians in motion. They shook, gyrated, and screamed in a pantomime of their heroes. The girls squealed. The boys clapped in time to the beat. People started to dance. By the third song the room was thick with excitement.

Side one ended and an awkward silence settled in. Everyone squinted as the lights switched on abruptly.

"Boys and girls!" called a familiar voice. "Come upstairs to the kitchen. I've got refreshments for you all." Mrs. Fleming beckoned from the foot of the basement stairs.

The Box Men followed the crowd of about twenty to the roomy kitchen, where milk and cookies awaited them. Mrs. Fleming motioned the trio of musicians through the adjoining dining room to the front sitting room.

"Son, that was a good performance," said Mr. Fleming, a craggy, slightly bent man in a business suit sitting on the large couch that dominated the room.

"You saw?"

"We all did," he said, gesturing to his friends, the Fitzgeralds, who lived up the street. "We came down when the, um, music started."

Mrs. Grace Fitzgerald perched on the edge of an imitation Queen Anne chair, Mrs. Fleming's pride and joy. Mrs. Fitzgerald's graying hair was kept curly and short by her downtown stylist. Her clothes were demure but smart in design. She smiled in agreement, waiting for her husband to do the talking.

Detective John Fitzgerald shot the boys a grin from his slumped position within a too-comfortable armchair. The body cut in half, his six-foot height was imperceptible. The short mustache, the tightly cropped hair, the broad forehead, the muscular build gave him the air of authority needed to be a policeman. At the same time, his jovial air and easy manner afforded him the opportunity to roughhouse with the local kids. "Fitz" took every chance to pick up a hockey stick and join the kids in the street to take a few slap shots at a nervous goalie. He enjoyed wrestling with some, tossing water balloons at others, and joking with most. All the roughhousing reminded him of his three sons when they were young and playing in the street during the great days before World War II, before he left with the army for the South Pacific.

"You guys did all right with your *yeah, yeah, yeahs*!" Fitz laughed. "Ken, come here for a sec."

At that moment Mrs. Fleming excused herself to supervise the children in the kitchen. Frank and Mike moved to the middle room to help themselves to the sandwiches Mrs. Fleming had arranged for her adult guests. They remained within earshot.

Mike caught snatches of the conversation. "Why do you need that Japanese . . . brings you down . . . nobody wants to see . . ." The memory of a recent road hockey game came to mind as he turned away from Fitz and Ken.

Fitz takes command of the tennis ball with his stick. He looks for Frank, passes it to him. He turns and sees Mike watching the play develop. Fitz steps sideways and knocks him to the ground. He sniggers at the crumpled boy as he retrieves the ball-puck, takes aim, and fires a high shot at Ken in goal. Ken's glove sweeps up automatically and catches the missile.

Fitz slaps the startled goalie on the back, congratulating him. He grabs Frank around the shoulders at the same time. The other neighborhood players mill about the trio.

"Good play, guys. Well, I gotta go. The missus wants me in for dinner. I'll see you later."

Mike looks up from his prone position. Fitz lumbers up his walk, his jacket casually tossed over his shoulder, his hand wiping the sweat off his forehead with a handkerchief. The boy hears the mocking laughter of his cousins in Japan.

Mike and his fellow Box Men resumed with side two. The temperature and excitement of the room built faster this time, as if everyone knew the evening would soon be over. Ken and Mike, the two front men, began shouting the lyrics as Frank cranked up the record player as loud as it would go. The crowd jumped up and jerked and twisted in a frenzied dance.

• • •

The novelty wore off by spring. Life for the boys returned to normal. Fitz continued to join the daily street games after work. He joked with Ken, terrorized him with high-velocity slap shots, and generally clowned with the others. Mike moved to the fringe of the game to avoid catching Fitz's attention. When the boys weren't scuffling up and down the street, they played their favorite weekend game: guns. Influenced by television and the weekly features at the Eastwood Movie Theatre, they saw themselves as William Holden landing on the beaches of Normandy or John Wayne climbing the hills of Iwo Jima.

The local laneway, across from the Fleming house, ran from the street and met a large sandlot before curving away to run behind the houses. The dump, a junkyard paradise of rusting cars, exposed bedsprings and worn out appliances, was the ideal playground for boys with vivid imaginations. The sand dunes, jutting rocks, and sloping cliffs that climbed to the railway tracks resembled the landscape of movies with titles like *Battle Cry!* and *From Hell to Eternity*.

The D.W. Tomlinson Company owned the vacant land. Tomlinson, a grocer, had taken advantage of the prosperity of the 1950s and built several storage warehouses across the lane from the houses. The dump was land gone fallow, intended for later expansion.

The three boys thought of it as their territory. Armed with wooden sticks or plastic guns, they defended the land against intruders and pretenders.

"Frank, who's that?" Ken asked.

"Where?"

"Up on top."

Five figures combed the terrain like ants on an anthill.

"Looks like kids from across the tracks."

"C'mon."

Mike felt himself pulled along. "Where?"

"To get rid of those guys!" Ken yelled.

As the three scaled the heights, they taunted the enemy. "Hey you creeps, get outta here." "Who do you think you are?" "We're gonna get you guys!" Frank raised his imitation carbine and pulled the trigger. The caps sparked and the noise echoed.

A strange echo ricocheted. The sand near Frank's feet danced. A second later, Frank let out a cry, his gun flying down the incline. He fell to the dirt, his hands covering his face.

The tallest of the gang holding the high ground lowered his rifle and let out a whoop. The others picked up rocks and hurled them down upon their assailants.

Mike could see the smirk beneath the wire-rimmed glasses of the leader. He jerked the hands away from Frank's face and found his cheek bleeding. Ken soon reached them and hustled them down the precipice, rocks landing all around them.

Where the laneway joined the street, Ken decided that Frank had been hit by a BB from an air rifle. Mike wiped his dirt-smudged face before noticing the blood on his hand. Wounded by a rock.

A chorus of distant catcalls stabbed deeper into wounds and hearts.

The heat shimmered above the fire. Ashes flaked off the graying wood and floated midair, caught in the updraft. Buried in the nest of kindling and combustion were six potatoes covered with aluminum foil. They looked like the eggs of a storybook phoenix.

Two of the boys crouched by the fire, poking the potatoes from time to time. Ken stood to keep a lookout. He trained his new Winchester BB rifle on the cliffs of the dump.

"Will you sit down!" ordered Frank. His face seemed drawn, all lines converging on the slight scar on his cheek. "It's been two weeks and we ain't seen those guys."

"Yeah, but they're there," Ken answered self-consciously.

"So what?"

"So we'll be ready for them next time."

Next time? Mike shuddered at the prospect.

The potatoes were hot but crunchy. Mike didn't mind. He enjoyed the apple texture. His mother made them too soft on the rare occasion he had potatoes rather than rice for dinner.

The boys lay back on the ground after their meal and relaxed their guard.

Something occurred to Mike. "Ken, you ever think about your parents?"

"Yeah, sure, all the time, especially around allowance time," he said, laughing as he gave his rifle a pat.

"No, I mean seriously. You ever think about them croaking?"

"You mean dying? What're you talking about? Yours dying soon?"

"No . . . no, I mean it'd be awful if they did. I keep trying to talk to them about stuff but I can't get through to them . . . them being Japanese and all."

Ken jerked his head up and shushed Mike at the same time. He heard someone approaching. In the distance he saw Fitz walking up the laneway from the street. "Hey, hey, get your guns. I got an idea."

The other two crawled over to Ken.

"That's just Fitz," Frank said.

"Yeah, let's scare him."

"What?" asked the other two.

"C'mon, it'll be fun," Ken called as he crept quickly to where the laneway met the sand and hid among garbage cans destined for the dump. Behind him, Mike and Frank took up positions in nearby bushes. Fitz continued to walk up the lane on his way to his garage, unaware of any ambush.

At the crucial moment all three jumped from their hiding places, their cap pistols and BB rifle blazing. Fitz reared straight up and staggered in surprise. He recovered quickly.

In one swift motion he grabbed Mike, the closest to him, by the back of the shirt and pulled out his service revolver. He roughly placed the barrel right between the boy's eyes.

"So you think you got the drop on ol' Fitz," he spat, his voice quivering with adrenaline.

Time stood suspended. Mike's mind traced the circle of the barrel mouth. Electricity shot down his legs as if his self were draining from him. Death breathed in his face.

"You little Jap. I oughta pull the trigger. . . ." He pushed the boy to the ground. Still aiming the revolver, he growled with contempt, "I oughta, for the boys I left behind. Goddamn it, I oughta." Tears blinded him. He lowered the weapon and slouched his way up the back alley.

No one said a thing. No one could. When Ken and Frank saw Fitz pull his revolver, invisible hands grabbed their throats in a choke hold. Their hollow legs became weighed down with cement, their throats desert dry. Even as Fitz moved away, they couldn't move. Frank's left hand shook slightly.

Mike felt the sharp edges of the gravel. He scraped the ground with his hands. The charcoal roughness turned red with his blood.

The boy stood before his mother shivering, a mass of mixed emotions. He felt pulverized and scattered, like dust dancing in light. In his mind he could still hear his friends calling after him as he ran up the street, away from them. The raised eyebrows, the pained look in his mother's eyes spoke of her dismay at the condition of his clothes and the torn skin of his palms.

"Where have you been?" Mrs. Akamatsu barked. "Look at those dungarees. Do you know how much these things cost?"

As his mother spanked his bottom in an effort to punish him and to clean the fabric at the same time, Mike thought about telling her. He even saw himself breaking down and crying in her comforting arms.

He then imagined his mother wilting before Fitz's dismissive glare, contemptuous of her quaking English. In the rain of scolding Japanese words, he kept his mouth shut and stood silently, a burning ring pressing between his eyes.

Roots

Mark Halliday

How good is it to know where you came from,
what people you came from and what they believed?
My mother never spoke of her parents—
they had somehow seen her as a bad girl
and she left Canada forever.
My father occasionally spoke of his grandparents
but it never seemed as if I had to listen . . .
Michigan—

in a small Michigan town two horses clop along
the dirt street under a blue sky
and the riders in the buggy or wagon or cart
believe in Jesus Christ
and the grownups can remember England.
They must have ideas about Oliver Cromwell
and William Pitt and Napoleon
and Andrew Jackson.

But I just found myself alive
in Raleigh, North Carolina
with my Davy Crockett cap and my Fanner .50,
my mother gave me a milkshake with an egg in it
each day after first grade so I'd get strong,
because you need to be strong to do things, to live,
and you just want to live.
I learned the word "agnostic" to tell what I was,
and my father's friend Jack Suberman chuckled when I said
"McCarthy is an alligator,"

soon I had ideas about Mickey Mantle and Roger Maris—
men who came from nowhere, who had always been Yankees,
who stepped from nowhere to the plate and clobbered the ball.

Then in 1964 in the ping-pong room in Connecticut
what mattered to Trey and Jon and me was the Beatles,
their every syllable: brown-haired angels,
the radiant big boys that we might become.
They were British, well, wasn't I sort of British
with a name like Halliday? It was good not to be
faintly peculiar like a Jew or a Catholic;
at the same time we were all Americans and that was good too
for freedom, freedom from old dark worries and popes and kings.
We sang "It Won't Be Long" and "Any Time At All"
in our church of albums . . .
Upstairs, Daddy was an expert on Hemingway's heroes.
He got me to read stories about Nick Adams—
you had to be brave because you would be alone
some day in the forest or in a big city.
And it was important to work hard in high school,
the quadratic theorem and molecules
and the Reign of Terror leading to Napoleon
then go to a famous college.
It was just important.
                                        With no God or Bible
there was sometimes a funny emptiness
in the car on North Avenue

but I had the Beach Boys, I had the Byrds,
I had the Lovin' Spoonful in a world all new;
one day in twelfth grade suddenly there was *Rubber Soul*
proving forever what you needed for the right life:
romantic love, humor, brilliant freshness—
that was it!
The universe had given *Rubber Soul* into our chosen hands.

A Different Bag

Larry Neal

Memory. If you is looking for lo-jik in a world that oppress you, den yr out out of yo head boy. He say. De winds was speakin' to him also and dere were spirits in it, in de sound; and durin' the voyage, while chains clinked he did ju-ju and called up the best that was within his-self; de words came forth from the deep well full of swirlings and hoodoo glimpses of the infinite wisdom of de universe. Dey spoke of natural things, of the ways that men must finally be, de pure strength inside of them. Not the dead. Not the dead rhythms they were to encounter later in the spiritless West. Down in the creativity of them, this substance; a prelude to the blues, the dance informed by the drum and song, and the Spirit hovering over. It was here in the dead valleys of the West that we re-created ourselves; and the slave merchants lurked in the shadows gaining strength from our creations.

But it bees that way when yr a nigger slave, brother, dig? And when yr such, expect to be used and abused (aha)! Daddy Cracker Rice puts on his blk. face, does the turn-around-jump-jim-crow-dance. And the jass imitators came. And the imitators of the imitations, and then the, and then the, and . . .

Because of the weight of his history, the black man responds to the world differently from the white man. It is a history weighted in oppression. Counterpoised against this oppression is a fantastically dynamic culture. The chief purpose of which is not only to provide "entertainment" but also to make possible the survival of one's soul in an essentially soulless world. The roots of our music therefore are very profound and are in no sense the expression of an elite orientation in social and religious life. Our songs are the closest thing that America has to a mythic cycle. The blues. The blues are like a string of folk narratives reflecting the myriad lives that birthed them and gave them shape. They are the creations of a collective psyche; and it was very necessary to create them. For the creation of the blues was a ritual act whose purpose was to make the race better able to survive. And, regardless of what my friend Al Calloway says in *Esquire* magazine, soul is not at all about being "hip." Soul is about survival. What you need. What you need to live in a world dominated by an aspiritual sensibility; that is, we are now living in a world that sees power in the hands of the *beast* of the planet. What you need to feel more alive inside of the inside of yourself. It is a need. It is acquired by need, by going through changes, paying one's dues, so to speak. To pay our due is to undergo the rites of passage from boyhood to manhood; is to have been initiated by the fire and then perceive some essential aspects of truth.

Dig John Lee Hooker speaking to his audience:

> "To you and all of my friends . . . especially my fellow mens. I'm so glad that we're here . . . it's a big wide world . . . we come a long ways. We trying trying to throw a program, me, Brownie (McGhee), Sonny (Terry), everybody . . . all folk singers. We are here to pay our dues to the natural facts. You know . . . we have come a long ways . . . we all . . . we entertainers trying to reach you to bring you the message of the blues . . . and folk . . . sometimes we traveling late at night. We are trying to reach you . . . to pay our dues to the natural facts . . . to you, for your enjoyment. All entertainers . . . sometimes you tired when you reach your destination. But you're paying your dues to the facts. We are here to please you the best we know. I hope you accept . . . thanks."

Hooker gives this monologue while running short riffs on his guitar. Each riff is a comment on his verbal statements and a kind of musical extension of the idea of struggle that he is trying to convey to his audience. Hooker's world is decidedly different from the zany world of *A Hard Day's Night*. His voice echoes chain gangs, steel mills, railroad yards, Southern cracker sheriffs, joblessness, and the most intense kinds of personal tragedies imaginable. His is not the world of little English boys with long hair. No. His is about something else. There are no blues in the land of Sergeant Pepper. And the British, like the Americans, are just beginning to know what it is to really pay some dues. Therefore, the emotional references we find in works by the Beatles are only vaguely interesting to black people. White emotional references can only be made meaningful by twisting them all out of shape; the word-images becoming something else—something closer to a black sensibility. Like suppose *Hard Day's Night* was about Billie Holiday, Charlie Parker, or any number of blues singers on the road. We would be all up into something else then, a whole 'nother universe.

To the black community, the Beatles come across as young boys. Everything about them smacks of boyhood. The most consistently asserted value in the black community is the necessity of maintaining one's manhood. In terms of the collective perception, the long hair of the Beatles and other white rock groups gives hints of femininity. In a world where a manly image is highly valued there is no place for little boys. Sam and Dave sing, "I'm a soul man." James Brown sings, "It's a man's world." These are necessary assertions in an emasculating world. The singer posits for his community and for himself the desired goal—manhood. Male vibrations are spiritual forces, weapons, and defenses against the imperial castraters. Black men, therefore, assert manhood. Black women demand it. And they sing the praises of men who have it. And they denounce them that don't. It has been this way a long time; back when John Henry did his thing, and when Stagolee shot Billy Lyons. All of those had niggers informing the blues. Some of them were "Mack Daddys." Others worked on chain gangs. They metamorphosed in the North and became hustlers and warriors. The women demand it. Denounce them that don't have it. And this is as it should be.

The Beatles exist outside of this world view. It's not their fault. They are little boys. They are not Frank Sinatra even. At least he *does* have machismo. The Beatles are neither liked nor disliked in the black community, but rather they are ignored.

What we are finally talking about are different ways of looking at the world. That is, the way in which the world is felt and the weight of that feeling in the scheme of things. And on a more profound level it is about place. Where you are in the world. Sergeant Pepper is not in the world as black people see it. No doubt about it. It's even ridiculous to speak about it. I mean, this is all bullshit intellectualism anyway. I mean, if you really want to know, *go* to the Apollo. Another place. Harlem. About another sensibility. Blues people cannot afford to fantasize too long or they will be summarily taken off the planet. Are there really diamond ladies floating around in the sky? In whose imagination? To propose this kind of multicolored nightmare to black people is to propose the death of the spirit. And that is why. In terms of standard Western sociopolitical analysis, the ideas of the Beatles issue forth from an essentially middle-class sensibility. Some black folk have similar hang-ups, but black music is about things more fundamental. Could I love and only want to dance with you, baby, as Lennon and McCartney write:

> "I don't wanna kiss or hold your hand
> I don't need to hug or hold you tight
> If it's funny try an' understand
> I just wanna dance with you all night."

This is cute schoolboy morality. Compare it to Aretha Franklin's "Respect," where sound moral principles are linked to the concrete demands of daily survival. Aretha's placement, however body-oriented, is finally more spiritual than the false platonism of the Beatles song.

Black music is essentially informed by a religious sensibility. The music has its roots in ritual and spirit worship. Except for the folk impulse, Euro-American music has ceased to be ritualistic. However, black singers like Aretha Franklin, Ray Charles, James Brown, Stevie Wonder, and Percy Sledge are straight out of the church-gospel thing. It is the emotional energy of the churches that shapes and informs black music. No such analogy exists in white popular music. Correspondingly, the music of white Christianity is a dead music.

And it is very difficult to find any source of creative inspiration in it. Under these conditions it is no surprise that a rebellion is occurring in many areas of orthodox Christianity. White Christians now find their lives bereft of intense spiritual feeling. They now want to get back to the spirit of the "primitive" church, back to the early pentecostal energy of the Holy Ghost. The black community is in need of no such movement. Art and ritual are still closely linked to the collective aspirations of the community.

James Brown screams joy-pain and slides across the stage. There is a flashing of bright colors. The band sways also. A sister boogaloos atop the rhythm. He calls out to his audience. They answer. He screams. They scream. He dances with the mike, falls caressing it, a lover. Soon the whole theater is in motion. He screams again, falling to his knees: Baaa-by, baaa-by, pleeze don't go! *Damn near exhausted, slithers offstage. We scream. We scream. He returns. Picks up the tempo and begins wailing again. He calls out to us. We answer. He does a hip spin that ends in a split. Screams. We scream—the pain. Suddenly the entire audience breaks into a boogaloo. The ritual cycle complete, the song-god fades, as if gliding . . .*

Here the style is ritualistic. The way you move across the stage, the bizarre and subtle executions, the way you ride the mike. Underneath are the blues. Black musical styles, the most unwhitened, are either blues oriented or energy oriented. At one end of what LeRoi Jones calls the blues continuum are singers like B. B. King and T-Bone Walker. In between are singing groups like the Temptations, the Miracles, and the Impressions. On this end of the continuum (spectrum) is the energy-music of John Coltrane, Cecil Taylor, Archie Shepp, and Milford Graves. The sub-base of all the music is black religious music. No such relationship exists in white popular music. And it is the absence of the blues gospel dynamic that obviates black appreciation of most white music. The Beatles initially tried to imitate the blues quality of black music; the end result proved not only to be a poor imitation of the music, but was, in fact, an insulting parody of the black lifestyle.

Therefore, the Beatles joined in the historical bastardization of black art at the hands of white musicians and entertainers. The Beatles, however, unlike many performers who have utilized Afro-American cultural expression, were honest enough to admit their debt to singers like Muddy Waters and Chuck Berry. These are the debts overlooked by the white critical establishment. But it is obvious that white cultural expression owes a tremendous debt to black creativity. Such has been the case, not only in the popular arts but in the so-called higher art forms as well. Picasso and Modigliani borrowed freely from African plastic forms. White actors of the late nineteenth century painted their faces black and did racist imitations of black folk drama. It is ironic that Paul Whiteman could be dubbed the "King of Jazz" at a time when Sidney Bechet, Louis Armstrong, and Kid Ory were still living. In the twenties, black musicals like *Shuffle Along* helped to change the entire character of the Broadway musical. *Porgy and Bess* owes what little musical power it has to black folk music. And so the story goes. The black man's creativity has economically benefited everyone but the black man himself. Because America is a racist society, black creative expression is feared and rarely accepted on its own terms. There must always be some "white hope" to make it more palatable. The Beatles and other white rock groups are merely modern examples of a pattern of cultural co-option that started years ago. But the Beatles are not the bad guys. They just doing what comes naturally in white culture. Further, considering the sterility of much of white culture, we could hardly blame them for trying to cop something meaningful.

But in America it is very difficult to separate the good guys from the bad guys. They all wear Brooks Brothers suits anyway; or they hang out on Broadway laid out in Italian knits and chewing stubby cigars. Or they're the clean-cut apple pie types like Dick Clark who make jive white boys like Elvis Presley rich.

Presley, who imitated blues-shouting Big Mama Thornton and Fats Domino, was the forerunner of the Beatlemania of the early sixties. His style is directly traceable to the rhythm 'n' blues singers of the late forties and early fifties. Singers and groups like Ivory Joe Hunter, Ruth Brown, Sonny Till, Chuck Willis, LaVerne Baker, Clyde McPhatter, the Ravens, the Orioles, the Drifters, the Clovers, and the Coasters represent the rhythm 'n' blues tradition at its best. They were the voice of black America, the poets of an oppressed people. They were great, but most of them were never allowed to break into the larger commercial market. This was the "race" music that was rarely heard by the white public. In a sense it was an underground art. And it was not even considered marketable. All of that changed with the advent of Elvis Presley (the White Hope) and the communications explosion. Therefore, in a perverse kind of way, white imitations helped to open up some employment for black singers. But the real money was made by the white recording companies. The so-called rock explosion sent white entrepreneurs in search of more black talent to exploit.

Suddenly the youth market came to represent a large part of the economy of the country. And they were demanding a more exciting music. The Lawrence Welk–type cornball of their parents had to go. The country needed energy. White singers began digging black music, the most clearly identifiable music in America. They began to sing folk songs and they came to understand that much of what passed for culture in white America was dead. The black man is what's happening because he is in motion. He is about change. So white Americans began trying to sing his blues and folk songs. They tried to sing them even though they did not understand the sensibility that produced them. But they knew that whatever that sensibility was, it was more profound than the sensibilities of their parents.

The so-called Beat movement found white dudes getting high and trying to talk and walk like the black hipster. Norman Mailer dug it. The "white negro" is a prelude to the hippie. Meanwhile, the upper classes, always the last people to get hip, started doing African dances like the Twist, the Fish, the Jerk, the Madison, the Hully-Gully. It was clear to any keen observer of the social scene that something of profound implications was happening in America. Most liberals did not understand it. But the American right wing did. They saw their sons and daughters doing nigger dances and claimed that there was a communist plot afoot to destroy American morality (as if the country were moral). They found all kinds of subversive allusions in the lyrics of rock 'n' roll songs. Bob Dylan and Pete Seeger came under special attack in a West Coast anticommunist film. This film attempted to illustrate the evil influences of rock 'n' roll on white youth. But its primary motivations were racist. It was essentially an attack on what the filmmakers described as the junglelike qualities of the music.

But these kinds of attacks could not stop the revolution in pop culture. The wellsprings of America's popular art had run dry. So her singers and entertainers dipped into the culture of the underclasses in an attempt to inject some vitality into American national life. The country even wanted a swinging president, at least one with style. Enter JFK, the first president to try to be hip. Discotheques opened. Jackie Kennedy was photographed doing the Twist.

The emergence of the Beatles is linked to the epoch's rejection of squaredom as the normal way of life. For the Beatles, however square themselves, had found the formula. They "cleaned" up the lyrics and used the most obvious aspects of black music: the big beat, amplification (picked up from Chuck Berry), ensemble singing, and a vague hint at blueness. But they were kids, and emotional subtleties eluded them. Even their ejaculation *Yeah! Yeah! Yeah!* was awkward and bland; mainly it lacked the conviction that blues singers infuse into it. "Yeah" is one of those bridge words found in black music. It is both a technical and an emotional device. It may be shouted in strong affirmation of the positive. Or it may be moan-sung, the way Smokey Robinson sometimes sings it. It definitely has meaning. It is one of the poignant words in the blues' lexicon. But who could really believe the Beatles when they sang, "She loves you, yeah, yeah!"? Only the white audience to which the song was addressed. No black person would want to be loved with so little conviction and feeling. We hear the world differently. The Beatles sounded absolutely ludicrous to us.

I am certain that the Beatles were not trying to be black. The whole thing may have, at first, been a joke.

Even though the initial ingredients of the Beatles' music are rooted in Afro-American and even some West Indian music, there is very little relationship between that music and the music of the black community. This statement is not tantamount to a put-down. That's just the way it is; it bees that way. What we are really talking about are the different ways artists relate to their communities. In the black community the singer is the ritual embodiment of the aspirations and sufferings of the people. He is the tribal poet. The collective voice. His power derives from his ability to articulate and fortify the conscious and unconscious urges of his community. The primary point of focus for the black singer must be the black community. Not only because racism forces him there, but also because, very often, that is where he *wants* to be. He represents specific points of identification. And this identification, as we have noted, is linked with the black man's profound spirituality. Further, the most important feature of Afro-American culture is that it places a great deal of importance on experience—more precisely, on experience as it is felt. This is how Julius Lester runs it down:

> In black culture it is the experience that counts, not what is said. The rhythm-and-blues singer and the gospel quartets know that their audiences want to feel the song. The singers are the physical embodiment of the emotions and experiences of the community. They are separate from the community only in that they have the means to make the community experience through music that no-good man who left, the pain of loneliness, the joy of love, physical and religious.

Neither the Beatles nor any other white group brings to the black community any experiences that are finally meaningful. There is no pain inside them. Or at least it is a pain that we cannot perceive. You may ask, then: How is it that several of Lennon and McCartney's songs are sung by black singers? First, on the level of abstract lyric, many of the songs are quite interesting. But primarily it's not the lyrics that count; it is rather what black singers *do* to them. Black singers do what is called "bending" a white song. They bend it all out of shape, emphasizing certain things and deleting other things. Bending consists primarily of expanding the song's emotional values. The black singer will invariably use more blue notes, slurs, glissandos, moans, and shouts. The song, if it is not too tacky, actually becomes a new song. Ray Charles' interpretation of "Eleanor Rigby," for example, barely hints at the song's baroque structure. His version is gospel-blues-oriented. The same hold for the Temptations and Ray's rendition of "Yesterday." It is the emotional expansion that makes the songs go for black listeners, many of whom don't even know that the Beatles wrote these songs.

Therefore, what amounts to a generalized expression of the love-need is made more specific. In that instance the singer brings to the song the full weight of his emotional history. And that history is quite different from the history of most white men.

There is then a difference between black art and white art. Not only do we determine this difference in the gesture and the manner of art, but also in the function and the nature of art in the universe. The Western (Euro-American) sensibility attempts to freeze art, to make it *a* forever. But man cannot create *a* forever. He can only create as change. Nothing is permanent but change itself. The nature of the universe is change. A classic is not a classic if no one sings or reads it. When the Beatles said that they were more popular than Jesus, they had a good point. If people were really still digging J.C. today, the Beatles could not have made that statement. Black art is directed at specific realities, the black audience swirling out there. It proceeds later to make itself more general.

Ironically, black culture is able to absorb certain features of white culture and not lose its essential integrity. But the process is not strictly reversible. Or at least it is rarely accepted by the black community. Bobbie Gentry's "Ode to Billie Joe" is one notable exception. Mose Allison and Herbie Mann are two others from the jazz bag.

However, white people with their stale lives need black culture, while black people rarely need white culture. As James Baldwin once said, the only thing white people got that black people should want is power. White culture is so corny and soulless that no black man who knows where it's really at wants any part of it. Even white youth are rejecting it. The hippie movement is a reaction against a dead culture. I can readily understand why some Americans want to be high all the time. I can understand why white people are turning on with LSD. This is a cold scene. But black people don't need LSD. LBJ could use some, perhaps. But the brothers have James Brown, Wilson Pickett, and John Coltrane behind which to blow their minds. And dat do make a difference. Like you can feel pretty spiritual and powerful digging James Brown or Coltrane.

The latest thing with the whiteys is the guru bag. Well, I can dig it. There ain't no real spiritual force operative in the West, save that of the oppressed peoples. So the Beatles get interested in Indian music and culture. That's more like where it's at. Hell. The West is spiritually dead, and what "hip" white boy wants to be dead? I mean, really. The Beatles are OK, I suppose. I mean, we could care less. They just bees in another bag, that's all.

He Loves You (Yeah, Yeah, Yeah)

Hillary Rollins

When I was in third grade, the Beatles appeared on *The Ed Sullivan Show*. I was called into the living room to witness this phenomenon by my parents, who were in show business and therefore believed that while they themselves had little use for the Fab Four (my father, a professional manager and judge of talent, thought the band would "never make it"), I ought to be kept abreast of whatever was "happening," even at the tender age of eight. I watched without judgment—the Beatles seemed neither good nor bad nor even especially interesting. What did any of this have to do with me? I was still listening to a bright red vinyl LP of "Peter and the Wolf" with "Tubby the Tuba" on the B side. But the day after the Sullivan broadcast, Emily C.—nine and a half and the center of my universe—taught me the drill: Put "She Loves You (Yeah, Yeah, Yeah)" on the record player, kiss the oversized areola of a Beatles button she'd purchased at Cheap Charlie's along with several packs of Beatles cards and a not-so-cheap Beatle's lunch box, then faint. That's what the grown-up girls did—scream and faint. But try as I might, I just couldn't seem to pass out over Paul ("He's cute"), or George (Shy? Sweet? Mysterious? Eventually we'd learn the word was *spiritual*), or Ringo ("I guess he's supposed to be funny"), or even the smart, the serious, the witty, the intellectual, the "writer of wrongs," artist, poet, and guy who would eventually publish a tiny, incomprehensible book of scribbles which proved that he was more than just a wizard of rock 'n' roll music, that he was some kind of a goddamned visionary genius—John Lennon. Even Lennon's soon-to-be-legendary soulfulness could not fell me. No matter how dedicated my efforts, I simply didn't get that rush of

Moog-synthetic music in my ears which precedes a bona fide faint.
"Fake it," said Emily.

The following August I went to the Beatle's concert at Shea Stadium. In the months between *The Ed Sullivan Show* and the live event at Shea, I had mastered the art of deception, or should I say theatrical illusion, by dramatically and convincingly pretending to swoon on the living room carpet in homage to the Liverpudlian lads. Of course, lying on the floor in a feigned faint was far too passive for the energy of an eight year old, and I secretly preferred the sessions of learning to dance to the Twist under the recorded tutelage of Chubby Checker: "Move like you're drying your back with a giant bath towel while stamping out a cigarette with your foot." But if fake fainting was what it took to honor the Brits, who was I to swim against the tide?

My folks knew a bigwig in the music industry who offered us tickets to the concert. Because it was to take place in August, we would have to make an unscheduled trip from our upstate vacation home into the sweltering city; my father wanted no part of it. But Mom, bless her acculturated heart, recognized the magnitude of the event and agreed to take me and my eleven-year-old sister into town to witness history. Alas, the baby—our younger sister who was then three years old but destined to be forever dubbed "the baby"—was farmed out to Grandma's for the day. She cannot now lay claim to the minor celebrity that attendance at a Beatles concert affords her two elders (which may, in part, explain thirty years of sibling hostility).

When the auspicious afternoon arrived, we rode the subway to the outer borough of Queens for my first rock concert. I was not sure if this was going to rival that borough's prior event—the 1964 World's Fair, where you could wait on line all day just to eat Belgian waffles and listen to "It's a Small World After All" sung by midget puppets of many lands—but the envy of my peers gave me hope and a sense of personal panache I'd longed for. Emily seethed.

I'd never been to Shea Stadium. I'd never been to any sporting arena except Madison Square Garden to see the circus because, my father notwithstanding, we were an all-girl family with little interest in team sports. I was shocked by the size of the place. Enormous concentric ovals of seats ringed the giant playing field. In the three-o'clock quadrant stood a platform that by today's concert standards seems barely adequate: no rear-projection video screens, no eye-popping laser shows—just a simple, functional riser, small as an airmail stamp against the expanse of the field. I was skeptical. I'd seen a Broadway show or two in my time, I knew that the magic was made with fancy sets, velvet curtains, amber lighting, a strobe. Even the "Small World" puppets rated some pop-art flowers and touch of Day-Glo acrylic to tart up their performance space. But if the stage for this event was a flat-chested Plain Jane, the bleachers were dressed to the nines, as swollen and pulsing with freshly minted estrogen as Ann-Margret's pout. It seemed there were at least a million girl-women writhing in the urban heat, shifting from side to side on impatient pelvic bones or rolling the muscles of their bellies like Sultanas preparing for a birth. And not one of them had come with their mother.

When the Beatles finally made their appearance, I could barely make out their faces. They were tiny, distant figures marooned on the makeshift stage. How could this be? The Beatles I knew were larger than life—the Beatles of the TV screen and the album cover, the Beatles of mass marketing and mass hysteria, warriors of the British Invasion who had come to reclaim the colonies one teenager at a time. And wasn't that the whole point of the Beatles—that they *loomed*? But here were four little dots, bobbing on a life raft, as impersonal and indistinguishable as a set of tin soldiers. The moment they made their way from the bowels of stadium into the blinking August light, the screaming, sobbing, and yes, fainting, began. Still, I was able to recognize the opening chords of "She Loves You" before the din became deafening. From then on I heard not one note of any song. The Beatles might have been playing "Tubby the Tuba" for all I knew. The real show wasn't on stage, but at the edge of the bleachers where a not-so-thin blue line of New York's finest made a human barricade between the fans and the playing field. Tidal waves of girls wailing like mourners at a jazz wake rolled down from the stands to heed the call of their own private Sirens and throw themselves against the rocks of the policemen's chests and outstretched arms. But not one reached the laden oasis in the center of the field. With work-a-day calm and precision, the cops scooped up the girls in a counterwave, deposited them back into the stands, and awaited the next onslaught.

I wondered what, exactly, these fanatical devotees would have done if they'd reached their goal? What was a brief moment in proximity with a real live Beatle actually going to achieve? Sure, one might grab a thread from George's velvet collar or wipe a swath of magical mystery sweat off of John's brow for use in a poultice or potion. But why go to all the trouble of attacking your obsession if it's unlikely to yield, say, a proposal of marriage? Or at the very least an invite to a Mod party somewhere off of Carnaby Street the next time you happened to be passing through London town? And surely throwing oneself, beet-faced and sloppy, onto the stage in the middle of a concert was no way to get Pauly to pop the question. With the cool and jaundiced eye of youth, I could see that. Even a few years later, when the dark skepticism of childhood was lifted by my sudden realization that James Taylor was going to marry me, when I used my copy of *Sweet Baby James* to do the closest thing to French kissing one can approximate with a two-dimensional photo on an album cover, when I realized that we were destined to live in deeply meaningful wedlock because I was the only female he'd ever come across with sufficient poetry in her soul—even then, I had the sobriety to know we'd have to be formally introduced.

Straining in the bleachers at Shea, I was more than a little annoyed that I couldn't hear anything except the hoarse cry of a generation. I liked the Beatles for their songs. I knew all the words, I could sing the exact harmonies, which I'd surreptitiously studied while enacting unconsciousness on the living room rug or during times when Emily wasn't around and I sat hunched over the built-in speakers of my low-tech record player—I couldn't understand why these girls wouldn't want to hear the music! But as I watched them manufacture tears on cue and transform their baby faces into masks of rapture and pain, I realized they knew something I didn't. Something essential and frightening and glamorous and just outside my reach. While I was critical, I was also envious. At eight, poised not quite at but near the edge of that cliff, I yearned to inherit this world of Eros and its many manias, Beatles and otherwise.

I tried to run down to the edge of the bleachers on the next pulse of hysteria, but wouldn't you know it? My mommy stopped me. Which may, in part, explain thirty years of mother/daughter hostility.

Today I am sitting in my apartment watching the much touted television event *The Beatles Anthology*, with another in a long line of men-I-sleep-with-who-like-me-a-lot-but-don't-want-to-be-my-boyfriend. This one is a professional musician and a self-proclaimed Beatles expert. The Beatles changed his life, he tells me; they are the whole reason he became a musician. I ask him what it was about their music that inspired him to his chosen profession.

"A few of my friends and I cut school and went to see *A Hard Day's Night*. All the screaming teenage girls throwing themselves at those guys? Man, we said, this is the life!"

The Beatles—unlike the compulsory swoons of prior generations such as Frank Sinatra and Elvis Presley—had the distinction of stealing the hearts and awakening the libidos of scores of young women while at the same time managing to *not* alienate the guys. On the contrary, my subjective memory of Shea as having been awash in nothing but weepy femininity aside, the boys often were—and are—bigger Beatlemaniacs than the girls. But in demonstrating their fervor for the holy quadrangle, they didn't learn to "fake it." They learned the guitar.

• • •

Several years after the August '65 concert, as I entered the morass of adolescence, I bought a beautiful Martin D-35 steel-string acoustic. I learned enough chords to play some tepid folk songs and tried to join in the fun. But not long after having discovered it was my fate as a girl to have to feign a form of *le petit mort* in the service of Beatlemania, I discovered another trait apparently associated with the inheritance of multiple X chromosomes: Girls could only play tambourine. Not the guitar, not the bass, and certainly not the drums, God forbid. If you really had to be part of the band instead of simply *with* the band . . . well then, you could shake a tambourine. Just as I'd sat in kindergarten ten years earlier being told "any one of you can grow up to become the President of the United States," all the while knowing only half of us *really* could (and then only if they were white), I now understand that even though I was the owner of my own spectacular Martin D-35, there was no point in trying to use it to live the Life of Riley the Rock Star. Sure, Jefferson Airplane had a lead singer who was a woman, but she didn't make the *music,* she didn't wail acid riffs on an electric "ax" slung low on presumably well-hung hips. Sure, Joni Mitchell was brilliant, successful, and respected, but her métier was more folk than rock—delicate, elegant, and soulful. Did anyone ever catch Mitchellmania? The message was clear: Unlike Hendrix or Clapton or JohnPaulGeorge&Ringo—in fact, unlike almost any idiot boy who could manage to strum a six-string in these United States—playing the guitar would not make me sexy.

Having the guitar, *providing* the guitar, was another story. Boys followed me home from school begging for a chance to finger its mother-of-pearl-studded neck and pick out the opening bars of "Blackbird" on my shapely Martin, which had more sensual proportions than did I. I learned to lend them the thing whenever they asked, to hang out nearby striking suggestive poses, to hum a timid harmony. But I never tried to play "Blackbird" myself—at least not in their presence. In 1972 the rules for playing music with the guys were analogous to those for playing cards or chess or sports in my mother's day: If you want them to like you, let them win. I was already a committed feminist on a political and social scale, yet somehow this did not extend to interpersonal dynamics or the sacred realm of rock 'n' roll. Sitting at a boy's feet, feigning adoration for his shut-down, distant, self-involved brand of sexuality, I accepted instrument worship as the closest I would ever come to love. Occasionally I shook a tambourine.

All of which may, of course, in part explain thirty years of male/female hostility.

The Beatles Anthology continues, as my ersatz paramour and I drink French wine and engage in three-dimensional French kissing. Here's the appearance on *The Ed Sullivan Show*. There's the clip from *A Hard Day's Night* which so inspired my spark. Now the concert footage from Shea Stadium . . . I fancy I hear more than he does in the rhythm and cadence of the crowd, that something about this mélange of screams is more specific to my ear because I haven't simply acquired it through the pale facsimile of film; I was there, I heard the real thing—this soundtrack isn't my source of information, it's the playback button for a live memory. This thought emboldens me and I begin to wonder if perhaps the camera that day, in documenting what seemed a modern mass miracle, happened to capture my own tiny epiphany on film. I search for a shot of myself among the throng. I don't find it, but I find again my wonder at the aching virgins who surrounded me with their wall of sound some thirty years ago, blotting out the songs of the Beatles but forcing my consciousness to a more ancient tune. Glancing sideways at my companion-of-convenience, I yearn for a dose of the fever which happily poisoned their blood, so that I might now be transported and anointed by that kind of suffering, so that I might finally, genuinely faint.

Dizzy Girls in the Sixties

Gary Soto

Back then even the good girls got dizzy
When you dropped an aspirin into a Coke,
Spoke with an English accent,
Or flickered a cut-out photo of Paul McCartney.
They got dizzy and dropped into your arms,
Brother said. And he said two guitar chords helped,
And the theme song to *Bonanza* made them walk
Backwards and wonder about the talent
That lay under a boy's black fingernails.
I played these chords. And when I could,
I shuffled my deck of cards and said,
"Let's get naked, *esa*. I won't tell—honest."
They didn't listen. Mostly they thumbed
Through magazines while teasing their hair
Into a nest of trouble. By seventh grade,
I was regrouping my hormones into one hard muscle
And no longer went around with my hands
Cupped in the hollow of my arms, the intentional farts
Cutting the classroom air.
It was a hit in fourth grade
But didn't work after the Beatles docked
In the hearts of girls and young mothers.
The aspirin didn't work either,
Or the English accent from a brown face,
Or the chords on a Sears guitar.
I was nowhere, really, the cafeteria helper
Scooping chile beans into a plastic dish.
I was deeply troubled by high math

And such parables as the ark
And every beast in twos. One Saturday
I floated on an inner tube in a canal
And the best-looking girls at the end of our universe
Were on shore, peeling back
the wrappers of Butterfingers. Right there,
With sweetness greasing up their thighs,
I understood that I was too old to captain
An inner tube down a canal. I needed an ocean liner
On a sea splintered with sunlight,
Some stretch of watery romance. When I waved,
The girls barely looked
As I bobbed over the current.
The green cool water had shrunk my desire,
Thumb-long flesh just beginning to steer me wrong.

America the Beatle-full

Jacques Wakefield

Dianne Cedrone "went with" Manny, a Black man who'd spent considerable time in prison and learned a little guitar. She was white and obviously willing to be his lover. I met them as a teenage singer in a local rhythm-and-blues band playing Harlem clubs for $25 a night. Manny was the lead guitarist. "White guilt" was rampant then. Dianne was more intelligent than she showed in her innocuous playfulness around Black patrons. Revealed in the many conversations I overheard: she making sense in petty arguments, he ultimately suggesting silence and or/violence when her behavior became obnoxious-flirting like she was a Black woman on the loose, complete with a Hollywood southern accent.

There was something about her. When I first met her she'd smile at me with a particular concern that kept me apprehensive as to her intention. Sex or violence (the Panthers or King). If she had any idea that I could save her from the problem she was having with her man, no, I was just a kid with a truth of expression come by the Baptist Church and capable of imitating the sounds of Sam and Dave, James Brown, Wilson Pickett; a talent to improvise on that ability for Harlem audiences wanting the taste of memories from "down home." How I came to know the Beatles as a personal affront?

Dianne invited me. (Since she was the only white girl who dared to be around us for long, it was big news that her man was not her man anymore). She gave me that mysterious wide and knowing smile and told me to meet her at the Addie Mae Collins Community Center on 127th and 5th—turned out to be a funded program where Black children were learning to read and being exposed to life outside the ghetto. (Addie Mae Collins was one of the Black children killed in the Alabama church bombing.)

I met her. She and I and a Black male friend (oh) of hers went to an apartment in Harlem. I loved this woman, but I was too young to know how to love her except by trust.

She and her friend laughed in the kitchen as I sat looking at the furniture in the living room, wondering how it must feel to be in the position of living life not as desperation choices but as priorities for happiness. To be in control. The word *free,* thrown around like surplus ignorance in those days—free. Exploited—the word became *enslaved.* I sat and assumed Dianne was giving me the opportunity to see a better side of life. I was satisfied on the sofa; evaluating the conditions of my life in contrast to that of a white woman who I loved maybe because she was white/different or maybe because of the difference it made; the ability to choose, so drastically, what I wanted in the white world, to be approved of, my humanity. In the eyes of political/cultural negligence I was nothing but music. I needed more from this world.

Dianne and her companion strolled from the kitchen. They looked at me like I was a mindless breath of hope. They kissed passionately, to draw my jealousy (I imagined), and Dianne went to a stack of records piled against the wall next to the phonograph. She pulled two Beatles LPs from a white painted metal milk crate. Then she went to another painted milk crate bookshelf and retrieved a book while pushing a lamp table toward me with the book placed upon it like it was an impromptu meal. There was a long look that registered on my already mossed rock for a brain, and then they walked away whispering and kissed again. They came back to me suddenly. Dianne had a small dot of paper on her index finger and like a breast-feeding mother, with the same loving consideration for nutrition, said, "Put this in your mouth and suck it." I did. I sat there sucking on this little piece of paper for a few minutes as they drank wine and looked at me curiously, as if I were going to fall apart or run.

Soon, Dianne approached me, knelt, lifted the book from the table to my chest, Kahlil Gibran's *The Prophet*. "Read this." I obediently read, to avoid offending her and to discover the mystery behind sucking the paper. What was it all about? Didn't Dianne know by now that I loved her—a Black kid from the ghetto who needed her interest in me? The world was contained in ignorance and stale history, remade to make revenge rather than rebirth (so I thought). Didn't she know I loved her more, compared to the Beatles?!

She put on a Beatles album. Something about a love only the imagination could imagine stuck to me in the imagery of grasping memories of childhood nursery rhymes—not of this flesh and blood. The lilt of poetry and the clearness of chord changes in the accent of British wit—meant to be entertainment for novelty. I lived the Beatles soundly, the spirit of their message tripping, overwhelmed in their alternative simplicity. Cruelly, Dianne played every record the Beatles ever made as I purged myself of the poison of ghetto life. Strange. That was the environment in which the Beatles' sound compromised my spirit as purposeful music! I was vulnerable to simplicity, even when they got "heavy"; it was simple, bearable, even beautiful. Innocence.

I was captured on the sofa. Dianne and her friend walked silently out of my presence, kissing not each other but the music. I continued to read because I felt like living, I felt like life. I mean, life was living. I mean, I didn't have to Be. I mean, meaningless . . . oh shit, nevermind, yeah, that was the feeling! Being everything and nothing. Nevermind. Yes. That's it— Nevermind! Love.

don't let me down

The Endless Days of Sixties Sunshine

Dave Smith

Throbbing and gurgling, my engine might have been
the coveted Olds, chromed bald, Republican.
But I got my first ticket in a friend's Ford,
hot night, Elvis thumping hard. Born to Chevies,
tri-carbed V-eights, like hope's big dog loping off,
we vacuumed for scent. My chariot was gold,
same as evening sun that sent me for my baby.
We'd ride through valleys of years, Little Richard,
Sam Cooke rocking between her half-opened knees.
Passing town's bullet-dimpled sign, she made me squeal.
What arias with our kids. Then her tumor therapy.
Trust no old bastard, she'd shriek. That's how we lived.
Then we had war, dead President, dead King, no Beetles.

The Girl Who Sang with the Beatles

Robert Hemenway

Of course their tastes turned out to be different. Cynthia was twenty-eight when they married, and looked younger, in the way small, very pretty women can—so much younger sometimes that bartenders would ask for her ID. Larry was close to forty and gray, a heavy man who, when he moved, moved slowly. He had been an English instructor once, though now he wrote market-research reports, and there was still something bookish about him. Cynthia, who was working as an interviewer for Larry's company when he met her, had been a vocalist with several dance bands for a while in the fifties before she quit to marry her first husband. She had left high school when she was a junior to take her first singing job. She and Larry were from different generations, practically, and from different cultures, and yet when they were married they both liked the same things. That was what brought them together. Thirties movies. Old bars—not the instant-tradition places, but what was left of the old ones, what Cynthia called bar bars. Double features in the loge of the Orpheum, eating hot dogs and drinking smuggled beer. Gibsons before dinner and Scotch after. Their TV nights, eating delicatessen while they watched *Mr. Lucky* or *Route 66* or *Ben Casey,* laughing at the same places, choking up at the same places, howling together when something was just *too much.* And then the eleven o'clock news and the late and late late shows, while they drank and necked and sometimes made love. And listening to Cynthia's records—old Sinatras and Judys, and Steve and Eydie, or *The Fantasticks* or *Candide*. They even agreed on redecorating Cynthia's apartment, which was full of leftovers from her first marriage. They agreed on all of it—the worn (but genuine) Oriental rugs; the low, carved Spanish tables; the dusky colors, grays and mauve and rose; the damask sofa with its down pillows; and, in the bedroom, the twin beds, nearly joined but held separate by an ornate brass bedstead. Cynthia's old double bed had been impractical; Larry was too big, and Cynthia kicked. When they came back from their Nassau honeymoon and saw the apartment for the first time in ten days, Cynthia said, "God, Larry, I *love* it. It's pure *Sunset Boulevard* now."

The place made Larry think of Hyde Park Boulevard in Chicago, where he had grown up in a mock-Tudor house filled with the wrought iron and walnut of an earlier Spanish fad. Entering the apartment was like entering his childhood. "Valencia!" sang in his head. "Valencia! In my dreams it always seems I hear you softly call to me. Valencia!"

They were married in the summer of 1962 and by the spring of 1963 the things they had bought no longer looked quite right. Everyone was buying Spanish now, and there was too much around in the cheap stores. Larry and Cynthia found themselves in a dowdy apartment full of things that looked as if they had been there since the twenties. It was depressing. They began to ask each other what they had done. Not that either of them wanted out, exactly, but what had they done? Why had they married? Why couldn't they have gone on with their affair? Neither had married the other for money, that was certain. Larry had made Cynthia quit work (not that she minded), and now they had only his salary, which was barely enough.

"We still love each other, don't we? I mean, I know I love you." Cynthia was in Larry's bed and Larry was talking. It was three in the morning. They had come back from their usual Saturday night tour of the neighborhood bars. "I love you," Larry said.

"You don't like me."

"I *love* you, Cynthia."

"You don't like me." Propped up by pillows, she stared red-eyed at a great paper daisy on the wall.

"I love you, Cindy."

"So? Big deal. Men have been telling me they loved me since I was fourteen. I thought you were different."

Larry lay flat on his back. "Don't be tough. It's not like you," he said.

"I *am* tough. That's what you won't understand. You didn't marry *me*. You married some nutty idea of your own. I was your secret fantasy. You told me so." Cynthia was shivering.

"Lie down," Larry said. "I'll rub your back."

"You won't get around me that way," Cynthia said, lying down. "You tricked me. I thought you liked the things I liked. You won't even watch TV with me anymore."

Larry began to rub the back of Cynthia's neck and play with the soft hairs behind one ear.

"Why don't you ever watch with me?" Cynthia said.

"You know. I get impatient."

"You don't like me." Cynthia was teasing him now. "If you really liked me you'd watch," she said. "You'd *like* being bored."

Larry sat up. "That isn't it," he said. "You know what it is? It's the noise. All the things you like make *noise*."

"I read."

"Sure. With the radio or the stereo or the TV on. I can't. I have to do one thing at a time," Larry said. "What if I want to sit home at night and read a book?"

"So read."

"When you have these programs you quote, have to watch, unquote?"

"Get me headphones. That's what my first husband did when he stopped talking to me. Or go in the bedroom and shut the door. I don't mind."

"We'll do something," Larry said, lying down again. "Now let's make love."

"Oh, it's no use, Larry," Cynthia said. "Not when we're like this. I'll only sweat."

And so it went on many nights, and everything seemed tainted by their disagreements, especially their times in bed. After they had made love they would slip again into these exchanges, on and on. What Cynthia seemed to resent most was that Larry had not been straightforward with her. Why had he let her think he cared for her world of song and dance? She knew it was trivial. She had never tried to make him think she was deep. Why had he pretended he was something he wasn't?

How was Larry to tell her the truth without making her think he was either a snob or a fool? There was no way. The thing was, he said, that when they met he *did* like what she liked, period. Just because she liked it. What was wrong with that? He wanted to see her enjoying herself, so they did what she wanted to do—went to Radio City to see the new Doris Day, or to Basin Street East to hear Peggy Lee, or to revivals of those fifties musicals Cynthia liked so much. Forget the things he liked that she didn't—foreign movies and chamber music and walks in Central Park, all that. She must have known what he liked, after all. She had been in his apartment often enough before they were married, God knows. She had seen his books and records. She knew his tastes.

"I thought you gave all that up," Cynthia said. "I thought you'd changed."

I thought you *would* change," Larry said. "I thought you wanted to. I thought if you wanted to marry me you must want to change."

"Be an *intellectual*?" Cynthia said. "You must be kidding."

No, he was serious. Why didn't she get bored with the stuff she watched and the junk she read? *He* did. When you had seen three Perry Masons, you had seen them all, and that went for Doris Day movies, the eleven o'clock news, and *What's My Line?*

"I know all that," Cynthia said. She *liked* to be bored. God, you couldn't keep thinking about *reality* all the time. You'd go out of your mind. She liked stories and actors that she knew, liked movies she had seen a dozen times and books she could read over and over again. Larry took his reading so seriously. As if reading were *life*.

Larry tried to persuade himself that Cynthia was teasing him, but it was no use. She meant what she said. She liked *East of Eden, Marjorie Morningstar, Gone with the Wind.* She liked Elizabeth Taylor movies. She found nourishment in that Styrofoam. He could see it in her childlike face, which sometimes shone as if she were regarding the beatific vision when she was under the spell of the sorriest trash. What repelled him brought her to life. He could feel it in her when they touched and when, after seeing one of her favorite movies, they made love. How odd that he should have married her! And yet he loved her, he thought, and he thought she loved him—needed him, anyway.

Sometimes they talked of having a child, or of Cynthia's going back to work, or of attending night classes together at Columbia or the New School, but nothing came of it. They were both drinking too much, perhaps, and getting too little exercise, yet it was easier to let things go on as they were. Larry did set out to read Camus, the first serious reading he had done since their marriage, and in the evenings after dinner he would go into the bedroom, shut the door, turn on WNCN to muffle the sounds from the living room, put Flents in his ears, and read. Although the meaningless noises from the TV set—the not quite comprehensible voices, the sudden surges of music—still reached him, he was reluctant to buy Cynthia the headphones she had suggested. They would be too clear a symbol of their defeat.

Cynthia often stayed up until three or four watching the late movies or playing her records, and Larry, who usually fell asleep around midnight, would sometimes wake after two or three hours and come out of the bedroom shouting, "Do you know what *time* it is?" and frighten her. Sometimes, though, he would make a drink for himself and watch her movie, too, necking with her the way they used to do, without saying much. They were still drawn to each other.

Sometimes very late at night when she was quite drunk, Cynthia would stand before the full-length mirror in their bedroom and admire herself. "I'm beautiful," she would say. "Right now, I'm really beautiful, and who can see me?" Larry would watch her from the bed. Something slack in her would grow taut as she looked in the mirror. She would draw her underpants down low on her hips, then place her hands on her shoulders, her crossed arms covering her bare breasts, and smile at her reflection, a one-sided smile. "I'm a narcissist," she would say, looking at Larry in the mirror. "I'm a sexual narcissist. How can you stand me?" Then she would join Larry in his bed.

Larry couldn't deny Cynthia anything for long. If he insisted on it, she would turn off the set, but then she would sulk until he felt he had imposed upon her and he would turn the set back on or take her out for a drink. How could he blame her? They had so little money. What else was there for her to do?

One Saturday night after their tour of the bars, Cynthia changed clothes and came out of the bedroom wearing a twenties black dress and black net stockings and pumps. The dress was banded with several rows of fringe and stopped just at the knee. She had added the last row of fringe, she told Larry. Her first husband had made her, just before they went to a costume party, because the dress showed too much of her thighs. Larry knelt before her and tore off the last row. Cynthia danced for him (a Charleston, a shimmy, a Watusi), and after that she sang. She had sung to him now and then late at night before they were married—just a few bars in a soft, almost inaudible voice. Tonight the voice seemed full and touching to Larry, and with a timbre and sadness different from any voice he had ever heard. "*Like* me. Please like me," the voice seemed to say. "Just like me. That's all I need. I'll be nice then."

She might have been the star she wanted to be, Larry thought. She had the charm and the need for love, but perhaps the voice was too small and her need too great. She had told him that twice while she was singing with a band in Las Vegas she had been "discovered" by assistant directors and offered a movie audition, and that each time she had been sick in the studio—literally sick to her stomach—and unable to go on. She had been too scared. Yet she still might have a career somehow, Larry thought. He would encourage her to practice. It would be an interest for her—something to do. She was barely past thirty and looked less. There was time.

Larry decided to read Camus in French and to translate some of the untranslated essays, just for practice, into English. One night he came home with the headphones Cynthia wanted, the old-fashioned kind made of black Bakelite, and hooked them up to the TV set through a control box that had an off-on switch for the speaker. Now that he could blank out the commercials, Larry would watch with Cynthia now and then—some of the news specials, and *Wide World of Sports*, and the late-night reruns of President Kennedy's press conferences, one of the few things they both enjoyed. They acknowledged his power, pulsing in him and out toward them—that sure, quick intelligence, and that charm.

Cynthia was happier now, because with the headphones on and the speakers off she could watch as late as she wanted without being afraid of Larry. When the phone rang she would not hear it. Larry would answer, finally, and if it was for her he would stand in front of the set gesturing until she took the headphones off. She would sit on the sofa for hours, dressed as if for company, her eyes made up to look even larger than they were. She wore one of the at-home hostessy things from Jax or Robert Leader she had bought before they were married, which hardly anyone but she and Larry had ever seen—looking so pretty, and with those radio operator's black headphones on her ears.

The sight made Larry melancholy, and he continued to work lying on his bed, propped up with a writing board on his lap. He would hear Cynthia laughing sometimes in the silent living room, and now and then, hearing thin sounds from her headphones, he would come out to find her crying, the phones on her lap and the final credits of a movie on the screen. "I always cry at this one," she would say. With the headphones, Cynthia was spending more time before the set than ever. Larry encouraged her to sing—to take lessons again if she wanted. But she did sing, she said, in the afternoon. She sang with her records, usually. There were a few songs of Eydie's and Peggy's and Judy's she liked. She sang along with those.

In spite of everything, when Larry compared his life now with his first marriage or with the bitter years after that, he could not say that this was worse. Cynthia seemed almost content. She made no demands upon him and left him free to think or read what he pleased. But there were nights when he would put his book aside and lie on his bed, hearing Cynthia laugh now and then or get up to make herself another drink, and ask himself why he was there. Little, in his job or in his life, seemed reasonable or real.

Why had he fallen in love with Cynthia? It was just because she was so *American,* he decided one night. She *liked* canned chili and corned-beef hash, the Academy Awards, coleslaw, barbecued chicken, the Miss America contest, head lettuce with Russian dressing, astrology columns, *Modern Screen,* takeout pizza pies. She liked them and made faces at them at the same time, looking up or over at him and saying, "Oh, God, isn't this awful? Isn't this vile?" Everything he had turned his back on in the name of the Bauhaus and the Institute of Design, of Elizabeth David and James Beard, of Lewis Mumford, Paul Goodman, D. H. Lawrence, Henry Miller, Frank Lloyd Wright—here it all was dished up before him in Cynthia. All the things that (to tell the truth) he had never had enough of. He had lost out on them in high school, when he had really wanted them, because he was studious and shy. He had rejected them in college, where it was a matter of political principle among his friends to reject them, before he had the chance to find out what they were like. At thirty-eight, when he met Cynthia, what did he know? Weren't there vast areas of the American experience he had missed? Why, until Cynthia he had never shacked up in a motel. Nor had he ever been in a barroom fight, or smoked pot, or been ticketed for speeding, or blacked out from booze.

What had he fallen in love with, then, but pop America! One more intellectual seduced by kitsch! He could almost see the humor in it. It was the first solid discovery about himself he had made for years, and he lay back in his bed, smiling. How glittering Cynthia's world had seemed, he thought. The sixties—this is what they were! Thruways, motels, Point Pleasant on a Saturday night twisting to the juke! That trip to Atlantic City in winter when, at Club Hialeah, the girls from South Jersey danced on the bar, and in the Hotel Marlborough-Blenheim he and Cynthia wandered through the cold deserted corridors and public rooms like actors in a shabby *Marienbad.*

And the music! Miles, Monk, Chico, Mingus, the M. J. Q., Sinatra and Nelson Riddle, Belafonte, Elvis, Ray Charles, Dion, Lena Horne—all new to him. He had stopped listening to music before bop, and with Cynthia he listened to everything. Progressive or pop or rhythm and blues, whatever. Did he like it all—how was it possible to like it *all*?—because Cynthia did, or did he fall in love with Cynthia because she liked it all? What difference did it make? It was all new—a gorgeous blur of enthusiasms. For the first time in his life he had given himself away. How wonderful it had been, at thirty-eight, on the edge of middle age—*in* middle age—to play the fool! This was experience, this was *life,* this was the sixties—*his* generation, with his peers in charge, the Kennedys and the rest. Wasn't that coming alive, when you were free enough to play the fool and not care? And if there had been enough money, he and Cynthia might have kept it up. . . . They might.

Yet hardly a moment had passed during the first months with Cynthia when he did not know what he was doing. He had gotten into a discussion of pop culture one night in the Cedar Street Tavern not long after he and Cynthia were married. "You don't know what you're talking about," he had said to the others while Cynthia was on a trip to the head. "You only dip into it. Listen. You don't know. I've *married* it. I've married the whole great American schmear."

But how nearly he had been taken in! Cynthia never had. She knew show business from the inside, after all. She dug it, and liked it, and laughed at herself for liking it. She knew how shabby it was. Yet it did something for her—that trumpery, that fake emotion, that sincere corn. Once he found out something was bad, how could he care for it any longer? It was impossible. If he had gone overboard at first for Cynthia's world, wasn't that because it was new to him and he saw fresh energy there? And how spurious that energy had turned out to be—how slick, how manufactured, how dead! And how dull. Yet something in it rubbed off on Cynthia, mesmerized her and made her glamorous, made her attractive to him still. That was the trouble. He still wanted her. He was as mesmerized as she. Wasn't it the fakery he despised that shone in

Cynthia and drew him to her? Then what in their marriage was real? He felt as detached from his life as a dreamer at times feels detached from his dream.

Quiet and sedentary as it had become, Larry's life continued to be charged with a forced excitement. The pop love songs, the photographs of beautiful men and women in the magazines Cynthia read, the romantic movies on TV, Cynthia herself—changing her clothes three or four times a day as if she were the star in a play and Larry the audience—all stimulated him in what he considered an unnatural way. He recognized in himself an extravagant lust that was quickly expended but never spent when he and Cynthia made love, as if she were one of the idealized photographs of which she was so fond and he were returning within her to the fantasies of his adolescence, their intercourse no more than the solitary motions of two bodies accidentally joined.

"We shouldn't have gotten married," Cynthia said one hot Saturday night in the summer of 1963 as they were lying in their beds trying to fall asleep.

"Maybe not," Larry said.

"Marriage turns me off. Something happens. I told you."

"I didn't believe you," Larry said. "And anyway, we're married."

"We sure are."

"I picked a lemon in the garden of love," Larry said. Cynthia laughed and moved into Larry's bed.

Late that night, though, he said something else. "We're like Catholics and their sacrament," he said. "When you're married for the second time, you're practically stuck with each other. You've almost got to work it out."

"You may think you're stuck, but *I'm* not," Cynthia said, and moved back to her own bed. The next Saturday night she brought up what Larry had said about being stuck. Why had he said it? Didn't he know her at all? Whenever she felt bound she had to break free—right out the door, sooner or later. That was what had always happened. Was he trying to drive her away? He knew how independent she'd been. That's what he liked about her, he'd said once. All that talk about protecting each other's freedom! What a lot of crap. Look at them now. Two birds in a cage, a filthy cage.

Cynthia's anger frightened Larry, and, to his surprise, the thought of her leaving frightened him too. But nothing changed. There wasn't much chance of her breaking away, after all. They didn't have enough money to separate, and neither of them really wanted to—not *that* routine, not again.

More and more often now, Larry would sit in the living room while Cynthia watched her programs, headphones on her ears. He would look over at her, knowing that at the moment she was content, and feel some satisfaction, even a sense of domestic peace. At times he would lie with his head on Cynthia's lap while she watched and she would stroke his hair.

One payday Larry came home with a second pair of headphones, made of green plastic and padded with foam rubber, the sort disc jockeys and astronauts wear, and plugged them into the stereo through a box that permitted turning off the speakers. Now he, like Cynthia, could listen in silence. He stacked some of his records on the turntable—the Mozart horn concertos, a Bach cantata, Gluck. It was eerie, Larry thought, for them both to be so completely absorbed, sitting twenty feet apart in that silent living room, and on the first night he found himself watching Cynthia's picture on the TV screen as the music in his ears seemed to fade away. Finally he took off his earphones, joined Cynthia on the sofa, and asked her to run on the sound. After a few nights, however, the sense of eeriness wore off, and Larry was as caught up in his music as Cynthia was in her shows. The stereo sound was so rich and pure; unmixed with other noises, the music carried directly into his brain, surrounding and penetrating him. It was so intense, so mindless. Listening was not a strong enough word for what was happening. The music flowed through him and swallowed him up. He felt endowed with a superior sense, as if he were a god. Yet there was something illicit about their both finding so intense a pleasure in isolation. He was troubled, off and on, by what they were falling into, but their life was tranquil and that was almost enough.

• • •

One night when Larry was reading (something he rarely did now) and there was nothing on TV she cared for, Cynthia put some of her records on the turntable and Larry's headphones on her ears and listened to Eydie and Judy and Frank, dancing a few steps now and then and singing the words softly. "Why didn't you tell me!" she said. It was *fantastic*. She could hear all the bass, and the color of the voices, and things in some of the arrangements she had never known were there. More and more often as the summer wore on, Cynthia would listen to her music instead of watching the tube, and Larry, thinking this was a step in the right direction—toward her singing, perhaps—turned the stereo over to her several evenings a week and tried to concentrate again on his reading. But music now held him in a way books no longer could, and after a few weeks he bought a second stereo phonograph and a second set of headphones. By the fall of 1963, he and Cynthia had begun to listen, each to his own music, together. "This is really a kick," Cynthia would say. The intensity of it excited them both.

On the day President Kennedy was assassinated, Larry and Cynthia were having one of their rare lunches in midtown at an Italian place near Bloomingdale's, where Cynthia planned to go shopping afterward. There was a small television set above the restaurant bar, and people stood there waiting for definite news after the first word of the shooting. When it was clear that the President was dead, Larry and Cynthia went back to their apartment. Larry didn't go back to work. They watched television together that afternoon and evening, and then they went to bed and began to weep. When Larry stopped, Cynthia would sob, and then Larry would start again. So it went until after four in the morning, when they fell asleep. Until the funeral was over, Cynthia sat before the set most of the day and night. Much of the time she was crying, and every night when she came to bed the tears would start. Larry, dry-eyed sooner than she was, was at first sympathetic, then impatient, then annoyed.

"He was such a *good* man," Cynthia would say, or, "He was *ours*.

He was all we had," and after the burial she said, half smiling, "He was a wonderful star." Nothing in her actual life could ever move her so deeply, Larry thought. How strange, to feel real sorrow and weep real tears for an unreal loss! But she was suffering, no question of that, and she could not stop crying. The Christmas season came and went and she still wept. She had begun to drink heavily, and often Larry would put her to bed. On the edge of unconsciousness, she would continue to cry.

What was she, he thought, but a transmitter of electronic sensations? First she had conveyed the nation's erotic fantasies to him, and now it was the national sorrow, and one was as unreal as the other. But there was more to it than that. John Kennedy had been a figure in her own erotic fantasies. She had told Larry so. She wept for him as a woman would for her dead lover. She was like a woman betrayed by Death, Larry thought, when what had betrayed her was the television set she had counted upon to shield her from the real. It had always told her stories of terror and passion that, because they were fictitious, might be endured, and now it had shown her actual death and actual sorrow. There was no way to console her, because her loss was not an actual loss, and Larry began to think her suffering more than he could endure. He began to wonder if she might not have lost her mind.

Cynthia read nothing for weeks after the assassination but articles on it, and so she did not hear of the Beatles until Larry, hoping to distract her, brought home their first album. She thought little of it at first, but after the Beatles appeared on *The Ed Sullivan Show* in February, she became an admirer and then a devotee. Larry brought her the new Beatles 45s as they came out, and he stood in line with teenage girls at the newsstands on Forty-second Street to buy the Beatles fan magazines. "I guess the period of mourning is over," Cynthia said one Saturday night. She still saved articles about the assassination, though, and photographs of Jacqueline in black.

When Cynthia began to sing as she listened to the Beatles late at night, Larry, listening from the bedroom, was pleased. She would play their records over and over, accompanying them in a voice that seemed flat and unresonant, perhaps because with the headphones on she could not hear the sounds she made. She no longer wept, or Larry was asleep when she did.

One night Larry woke around three to the tinny noise of "I Want to Hold Your Hand" spilling from Cynthia's phones and found he was hungry. On his way to the kitchen he stopped in the dark hall to watch Cynthia, who stood in the center of the living room with the astronaut headphones on, singing what sounded like a harmonizing part, a little off-key, holding an imaginary guitar, swaying jerkily, and smiling as if she were before an audience. Her performance, empty as it was, seemed oddly polished and professional. Afraid of startling her, he stood watching until the end of the song before he entered the room.

"How much did you see?" Cynthia said.

"Nothing," Larry said. "I was going to get a glass of milk, that's all." The look on Cynthia's face as she stood before him with those enormous headphones clamped to her ears troubled him, as if he had discovered her in some indecency better forgotten. "After this I'll flick out the lights and warn you," he said.

And he said no more about it, though often now he awoke during the night to the faint sounds from Cynthia's headphones and wondered what she was doing that held her so fast. He was jealous of it in a way. She was rarely in bed before four, and always in bed when he left for work in the morning. In the evening, though, as she watched television, she seemed happy enough, much as she had been before Kennedy's death.

For some time after the assassination they gave up their Saturday nights in the bars, but by April they were again making their rounds. Once, when they came home higher and happier than usual, Cynthia danced and sang for Larry as she had before, and for a while Larry danced with her, something he did not do often. They were having such a pleasant time that when Larry put on a Beatles album and Cynthia began her performance for him, she explained, "We're at the

Palladium in London, you see," she said. "The place is mobbed. . . . The Beatles are onstage. . . . I'm singing with them, and naturally everybody loves us. I work through the whole show . . . playing second guitar. I back up George." And then she sang, a third or so below the melody, "'She was just seventeen, if you know what I mean . . .'"

"I never sing lead," Cynthia said when the number was over. "I play a minor role."

"Is this what you do at night?" Larry asked her.

Cynthia was breathing heavily. "Sure," she said. "It sounds silly, but it's not. Besides, it's possible, isn't it? It *could* happen. I can sing." She looked at Larry, her eyes candid and kind. "Don't worry," she said. "I'm not losing my grip."

"It's a nice game," Larry said later when they were in bed.

"Oh, it's more than a game," Cynthia said. "When I'm with them in the Palladium, I'm really *there*. It's more real than here. I know it's a fantasy, though."

"How did you meet the Beatles?" Larry asked her.

"D'you really want to hear?"

She seemed pleased at his interest, Larry thought, but then she was drunk. They both were.

"It's not much of a story," she said. "The details vary, but basically I am standing on Fifth Avenue there near the Plaza in the snow waiting for a cab at three in the afternoon, dressed in my black flared coat and black pants and the black boots you gave me, and I have a guitar. No taxis, or they're whipping right by, and I'm *cold*. You know how cold I can get. And then this Bentley stops with a couple of guys in front and in back is George Harrison all alone, though sometimes it's Paul. He gives me a lift and we talk. He's completely polite and sincere, and I can see he likes me. It seems the Beatles are rehearsing for a television special at Central Plaza and they'll be there the next day, so he asks me to come up and bring my guitar. I go, naturally, and it turns out they are auditioning girls, and I'm the winner. What would be the point if I wasn't? They want a girl for just one number, but when they see how terrific I am, of course they love me, and when they find out I've already worked up all their songs I'm in."

"You join them."

"Sure. They insist. I have to leave you, but you don't mind, not anymore. In one year we're the Beatles and Cynthia and we're playing the Palladium, and Princess Margaret and Tony are there, and Frank, and Peter O'Toole, and David McCallum, and Steve McQueen, and Bobby Kennedy. And all those men *want* me, I can feel it, and I'm going to meet them afterward at the Savoy in our suite."

"Our?"

"I'm married to a rich diamond merchant who lets me do whatever I want. Played by George Sanders."

"I thought you were married to me," Larry said.

"On, no. You divorced me, alleging I was mentally cruel. Maybe I was once, but I'm not anymore, because the Beatles love me. They're my brothers. They're not jealous of me at all."

"Are you putting me on?" Larry said.

"No. Why should I? I made it all up, if that's what you mean, but I *really* made it up."

"Do you believe any of it?" Larry said.

Cynthia smiled at him. "Don't you? You used to say I had a good voice and you used to say I was pretty. Anyway, I don't have fantasies about things that couldn't possibly happen. I could get a job tomorrow if you'd let me."

Cynthia's voice had the lilt Larry remembered from the days before they were married. The whole thing was so convincing and so insane. He began to indulge her in it. "I'm going to Beatle now," Cynthia would say nearly every night after dinner, and Larry would go into the bedroom. Whenever he came out he would flick the hall lights and she would stop. She was shy and did not let him watch at first. She seemed embarrassed that she had told him as much as she had—if, indeed, she remembered telling him anything at all.

Larry liked the Beatles more and more as the nights went by, and often he would listen to their records with the speakers on before

Cynthia began her performance. "Listen, Cynthia," he said one Saturday night. "The Beatles are filled with the Holy Ghost." He was really quite drunk. "Do you know that? They came to bring us back to life! Out of the old nightmare. Dallas, Oswald, Ruby, all of it, cops, reporters, thruways, lies, crises, missiles, heroes, cameras, fear—all that mishmash, and all of it dead. All of us dead watching the burial of the dead. Look at *you*. They've brought you back to life. I couldn't—not after November. Nothing could."

"You're right," Cynthia said. "I didn't want to tell you. I thought you'd be jealous."

"Jealous? Of the Beatles?"

"They're very real to me, you know."

"I'm not jealous," Larry said.

"Then will you read to me the way you used to? Read me to sleep?"

"Sure."

"Can I get in your bed?"

"Sure."

Before Larry had finished a page, he was asleep, and Cynthia was asleep before him.

For her birthday in September, Larry gave Cynthia an electric guitar. Though she could not really play it and rarely even plugged it in, she used the guitar now in her performances, pretending to pluck the strings. She began to dress more elaborately for her Beatling, too, making herself up as if for the stage.

She was a little mad, no question of it, Larry thought, but it did no harm. He no longer loved her, nor could he find much to like in her, and yet he cared for her, he felt, and he saw that she was too fragile to be left alone. She was prettier now than he had ever seen her. She *should* have been a performer. She needed applause and admirers and whatever it was she gave herself in her fantasies—something he alone could not provide. Their life together asked little of him at any rate, and cost little. By now he and Cynthia rarely touched or embraced; they were like old friends—fellow conspirators even, for who knew of Cynthia's Beatle world but him?

Cynthia discussed her performances with Larry now, telling him of the additions to her repertoire and of the new places she and the Beatles played—Kezar Stadium, the Hollywood Bowl, Philharmonic Hall. She began to permit him in the living room with her, and he would lie on the sofa listening to his music while her Beatling went on. He felt sometimes that by sharing her fantasies he might be sharing her madness, but it seemed better for them both to be innocently deranged than to be as separate as they had been before. All of it tired Larry though. He was past forty. He felt himself growing old and his tastes changing. Now he listened to the things he had liked in college—the familiar Beethoven and Mozart symphonies, and Schubert, and Brahms, in new stereophonic recordings. Often as he listened he would fall asleep and be awakened by the silence when the last of the records stacked on the turntable had been played. Usually Cynthia's performance would still be going on, and he would rise, take off his headphones, and go to bed.

One night Larry fell asleep toward the end of the "Messiah" with the bass singing "The trumpet shall sound . . ." and the trumpet responding. He woke as usual in silence, the headphones still on his ears. This time he lay on the sofa looking at Cynthia, his eyes barely open. She had changed clothes again, he saw, and was wearing the silver lamé pants suit, left over from her singing days, that she had worn the first night he had come to her apartment. He saw her bow, prettily and lightly in spite of the headphones on her ears, and extend her arms to her imaginary audience. Then he watched her begin a slow, confined dance, moving no more than a step to the side or forward and then back. She seemed to be singing, but with his headphones on Larry could not hear. She raised her arms again, this time in a gesture of invitation, and although she could not know he was awake it seemed to Larry that she was beckoning to him and not to an imaginary partner—that this dance, one he had never seen, was for him, and Cynthia was asking him to join her in that slow and self-contained step.

Larry rose and sat looking at her, his head by now nearly clear. "Come," she beckoned. "Come." He saw her lips form the word. Was it he to whom she spoke or one of her fantasies? What did it matter? She stood waiting for her partner—for him—and Larry got up, unplugged his headphones, and walked across the room to her. The movement seemed to him a movement of love. He plugged his headphones in next to Cynthia's and stood before her, almost smiling. She smiled, and then, in silence, not quite touching her in that silent room, with the sound of the Beatles loud in his ears, Larry entered into her dance.

The Ballad of Aunt Helen

Timothy McCall

My sister lifted the arm on the phonograph
and the 45 with the green apple spun
again and again. It was the summer
after 8th grade and Aunt Helen
was visiting us at the lake.
Diagnosed with her fifth cancer,
she'd left the Sisters of Charity,
given up her black-and-white habit.
Christ you know it ain't easy
John kept wailing.
I'd just bought the single
at the five-and-ten in Hardwick.
We weren't trying to hurt
her feelings, but sacrilege
is probably what she thought
and never said. She just smiled
that too-sweet smile, told us
she loved us so much. Over and over
the hi-fi hissed *the way things are going*
they're gonna crucify me.

Mr. Champinoux Meets the Beatles

Ellen Zabaly

Philomena took her albums with her when she moved to the dorm in Ann Arbor, a city she had never visited but which she was sure was vastly superior to her own hometown. As if you could call Hurleyville a town. Hurleyville, way at the top of the Upper Peninsula in Michigan, had a combination gas station/coffee shop that was only open when Jerry Shimmus, its owner, felt like working. There was a lumberyard, and the maximum number of taverns allowed by law, thirteen, which averaged out to one every square mile or so. Jerry Shimmus liked to say you could spit farther than the distance between bars in Hurleyville. Those old lumberjacks liked to drink—nothing else to do in the woods at night in the U.P.'s endless winters—and, though the trees were long gone, the alcohol flowed free as ever.

The town hadn't changed in the eighteen years Philomena lived there. No one ever moved in and no one ever moved away. People were born and there was a baby shower and people died and there was a funeral. Every once in a while there was a wedding at the town hall, and then the old ladies of Hurleyville cooked and baked for days to get the new couple off to a good hearty start. This is what there was to look forward to in Hurleyville, and the dullness of it had about driven Philomena crazy at least since she was in eighth grade. When she got into high school she bought a four-year calendar and began marking off the days until she could leave.

Mr. Champinoux was the math teacher at Hurleyville High School. He was the youngest teacher who ever taught in Hurleyville and he liked Philomena a lot. He had black hair and green eyes and a look about him that made you know he wasn't from Hurleyville.

Of course he didn't live in town. Where would he have stayed? There were no apartments or houses for rent, and Philomena could tell just by looking at Mr. Champinoux that he was not the type to buy, even if there had been a house for sale, which there wasn't. Some of the kids said that he lived in a reservation house down on the tribal land, forty or so miles from town, and of course no one lived there if they weren't Indian. Philomena didn't know what to think, except that in algebra and the next year in geometry and the year after that in trigonometry, Mr. Champinoux gazed at her in class and called her to his desk for extra help every day, and when he talked to her, which he did a lot, his voice sounded like the beating of a slow deep drum.

Mr. Champinoux reminded Philomena of one of the Beatles, but she wasn't sure which one. It wasn't that she couldn't tell them apart. Even in Hurleyville people had heard of the Beatles, although most of them didn't approve. To people in Hurleyville just the idea of England was offensive. In the bars and the coffee shop, when it was open, the men of Hurleyville liked to sit around over their beer, smoking cigarettes and rubbing the ashes into their greasy dungarees and loudly hating the fact that such a place as London actually existed and had the power to export unconventionality in the form of the Beatles.

But not Mr. Champinoux. Mr. Champinoux liked the Beatles. Most of the time when he called Philomena up to his desk, while the other students worked the extra problems he assigned them, Mr. Champinoux talked to her about the Beatles. And the thing that made it hard to tell which one of the Beatles he reminded her of the most was that Mr. Champinoux kept changing his mind. Every day a different Beatle would be his favorite.

"Take John," Mr. Champinoux would say on Monday. "He's a thinker, you can tell that straight off. Look at his eyes. He's smiling, but you can see how solemn he is even so."

He took a photograph of John from a folder he kept in his top desk drawer. The folder contained lyrics, photographs, news clippings, all about the Beatles. Mr. Champinoux evidently was gathering information for a thesis. Either that or he was seriously nuts.

After all, he wasn't a teenage girl. Philomena had seen on TV how they went crazy at Beatles concerts. She would have liked to go a little crazy over them herself, but she was waiting until she left Hurleyville.

Then on Tuesday, Mr. Champinoux favored Paul. "He might not have John's depth," said Mr. Champinoux, "but look at his energy! He's the one who keeps them going, you can see that." He smiled, an ardent, wistful smile, just like Paul's, filled with the desire to please, just like Paul, and his cheeks bunched up in that same cuddly way that Paul's did.

But it was his singing that was most amazing. He sang to her, low, under his breath, in a whisper, and his mouth smelled like sweet tobacco. "Half of what I say is meaningless," he sang, turning slightly from side to side in his swivel chair, marking time with his body. "But I say it just to reach you, Juuu-lee-eaaa."

He wasn't shy about it. He looked her in the eye every time he sang to her, throughout the whole song. He had a good voice, what she could hear of it, especially for someone from Hurleyville, where they didn't believe in singing, not for men anyway.

At least once a week Mr. Champinoux invited Philomena to his house. "I have all their records," he whispered. "You can come over and listen to them anytime you say."

Philomena considered the idea every time he brought it up, until one day she accepted. It was close to graduation and soon she would leave Hurleyville. Her mother—there was only her mom. Her dad had died when Philomena was four. He got drunk one night, as usual, and when he found that Philomena's mom had locked him out of the house—like a lot of the townswomen, she disapproved of alcohol—he fell asleep in his car with the engine running and the windows closed. They found his body in the morning. Philomena's mom never remarried. She had a series of boyfriends but they never lasted.

Her mom thought Philomena was going away to become a nurse, and that she would return as soon as she finished school. There was always a need in Hurleyville for someone to minister to the sick and elderly, and Philomena's mother had long envisioned her daughter in this role. But Philomena had other plans, which she kept to herself.

On a Friday after school, Philomena waited behind the soccer shed for Mr. Champinoux. He drove up in his green Ford pickup exactly at 5:30, just as he said he would. He took the back way out of town and they drove for a while without either of them saying anything. Friday had been a George day, so Mr. Champinoux was brooding. He looked intense as he gripped the wheel. His hair, combed back from his narrow forehead during school hours, fell forward over his thick brown eyebrows. Philomena glanced at him from time to time, then looked out the window. It was the third week of May and the snow was finally gone. Puddles of muddy water stood everywhere, and with the sunset came a still-wintry chill. She shivered and Mr. Champinoux turned on the heat.

"Philomena," he said. His voice was low. She could hear the drums. "You know that I want you. I want you so bad."

"I'm leaving," she said. "I'm not coming back, either."

"I know."

"How can you stand it? Why do you live here?"

"I don't live here. This is just a place."

"Yeah." Philomena looked out the window. They passed by the Tip Top Inn. The parking lot was full even though it was barely dark. Philomena saw Jerry Shimmus getting out of his truck. He looked like he was already drunk. He staggered inside just as Lenny Rayburn and Vernon Duck fell out the front door. All three of them rolled over one another and landed in a big mud puddle in the middle of the parking lot. It still got pretty cold at night and the puddle was covered with a thin layer of ice.

"God those guys are idiots," she said.

"They've got nothing better to do," said Mr. Champinoux. "They're just marking out their time until it's all over."

"Is that what you're doing, too? Well, not me. I was meant for better things."

"Everyone was."

He turned his truck off the highway into a narrow road. White pine mixed with spruce and balsam crowded right up to the faded blacktop. The road was old and bumpy. He slowed down. "Lots of deer in here," he said. "The highway department calls my uncle whenever somebody hits one. He goes out and picks it up and if it's not too beat up they eat it."

"Is this reservation land?"

"Why? Would it scare you if it was?"

"Not necessarily. I've never been here before. Not many people come here." She turned toward him but he didn't look at her. Through the back window she saw lights far behind them.

"Not many people. Just Indians, huh?"

"That's not what I meant." She unbuttoned her jacket. "Could you turn down the heat? Are we nearly there?"

"Lake Superior's just ahead. S'pose you've never seen that, either."

"No."

"Want to?"

"What about the records?"

"We can do that after."

He drove on without speaking. In a little while he turned off an even narrower dirt road and they bumped along for five or six miles before he rounded a curve and there in front of them was the lake, glittering in the moon that was just rising over the eastern horizon. He stopped the truck and pulled a blanket from behind the seat. He spread it over her and then he got under it himself. The lake was right there. He had parked with the front tires actually in the lake, and he rolled down the window a little so they could hear the waves splashing on the shore. The smell of big water filled the cab of the truck and Philomena breathed deep.

"I've met them, you know," he said, and Philomena heard the drums again. "I've met the Beatles."

"Get off it," she said. "When? The last time they came through Hurleyville?"

"There's lots of ways to meet somebody if you really want to do it."

"Yeah? Well how were they?"

"They're great. Like everybody else only more so. And not like anyone else at all."

The water splashed up against the tire rims. It seemed to be getting higher. "Don't you think you'd better back up?" Philomena asked.

"Why? Afraid you might get swept away?"

He put his arm around her and it felt good. She didn't try to make him move it. She wanted it to stay there. He put his other arm around her waist and pulled her closer. He was strong and he smelled like balsam and water.

"Girl, girl," he whispered. He took his hand from her waist, turned her face toward him, and kissed her lightly. "She's the kind of girl you want so much it makes you sorry." He kissed her again, deeper this time. "Was she told when she was younger pain would lead to pleasure, did she understand. . . ." The third kiss was deeper still. She felt his tongue on her lips and opened her mouth to let him in. His tongue was warm and smooth and seeking. She leaned back and he maneuvered her body so that she was lying across the seat. He took his place next to her.

"What about Ringo?" she asked. "He seems like the nicest one."

"He's sad. You can see it in his eyes. And it's not just because he's short. It's a whole different way of looking at the world. Of course he's not sad all the time, and he has fun like the rest of them. But he sees the sorrow of it, you know, not just for himself."

"I'd like it if you kissed me again," she said.

"Would you be more comfortable if I took you to my cabin?" he asked, lying on top of her. "It's not far."

"I like it right here," she said, and he kissed her again.

She heard something like a roaring coming closer. They both sat up in time to see the lights of a pickup bearing down fast on the narrow road behind them. It looked as if it would hit them but at the last moment it veered to the side. There was a crashing sound as the truck hit the trees and brush at the shoreline, and then it sailed on ahead right into the water. It didn't stop until it was about fifty feet out and then it began to sink fast. In a few minutes only the red roof was visible.

Mr. Champinoux was pulling off his shoes and pants. "The water's cold," he said. "They won't last long. Take the truck and go to my cabin. It's just there," he motioned to a driveway a few feet to the right. "Call my uncle. Joe Ackley. His number's by the phone." He ran into the lake. By the time Philomena turned into the drive he had almost reached the pickup.

She found the cabin, one big room made of massive logs. You could see the lake through the trees. Inside she found the phone and made the call. Then she got back in the truck and returned to the landing. There was no sign of Mr. Champinoux, but Jerry Shimmus lay coughing and retching on the beach.

"Where's Mr. Champinoux?" she asked, but he didn't answer. Philomena had heard lots of stories about him from the kids in school. How he hated Indians and made trips to the reservation just to harass them, especially the women when he knew the men were gone ricing or hunting.

"What are you doing here?" she asked, and this time Jerry Shimmus tried to speak but couldn't get the words out. He coughed and gasped and finally said, "Vernon's still out there."

"What about Mr. Champinoux?" Philomena asked again.

A black Chevy with a makeshift tow rig screeched up to the shore and a big man jumped out, Joe Ackley. "You Philomena?" he asked. "Where's Clement?" He turned to see Jerry Shimmus lying half in, half out of the water. "What're you doing here, Shimmus, you piece of shit!"

"His truck went in there," said Philomena, and she pointed into the lake where there was no longer a sign of anything.

Uncle Joe swam out. Philomena waited on shore, shivering. He was gone a long time and when he came back he was alone. "Nothing," he said. He picked up Jerry Shimmus and threw him onto the back of Mr. Champinoux's truck as if he were a sack of potatoes. "Take him to the sheriff," he said. "I'll get some more guys here and we'll keep looking."

A week later Vernon Duck's body washed up two hundred miles east. The next day was graduation, and the day after that Philomena planned to leave Hurleyville. While she was packing, Joe Ackley drove up in his black Chevy. He got up and came toward the house carrying a box. Philomena met him on the porch.

"These were his," Joe said, and he handed her the box. Inside were records. "Take them."

"Thanks," said Philomena, but Joe was already back in the truck and gone. Philomena took the box into the house and packed the albums into her suitcase.

"I'm ready to go, Mom," she called, and her mother helped her carry her things down to the car. At the Greyhound station Philomena kissed her mother, and when the bus drove out of town, Philomena didn't look.

"Nothing's gonna change my world," she sang softly. "Nothing's gonna change my world."

The Frisco Gigs

Susan Terris

A Hard Day's Night

Cow Palace, August 19, 1964

Beatlemania, first stop on their first tour:
four Liverpool boys
with Lord Fauntleroy hair,
suits with jackets snug in the armpits.
I was too old then, didn't see them,
hardly knew them. Not really too old,
of course; the boys and I
were of an age, but I was married,
mothering toddlers, plus a newborn
who made my nights into hard days.
As the Beatles, mobbed and smiling,
tasted caviar worldwide, I tasted tuna
and Wonder Bread from the Green Frog.
While John and the others rocked pelvises,
sang "I Want to Hold Your Hand,"
I—too tired to rock mine—sang
The little white duck is sitting
in the water . . . quack, quack, quack.

Revolver

Candlestick Park, August 29, 1966

In photos they looked wary,
facing the final gig on their final tour.
Hunkered in suites with guards
to shield them, they doped and dropped
acid while I traipsed the park
watching children drop Sno-Kones.
As we paused to let their limos pass,
we waved and sang "Yellow Submarine."
Back then before the losses began,
I hummed the Beatles and wrote,
busy yet not too busy to walk the Haight
and note graffiti in fresh cement:
John Lennon 8/66. The day John was shot
I went back, searched for his name.
As I knelt and traced it with my finger,
I knew—*words of wisdom,*
let it be, let it be—we were all older now.

1973

Susan Stemont

In the photograph, John Lennon
wears a New York City T-shirt
with the sleeves rolled up.
He leans against the brickwork
of a Manhattan rooftop,
the Big Apple spread out
in slices behind him.
You can't see past the dark
of his wire-rimmed shades.
This is the year
he will leave his second wife,
drink too much, hang out
with other rock stars,
show up at a party
with a Kotex on his head.

This is the year I get married
(the first time), stay stoned,
and watch talk shows.
Sex is easy. Fun.
We consider open marriage,
joke about exceptions to our vows—
Diana Rigg, John Lennon.
I am learning to make wine
from berries, honey, plums.
I can't imagine any other life.

In the photograph

John's mouth mocks the grief
that lines his forehead.

The note in my husband's coat
that seems to be incriminating
is easily explained.

Drive My Car

Tobi Taylor

As the airport shuttle turned down the road to Larry's house, Pamela felt like she'd ended up on an episode of Green Acres. There was Larry, standing in his front yard with a rake, fifteen years older and still slim and fit as the last time she'd seen him. Bob—her husband and Larry's brother—had always sworn that Larry never really got over Vietnam, that he had cartons of C-rations in his basement and kept himself in fighting trim in case the Democrats wiped out defense spending. Whatever his reason for keeping fit, Larry was alive. Bob, on the other hand, ate and drank and smoked like a twenty-year-old, and his heart had given out at forty. Pamela's friends at the wedding had called Larry a smaller, poorer quality Xerox of Bob. This was what Bob would have been if he'd never left Michigan.

When she alighted from the shuttle, Pamela threw her arms around Larry while the driver got her bags. She felt him stiffen and saw a flash of red on his cheeks beneath the beard. Still afraid of women after all this time. She pulled away and brushed back her hair from her face. Larry led her into the house.

"Did you have a good flight?" he asked, showing her the guest bedroom adjacent to his: it was green and yellow with black-velvet ship paintings on two walls and a biblical verse on a third.

"It was okay, but I'd rather stay closer to the ground."

"Like in your new Grand Am?" asked Larry. "It's in the garage."

Pamela set her suitcase on the bed. "I really appreciate this," she said. "I'll think of you every time I drive it."

They walked out to the garage, catching up on a decade and a half's worth of news, to find Pamela's new red Grand Am next to Larry's slightly older silver one. She marveled at the cleanliness of the garage and the house: it was as though no one lived here. Even the lampshades wore clear plastic covers. Larry himself was very clean; even though he'd said he was out in the yard all morning, he looked like he'd ironed all his clothes and hadn't sat down.

"Can we take it for a drive?" asked Pamela.

"Of course. Just a little spin to break it in won't hurt it."

Larry had said he'd pick Pamela up, but she'd insisted she would get a shuttle out to his house. She didn't want to put him out. He figured it was the Indian way. Or was it Native American? He'd heard that some of them wanted to be called that, like the African Americans instead of blacks, or Asian Americans instead of orientals. He himself was American, thank you very much, of German descent, the largest minority in the whole country. He'd have to ask her what she wanted to be called. Or was that rude? Maybe he would just call her Pamela and see what she said to other people.

Larry found the keys next to the paperwork he'd have to get Pamela to sign to transfer the car from his name to hers. He'd bought the car outright from General Motors because of a combination of factors: her residence in Arizona, her different last name, and the fact that they no longer were related. Buying Pamela's car also meant that he couldn't get himself a new Grand Am for another year, since his contract with GM allowed him only one car per twelve months. He hadn't planned on getting another car this year anyhow, he guessed; his Grand Am had only a little bit of rust and it ran great. He figured he could afford to wait.

When Larry emerged from the house, he saw that Pamela was in the passenger's seat. Wasn't she going to demand to drive the car ninety miles an hour up the road to Lansing, playing havoc with the drivetrain? "Would you like to see the University? It's a pretty drive, and nice and slow to get the valves seated properly."

"Sure." Pamela leaned forward and turned on the radio, a little too loud for Larry's taste, especially since the song was "Drive My Car."

"That station's having an all-Beatles weekend," he remarked. His brother had been a big fan, for some reason, but the band left Larry cold. Bob had tried to explain the so-called complexities of "A Day in the Life," but to Larry it always sounded like the warning signal before the national radio broadcasting test.

Pamela punched the seek button. "Hope you don't mind if I change it. I'm more of a seventies kind of girl." The next song was Linda Ronstadt's biggest hit, "When Will I Be Loved?"

"She was Bob's first love, you know," said Larry. "But he probably told you that."

"He only made me go see her four or five times. I was more into the Bee Gees and Abba."

"You *are* young, aren't you?"

"Nobody's said *that* to me in a long time. I think I'm going to like being here."

As they drove through the campus, Larry showed Pamela where he'd picked Bob up each day. He drove slowly past the slate-roofed buildings so that Pamela could admire them, all so different from the campus of Arizona State where she and Bob had met when Bob was a grad student.

Pamela hadn't been to visit for fifteen years; the first and only other time was a year after she and Bob had been married. Larry had gone to their wedding in Arizona as the sole representative of Bob's family. Everyone had warned him not to go, and maybe they were right: it was a circus, or perhaps, given the setting, a rodeo. Instead of white, Pamela had worn a black silk dress with green and pink flowers on it, sort of like rhododendrons, he guessed, and black stockings and black pumps. Bob had worn a short-sleeved shirt that was open at the collar. No morning coat, no tie. And there was no minister, either—it was a woman justice of the peace who said an Apache wedding prayer, something Pamela's grandfather had cooked up. Even though Pamela's parents were there, the father didn't give her away. Pamela didn't believe in being transferred from one man to another; she wasn't a cow or a house. He wondered if her father felt uncomfortable standing uselessly beside Pamela's mother as his daughter walked alone across the backyard, up the makeshift aisle, while a friend of the family played "If I Needed Someone" on a mandolin.

Larry saw the bride and groom briefly the next morning when Bob made him breakfast and Pamela appeared in the kitchen doorway hung over and listless. Later that day they were off on their honeymoon and he was left with Bob's new in-laws. Larry had scheduled his trip to include a few birding spots in Arizona—it was said to have more species than most of the other states, and he wanted to improve his life list. But he either didn't get to the right places or his books reflected different times, because he mainly encountered sparrows, hawks, and a cardinal, all close relations of birds you could see every day in Michigan. He went home feeling a little cheated in a lot of ways.

But that was years ago. So long ago, in fact, that when Pamela called it took him a minute to place her, especially since for some reason she'd kept her maiden name. But he had no trouble remembering what she looked like. She was what people on television called "striking." Larry's father had raised dairy cattle for several years and he was always interested in mating totally unrelated stock—he called it "outcrossing." Pamela was the happy result of human outcrossing: she had two white grandparents and two Indian ones and she was an exotic combination of Norwegian and Apache, with high cheekbones and eyes that were nearly amber and a thin, childlike body. She looked a great deal like the half-breeds he'd seen in Vietnam—beautiful outcasts. Was Pamela an outcast? He didn't know. Not many of her family had been at the wedding either, but no one he spoke with offered an explanation and Larry hadn't asked. At the time he thought it wasn't his business.

Larry watched her taking it all in, rolling down the window and sticking her head out to see past the tall old trees. Then they headed toward the agricultural station, where the students raised cattle, sheep, and pigs. Near the cattle barns was a stand of trees, the only bit of original timber for miles around. "Bob and I used to go birding in there sometimes," he told her. "But Bob was really allergic to poison ivy—he only had to look at it to get a rash."

Pamela laughed. "Yeah, he told me that one time he got it so bad he even got it on his . . ."

"I know. I was there, and I did too." Larry couldn't remember ever having talked about his privates with a woman, even in an elliptical way like this. "I didn't offend you just now, did I?"

"God, no—you should hear the women I hang around with. We talk about things that would blow men's minds!" Pamela smiled again.

Larry wondered what she'd be saying about him when she got back to Arizona, then decided he didn't want to know. "Would you like to go back home? I have to get ready for work tonight."

Larry worked third shift at the GM plant in Lansing, which took him out of the house until early the next morning. Pamela was glad for the chance to sit, rest, and snoop around. She'd always wondered if Bob's theories about Larry were true. Was he gay? Or Michigan's version of Jeffrey Dahmer? Or both?

Once Larry's Grand Am disappeared down the road, Pamela went in to take a shower. She found a towel and washcloth that looked like they had never been used and began to disrobe. In the back of her mind she wondered if he'd rigged the house with surveillance equipment: Was he taping her undressing right now? She clutched the towel to her and turned on the water, then slipped inside the shower quickly and threw the towel over the curtain. The water was much softer than she was accustomed to; it slipped off her body like baby oil and didn't make her feel much cleaner. She looked around the shower, amazed that there wasn't a hair anywhere and even the soap in the holder was new.

After she'd showered, quickly toweled off, and slipped into her robe, Pamela went from room to room. Larry's bedroom was a deep blue. He had a Bible, a Peterson's field guide to birds, binoculars, and an asthma inhaler next to the bed. Some handcrafted items she recognized as having been made by her ex-mother-in-law sat or hung in various parts of the room. There were no photographs, no personal treasures lying around.

The kitchen was from the 1970s; it had an avocado-colored refrigerator, stove, and countertop, dark wood cabinets, and plaid-covered bar stools. It was spotless, with few appliances sitting out. Those that were had handmade covers over them in the shape of geese or turkeys. On the wooden rack where Larry kept his keys, each ring was adorned with a copy of his dog tag.

She turned the corner and went down the basement stairs. Like the rest of the house, the basement was spotless. Larry had a little workshop in the corner, and his tools looked nearly new. He was working on some odds and ends, picture frames and things, all perfectly beveled. She laughed when she saw a Snap-on Tool calendar on one wall featuring an abnormally large-breasted youngster hefting some kind of wrench and desperately trying to keep her balance. Maybe he was more human than Bob had suspected.

She went back upstairs to explore the living room, the last on her tour. Hundreds of books that looked unread sat on shelves Larry had built himself. Mainly about birds but also about military history, Michigan, and the Bible. Pamela didn't see anything she wanted to read. Then she noticed a book sitting near Larry's TV chair: *Indians of North America*. He was probably studying up for her visit. Little did he know that she probably knew less about the Apache than he did. She flipped open the book to where he'd left off. It was near the beginning, when Paleo-Indians were crossing the Bering land bridge. He'd highlighted some parts about tooth and cranial similarities between Asian and Indian populations. She wondered if he'd been trying to brush up on his conversational skills. Bless his heart. He was really working at being a good host. She felt silly for wondering if he'd been filming her in the bathroom.

Pamela looked at her watch and converted the time to Mountain Standard. Even though it wasn't close to bedtime in Arizona, she yawned automatically and declared her investigation over. Larry was no Bob, but he wasn't Jeffrey Dahmer either. He was even kind of cute, for a Midwestern guy.

Larry could hear Pamela rustling around, even though he knew she was trying to be quiet for his sake. A while ago she'd taken the car someplace and now she was back with some plastic bags. He was surprised she didn't ask for paper instead of plastic; Indians didn't like anything synthetic, did they? He covered his head with a pillow and tried to sleep a while longer, but after ten minutes or so he decided to get up. There was something peculiar about having a woman around the house, an alien presence. He wrapped his robe tightly around him and slipped noiselessly into the bathroom to shower, shave, and wonder whether Pamela was a messy cook or if he'd end up with spicy food that wouldn't agree with him. Or both.

Pamela had her hair tied back and was wearing jeans. There were several bowls in various states of cleanliness sitting on the counter, and Larry noticed that there was a fine layer of flour on several of the barstools.

"Good morning!" she said, wiping her hands on the barely used apron he kept in the pantry. "I'm making you a hearty breakfast. We're going on a big adventure."

"It had better not be too big," Larry replied. "I've got to work later."

"No you don't. I called them. You're sick in bed."

"But I haven't missed more than a couple of days in ten years!"

"Then you've got plenty of time saved up. Now eat." Pamela pushed a plate of beans, eggs scrambled with chorizo, and newly fried flour tortillas toward him.

Larry tried not to count the fat grams that sat in front of him, picking up his plate and sitting down at the small dining table. "Is this—Apache food?"

"Nope. I've spent more time with Mexicans than anybody else. Even my Norwegian grandmother made tamales and chicken mole. Mexican food is inescapable out West. Hope you like it." She sat down across from him and tucked into her breakfast. For someone so delicate she certainly could eat. Larry played with his eggs for a while until he caught Pamela watching him. Then he heroically took a mouthful and ran to the sink for water.

"I think that's enough," he said after drinking two glasses.

"I'll eat it." Pamela picked up his plate and put it onto her now-clean one.

Larry sat back down. "That's interesting that you don't know any Apache foods."

"Well, Bob didn't know how to make sauerbraten or speak German, either."

"I heard where . . . your people walked over from Asia thousands of years ago."

"Some of them, I guess."

"I saw some girls in Vietnam that looked like you." Larry felt a little flushed. He got up and drank another glass of water.

"Well, I may be a mutt but I don't think I'm Vietnamese."

Larry was glad he wasn't facing her. "That's not what I meant. I just meant that I saw some pretty girls there and you look like them."

"You're sweet, Larry. I'm not a girl anymore."

"To me you are." They were quiet for a moment.

"Well, let's go," said Pamela. "We've got a lot of driving to do."

"Slowly," answered Larry. "We're still breaking it in."

"Yeah, whatever."

Before they left Lansing, Pamela stopped at a party store and bought some beer. She handed Larry one, knowing he would drink it out of politeness. When he finished it they were already on the interstate heading toward Chicago. She handed him another. By the time he'd had four beers he wasn't hounding her about the speed she should drive the Grand Am anymore. She let it out a notch and soon they were flying.

It took but a few hours to get to Chicago. Pamela didn't know where to go when she got there, she only knew she wanted to see the town. She wove in and out of the various expressways, getting off at an exit for Michigan Avenue. Larry hadn't recovered from the four beers and was turning the radio up rather loudly for moldy oldies like "Spirit in the Sky" and "Layla." Pamela found a parking lot with a few empty spaces and they left the Grand Am there.

"Isn't this great!" she remarked, not especially to Larry. All the buildings blazed with color and light. They paused by the shops, the offices, the library, the water tower. Pamela didn't care so much whether she went in a building as near it. Here she was in Chicago, a neon landscape instead of a desert. She noticed the skyscrapers creating a jagged canyon out of Michigan Avenue. It was a welcome change from the flatness of Phoenix, the green of Lansing, the sterile air of the plane.

Larry wasn't saying much; he was pretty buzzed, and she supposed she'd worn him out. After they'd walked a couple of miles up one side and down the other, with Pamela trying to keep him on a straight line, he became animated. "Can we go in there?" He nodded at Victoria's Secret, near Borders Books.

"Sure." She followed Larry into the store, the deep-pile carpeting a welcome change from the sidewalk.

"May I help you?" asked a tawny sales representative with a voice like cappuccino.

"I—uh—"

Pamela strolled forward, putting her arm through Larry's. "We're just looking, thanks." She guided him around from rack to rack and room to room. He picked up lotions and put them down. She watched him read the sign for lace underwear and then pick some up in wonder, letting it slip through his fingers and back to its mates. He held up sheer nightgowns and looked through them like a window curtain, his wide eyes meeting hers.

After the salesperson asked them for the third time if she could be of help, Pamela suggested to Larry that they ought to go.

"I really was looking for something."

Pamela first envisioned black leather or PVC, then shrugged it off.

Bob had called her "Polythene Pam." She wondered if Larry would be into that sort of stuff. "Like what?"

"I don't know. I'd know it if I saw it."

"And they say women are vague! Let's get out of here." They went out into the late afternoon. It was nearly dark inside the corridor of skyscrapers. "If you tell me what it is, we'll get it. I love scavenger hunts."

Larry thought for a moment as they walked along. "Asian imports."

"Back to the car then." They pulled out onto Michigan Avenue. Pamela pulled up next to a Pinto driven by a large black man wearing a Desert Storm T-shirt and asked for directions to Chinatown. After much gesticulating and misunderstood words, she waved him on and turned to Larry. "I don't know if I got all of that, but let's give it a try."

They zoomed over to Broadway, then north until the billboards for Burger King and Budweiser were written in Chinese. Pamela drove around until she found a parking lot that actually had an attendant on duty, at least for a little while longer. "You'd better know what you want 'cause we need to get in and out fast."

"I'll know it when I see it."

They passed a couple of restaurants and entered a few shops, but Larry evidently saw nothing he wanted. Pamela wondered if he really did know what he was looking for. Whatever it was, she hoped he found it quickly. Night was coming on and they had some ground to cover back to Lansing.

Almost before she noticed, Larry slipped into a small Vietnamese store with dry goods and various curiosities behind the barred windows. She followed him in but he sent her outside, saying he'd be with her in a moment. It was clear that he was buying her a present; what wasn't clear was whether she would pretend to like it if she didn't. Even though Bob hadn't liked his mother's taste in crewelwork or embroidery, he had became upset when Pamela made jokes about them.

Larry returned with a bag under his arm and they ran back to the car, the foreign surroundings turning sinister in the dusk. Pamela went around the town in a circle a few times before she found the correct freeway entrance, and then they lapped the miles through Indiana and across Michigan. From time to time she looked over at Larry, who'd fallen asleep. The bag was on his lap, but she curbed her urge to peek into it. Bob had always said she was bad about surprises. He'd almost killed her the time he caught her rewrapping all the Christmas presents he'd bought her. Larry was probably giving her a going-away present, something from Vietnam that, in his drunken confusion of Apaches and Asians, he thought she'd like. She made a point to like it no matter what. Larry was sweet: he'd gotten her a deal on a car, he'd studied up on Indians, he'd humored her while she drove the car across three states.

Somewhere outside of Kalamazoo she began to hear a noise. Looking over at Larry, she saw he was mouth breathing against the passenger window, and she turned up the radio until the noise went away. The Beatles station was playing the one song she liked: "Two of Us." It reminded her of Bob, and her mother—the Beatles were their favorite group, but they hadn't been part of Pamela's world. She'd actually preferred Sinatra. Then Bob came along. He and her mother swapped song titles until it drove her crazy. She wondered sometimes if the only reasons her mother had given her blessing to the marriage was that Bob had shown her exactly where the slow and fast versions of "Strawberry Fields Forever" were welded together and because he made her a tape of some rare Beatles demo disks, like "Bad to Me" and "Goodbye." Parents had given their blessings for worse reasons, she supposed. She caught herself singing along: *You and I have memories longer than the road that stretches out of here*. The noise was getting louder. She thought about pulling over, but they weren't that far from Lansing now.

Larry was dreaming that he was in a bomber again, only this time it was flying over Arizona. Instead of jungle and rice paddies he saw sand and rocks and roadside curio stands. Far below, children waved as the plane knifed across the sky, spilling its cargo out the bomb bay doors. The long, low sound of the blast forced him into consciousness, as it always did.

It took him a moment to recognize Pamela. In the moonlight, inside the car, she was almost a stranger, a girl he'd glimpsed in a Saigon doorway. She looked over at him and then turned down the radio. "I'm glad you're awake. I think there's something wrong with the car. Listen."

"Pull over."

Pamela veered around a dead deer in the emergency lane and brought the car to a halt. Larry told her to pop the hood and then jumped out to assess the situation. It was probably nothing. There wasn't enough moonlight to see anything, and he hadn't thought to bring a flashlight. He walked around to Pamela's side and motioned for her to roll down the window.

"Start it up."

There was only the steady *plonk-plonk-plonk* of the American-made engine, but Larry didn't want to take any chances. He carefully closed the hood. "I'll drive," he said. There wasn't much traffic on the interstate, and they glided out of the emergency lane and slowly accelerated. At fifty-five they looked at each other: the noise had begun again. "You like cornflakes?" asked Larry.

"Sure. Why?"

"Because it looks like we'll be spending the night in Battle Creek." He took the first exit and cruised through the town, past the factories that cranked out Grape-Nuts, and Mueslix, and Wheaties. There was only one motel that looked open, Yarnell's Motor Lodge, a relic from the 1950s. He'd get a room for Pamela and sleep in the Grand Am. It would be like car camping, like his folks had done when the family was too poor to stay in motels. "How's this look?"

"Okay. Stop here—I'll take care of it. It's the least I can do." Pamela slipped into the lobby. He saw her talking to the desk clerk and pointing at the car. Then he glanced down at the package and rattled its paper wrapper with his hand.

Pamela walked over to his side of the car, jingling a key. "Number nine," she said, nodding toward the far end of the building. "Meet you there."

Larry parked, stuffed his package under his arm, and picked up the remaining two beers. By the time he entered the room, Pamela had turned on the air conditioning, a rickety little unit that sounded worse than the car, and turned down the bed. He grabbed the package more tightly and sat on an old wooden chair with bite marks on the arms. "I'm going to stay in the car tonight."

"No, you're not," Pamela rummaged through her purse. "Now, I've got some toothpaste, and a little travel bottle of shampoo, and a comb. And you've got two beers and your secret package."

Larry knew he must look like the dead deer in the emergency lane just before it was hit. He saw Pamela smirking at him and he finally couldn't stand it. "I know what you're thinking. Bob probably told you a lot about me. But there's a lot he didn't know." He stood up. "I'm taking a shower and then going to sleep in the car." He took the toothpaste, shampoo, and comb from Pamela's outstretched hands and stalked into the bathroom, slamming the flimsy door. Inside were two little towels, a bar of soap sporting the name of another motel, and some shrink-wrapped drinking cups. The shower wasn't clean enough for his liking, but it would do.

As soon as she heard the water running Pamela turned the lights down and opened Larry's package. She withdrew a light blue silk pajama set; the top had black closures shaped like birds. It was beautifully made, and as she held it to her body she knew it would fit her perfectly. Kicking away her shoes and dropping her jeans and T-shirt to the floor, she slipped into the pajama bottoms and then the top, fastening the closures. She brushed her hair into a bun and stuck a black pen in it to keep it in place. In the half light she would look at least a little Vietnamese. Enough.

When Larry came out of the bathroom he had all his clothes on and was rubbing a towel vigorously over his head. Pamela didn't move, waiting for him to notice her. She had played a sex game like this with Bob. She couldn't move until he touched her; they called it freeze tag.

Pamela watched Larry combing his hair in the mirror, actively ignoring her, his eyes trained on making his part perfectly straight. She saw his eyes drop to the empty package. He spun around—the fastest she'd seen him move.

His voice was shaking. "Get out of that."

"Why?"

He walked toward her. "Take it off in the bathroom, and put your clothes on."

"But I need pajamas to sleep in—don't I?"

Larry stepped closer, clenching and unclenching a fist. "Get out of that. Now." He grabbed her shoulder and shoved her toward the bathroom, throwing her scattered clothes behind her. Pamela whipped the door closed and locked it. She pulled the pen out of her hair, which cascaded down around her, and looked at herself in the mirror. All she needed was an instrument and she'd be Yoko Ono in a Sgt. Pepper costume. She had to admit there was more to Larry than she'd expected. A lot of the men she'd been with had loved her to dress up, especially the ones that, like Larry, seemed to have had more than a little trouble relating to women. They could objectify you if you were in costume, give themselves some room.

She slipped off the pajama bottoms and then undid the closures. Fine, then. Larry would have to deal with her directly. Without dressing, she emerged from the bathroom holding the pajamas in front of her.

Larry was sitting on the scarred chair, crying openly. Pamela fished in her purse for some tissues, put them and the pajamas on his lap, and backed away. He didn't look up. She sat down on the bed across from him and leaned against the peeling wallpaper, listening to his jagged breath.

A long time passed and then Larry sought her out. His eyes narrowed as he took in her body. "Did you think I brought you here to sleep with you? I really was going to sleep in the car."

"Why'd you buy the pajamas then?"

Larry fingered the pile of silk on his lap. "They aren't for you. And remember, I didn't choose this motel room—or that bed."

Pamela smiled. "I like you. I thought you liked me. You remind me of Bob sometimes, especially when you drink. Part of me was starting to forget him."

Larry looked around the room and then directly at Pamela. He didn't seem to blink. "You remind me of somebody too. Somebody I haven't seen for twenty years. Somebody I've been starting to forget a little."

Pamela was almost whispering. "If you let me put those on, I can be anybody you want me to be."

"You can't be my daughter."

"Holy shit." Pamela pulled the covers up to her neck. Suddenly it made sense. Larry's questions about the Bering land bridge, and assimilation, and customs. And the trips to Victoria's Secret and the Vietnamese shop.

"I haven't told anybody that, ever. She has a new father and other brothers and sisters. They treat her well. But when she looks in the mirror, she's got to know she's different. I met some half-breeds there. They don't belong anywhere. Sometimes I wish she'd never been born and other times I'd give a million dollars to see her."

This was not the evening Pamela had expected. Men's fantasies she could handle. But this was reality, aged to perfection. "How much does she know about you?"

"They have photos of me. I send things—money, gifts—to her mother, but I don't know what happens once it gets there."

"She's lucky to have you as a father, even if she doesn't know you." She paused. "You're a good man. You didn't have to help me get the car. You don't owe me any favors."

"But you're family." He seemed to mouth the words as though they were a new kind of fruit. Then he glanced at the pajamas in his hands and tossed them to her. "I'm getting kind of tired. I don't like the idea of my sister-in-law sleeping in here naked when there are some perfectly good pajamas around."

Pamela ventured a laugh. He was coming around surprisingly quickly. "My ancestors didn't wear pajamas—or didn't you read that in your book?"

"Well, you at least need a loincloth, don't you?"

Under the bedspread, she slipped on the pajama bottoms, then turned away to put on the top and fasten the closures. "Don't forget, Larry, you probably know more about Apaches than I do."

He fished around for one of the two remaining beers, popped the top, and drank deeply. A kind of relief seemed to cross his face.

Timeline

Cortney Davis

It was 1970. He was out a year
at most. When fire trucks went by,
rattling our bed, he'd jump up,
his body bent, hazel eyes
flecked with green. I thought
I could see his soul. I was poor,
just starting nursing school.
Kennedy was dead, men walked
on the moon, and when the Beatles sang
Nothing's gonna change my world,
I actually believed them, graduated
with high honors, and took a job:
night shift in intensive care. My kids
grew up. Sometimes, when we
made love, my husband said
he thought about the women in Vietnam.
One December morning
we woke to hear that Lennon died.
I felt odd all day. I wasn't such a fan—
it had to do with what was shot
away: Kennedy, Martin Luther King,
Vietnam. For the first time, I felt
my generation as a living, breathing
thing. My daughter grew into a thin,
startled beauty and started using drugs.
My son escaped to college. I was divorced
in 1986. How to summarize?
I went to therapy. I got sane.

what do you see when
you turn out the light?

The Assassination of John Lennon as Depicted by the Madame Toussaud Wax Museum, Niagara Falls, Ontario, 1987

David Wojahn

Smuggled human hair from Mexico
Falls radiant round the waxy *O*

Of her scream. Shades on, leather coat and pants, Yoko
On her knees—like the famous Kent State photo

Where the girl can't shriek her boyfriend alive, her arms
Windmilling Ohio sky.
                                        A pump in John's chest heaves

To mimic death throes. The blood is made of latex.
His glasses: broken on the plastic sidewalk.

A scowling David Chapman, his arms outstretched,
His pistol barrel spiraling fake smoke

In a siren's red wash, completes the composition,
And somewhere background music plays "Imagine"

Before the tableau darkens. We push a button
To renew the scream.
                                        The chest starts up again.

Working at *Rolling Stone*: December 8, 1980

Lisa Clark

It was a thrill to say
I'd seen him in the hall.
He and Yoko
on the cover this time.
He was in and out
all week. The photograph
was settled, the one of him naked,
his arms and legs around her,
kissing her cheek.
She was fully clothed in black,
staring blankly at the camera.
Just before the deadline

we got a call—
redesign the magazine,
quickly. All of it would be
about him, every piece.
We slept on the floor,
cried and raced,
played *Double Fantasy*
as loud as we could.
We took separate shifts,
kept vigil until
it was laid out, over,
put to bed.

Liverpool Echo

Carol Ann Duffy

Pat Hodges kissed you once, although quite shy,
in sixty-two. Small crowds in Mathew Street
endure rain for the echo of a beat,
as if nostalgia means you did not die.

Inside phone-booths, loveless ladies cry
on Merseyside. Their faces show defeat.
An ancient jukebox blares out *Ain't She Sweet*
in Liverpool, which cannot say goodbye.

Here everybody has an anecdote
of how they met you, were the best of mates.
The seagulls circle round a ferry boat

out on the river, where it's getting late.
Like litter on the water, people float
outside the cavern in the rain. And wait.

Prologue from *Shout!* December 1980

Philip Norman

"He kept me from dying so many times."

In New York it was now just after midnight. The assassin and his victim had each been taken into custody. People were already massing, in an atmosphere of stunned quiet, opposite the big, old neo-Gothic archway into the Dakota building. Britain, five hours ahead over the time zones, still knew nothing. In Britain, only dozing security guards and predawn travelers heard, via the BBC Overseas Service, an announcement which even the clipped, old-fashioned newsreader's voice could barely authenticate. John Lennon had been shot outside his New York apartment. John Lennon was dead.

The shock, when Britain awoke to it, had an eerie quality, as of time cut suddenly from underfoot. It was the dubious achievement of the seventies to turn sudden, senseless murder into a commonplace, scarcely noticeable event. Yet here was an emotion, vast and simultaneous, felt in one kindred flow of horror by all for whom John Lennon's music, and the Beatles', had become a release—a refuge even—from the brutal recent decade. Strangers talked; old friends broke telephone silence to remind themselves when last they had felt at one like this. Not since Kennedy was killed, they said. Not since the murder of Martin Luther King. Not since a day back in 1967, that summer drenched in heat and acid sparkle, when a million heads swam together at the behest of Sergeant Pepper's Lonely Hearts Club Band.

In TV and radio newsrooms the tributes began to take hurried shape. Bulging file envelopes were brought up from cuttings libraries, their tattered contents spread and quickly sifted. Errors uncorrected fifteen years ago became brand new errors for tonight's bulletin and tomorrow morning's feature page: "At the age of eight, John Lennon saw his mother knocked down by a car and killed. . . . He was brought up by his Aunt Mimi in a tough working-class district of Liverpool. . . ."

Two hours had elapsed since Mark David Chapman—his full name in use, as with all notable killers—yielded up his signed autograph book, his cassettes of Beatles music, and his .38-caliber revolver. Across the time gap, near Bournemouth, Dorset, dawn was just breaking over Poole Harbour. The half-tame seagull that Aunt Mimi calls Albert strutted over the patio, waiting to be fed by the lean, practical, occasionally uproarious woman whom John resembled in so many ways and from whom he inherited not inconsiderable virtues.

John bought this harborside bungalow for Mimi long ago in the sixties, after fan madness had made Liverpool uninhabitable. He found her one night in tears, crumpled on the front staircase, and told her to choose a new house anywhere in England. Mimi lives alone, untroubled but for the occasional pleasure-launch microphone announcing, "There's John Lennon's aunt's house," and the regular sudden rings at her front doorbell. Mimi, seeing the shapes through the frosted glass, always knows what to expect. Another group of girls from America, Australia, or Japan is following the well-beaten trail of Beatle monuments and shrines. Brusque and softhearted, Mimi scolds them and invites them in, just as she once invited in Paul McCartney and George Harrison. Often she puts them up overnight, in the spare room with the little bed whose significance they do not dream. "I say quite casually, 'That used to be John's bed, you know.' Oh, you should *see* their faces!"

The bungalow is not luxurious. It is, like Mimi's house in Liverpool, a comfortable, spotless home where feet do better to be wiped. On the television set a photograph of John in his Quarry Bank school cap hides the place once occupied by his MBE medal. A bureau drawer still contains the little drawings and verses, written on the blue, ruled paper of childhood, which Mimi kept there even after the world had hailed their erratic brilliance. Near the patio window stands the room's single pretentious object: a cocktail cabinet shaped like an antique globe. Asprey's, the Bond Street silversmiths, supplied several such globes to Beatle households in the era when spending money had no limit and its charm was already dwindling fast.

Mimi awoke on December 9 and switched on her radio to hear someone talking about John on the *Today* show. She was not perturbed, not even surprised. She thought what she used to when he was at Quarry Bank and the headmaster's office would telephone; the same vexed, half-smiling thought as so many times down the years. "Oh Lord—what's he done *now*?"

The crowds that gathered the following Sunday, opposite Lime Street station in Liverpool, and in Central Park, New York, held a requiem for more than the thin-nosed, impudent boy whose wayward, soon-fatigued virtuosity jolted, entranced, and exasperated his generation. The vigil was for John; the farewell was to all the Beatles. A decade after their partnership officially ended and the magic entity split into four all-too-human fragments, rumors of a second coming had persisted—even strengthened. In 1980 even more than in 1963, the world seemed to be waiting for the Beatles.

The four had long since become reconciled within themselves. There were partial reunions, as when Ringo made an album with Paul and George playing on different tracks. Each year or so Sid Bernstein, the New York promoter, placed his familiar full-page newspaper advertisement, offering still more millions for a single concert by the Beatles reborn. It was an entreaty not just from fans; it came also from international charities and relief organizations, suspecting that in the Beatles lay a power greater than theirs to benefit mankind. This had its effect at last on Paul McCartney's tender social conscience, with the series of London concerts he organized early in 1980 for the Kampuchean refugees. George Harrison and

Ringo Starr were both reportedly willing to appear with Paul on stage. John, in New York, refused to be drawn, even after a personal appeal from the United Nations' Secretary General. To John, the Beatles had benefited mankind enough. He said as much, in the voice which so often used to bring Paul's schemes and fancies down to earth. "We gave everything for ten years. We gave *ourselves.* If we played now, anyway, we'd just be four rusty old men."

The crowds stood in Central Park, chanting songs that for thousands epitomized their youth, and for equivalent thousands predated consciousness, even birth. Some were here in February 1964, flinging themselves against similar police barricades, that day of snow and madness when the Beatles came to the Plaza Hotel. For some the climax was in 1967, when Sergeant Pepper's multicolored vaudeville show wove its way into a new American Dream. And there were the seventies children, nurtured on Beatles music despite the dynasties of glittering frauds that followed, despite the familiar yardstick of rock hype that this or that merely successful group was "bigger than the Beatles." Even when million-sellers became common currency, the Beatles outsold, as well as eclipsed all others. Their music, that vast, nonchalant treasury, pours out in undiminished strength on record, on radio, in supermarkets, in elevators; is hummed on the unconscious breath; is drummed by the fingertips of two continents. A New Yorker of twenty-one spoke for his whole insecure generation when he said: "I came here for John. I can't believe he's dead. He kept me from dying so many times."

In Liverpool, on that time-warped afternoon, thirty thousand people filled the piazza of St. George's Hall, around the equestrian statues commemorating Queen Victoria and Prince Albert. The ruined imperial city, its abandoned river, its tormented suburban plain, knew an anguish greater even than the recession and unemployment which have laid Merseyside waste under bombardments more deadly than Hitler's blitz.

This crowd, too, stood hour after hour, chanting "She Loves You" in the dialect it was written for, scarcely conscious what a part the soot-blackened colonnade before them played in their heroes' earliest history. Across this same piazza in 1959, John, Paul, George, and Stu Sutcliffe staggered with the carnival floats they had built for Allan William's Mersey Arts Ball. Downhill from here, a brand-new shopping precinct leads into Whitechapel. What used to be NEMS' shop is a branch of Rumbelows, still selling electrical goods and records, though shrunken by a false ceiling. At the edge you can see up to the old, high ceiling, still covered with Brian Epstein's tasteful collage of album sleeves.

It is just across the road, as Brian discovered, that Mathew Street begins. Some say the Cavern Club is down there even now, intact under the car park that abolished it. Farther along in a garage entrance rests a tribute which Liverpool, somehow, never got around to erecting—four bronze-laminated Beatle faces, left leaning behind the bumpers of an Austin 1100. There is only Arthur Dooley's inn-sign sculpture overhead, honoring FOUR LADS WHO SHOOK THE WORLD. Underneath, on this Sunday, little love notes were stuck to the wall. Single flowers lay sodden on the unchanging cobblestones.

The Beatles eventually ruled over time itself. Epoch after epoch is personified by a guitar chord they had discovered or a shirt collar with a new fastening; their album covers are the portrait gallery of an age. They could not, on their own, put an end to their existence. That required the strength of pure random lunacy, of a mind perhaps unhinged by worship of them. So now, suddenly, stunningly, in the death of their tetchy, honest, foolish, incorruptible soul, the Beatles were seen to be no more. As dusk fell, in New York and Liverpool, candles flickered and smoked in cupped-together hands.

When the candles blew out, only the music was left. Only myths and rumors, multiplying stronger than ever around this scarcely imaginable, true story.

Why I Didn't Like the Beatles

Priscilla Webster-Williams

Silly boys, loping like shaggy goats
out of airplanes, onto stages.
They weren't real men,
like Uncle Leon,
who sat beside me,
old enough to be my daddy,
holding my hand
on his pointed pink thing.

Other third-grade girls didn't know
what I did, that to please a real man
all you have to do is do what he wants
and he'll bring you a doll, call you
Princess, give you a sparkly ring.
And later on, gift-wrapped,
a box of rubbers, and say
the boys are really going to like you.

Except, when I got older,
I didn't like the goofy boys,
and the older girls always fixing
their hair, wondering what to wear next.
I could have told them
you don't have to buy tickets,
tease your hair, scream or faint
to be someone's special girl.

When Lennon got shot,
everyone standing around for days,
staring at the Dakota,
I think they realized what I'd known
since I was nine:
You don't have to do anything.
All you gotta do is
be at the right place at the wrong time.

Shake a Tail Feather

Lisa Williams Kline

I am picking up my daughter, who is nine, from a friend's house, and the mother and I talk in the kitchen while my daughter puts on her shoes. Our daughters had their first fight today, the mother tells me. I tell her something I heard about older students trying to sell a form of LSD called Blue Star to some fourth graders at our school. We shake our heads, the conversation moves on, and she gives me the name of a good piano teacher.

Then I see a framed poster over the breakfast table, in black and white, of the Beatles early on, with the black suits and bowl haircuts.

"Where did you get this?" I say, crossing her kitchen. Something about those four young faces causes emotion to rush over me.

"I saw it in an art store, already framed," says the mother, "and almost started crying right there. I had to have it."

"When I was in seventh grade they had a concert in my hometown," I tell her.

The year the Beatles came to Winston-Salem, I was writing a mystery novel with my best friend, Arlene. That year I saw *The Sound of Music* ten times. Once with my parents, and nine times with Arlene.

We were both twelve and ignoring the fact that we needed training bras. We spent our free time in Arlene's slope-ceilinged third floor bedroom plotting, writing, and acting out scenes for our mystery novel. Acting out scenes was very important because it provided the authenticity that all novels require.

For example, when one dies of marijuana poisoning, does one writhe on the floor for a long period of time or just keel right over?

If one lived in a tree house, how would one go to the bathroom? Discussions such as these consumed entire weekends.

Arlene was tall and gangly with limp hair and glasses as thick as Coke bottles. I was short and plump with limp hair and glasses as thick as Coke bottles. We did not care how we looked, nor did we have an inkling anyone would ever evaluate us based on our appearances. We were innocents. This was what our parents loved about us.

Our contemporaries, who were rolling their hair with puffy pink rollers and Dippity-Do, dabbing Clearasil on their faces, and almost letting boys touch certain areas of their bodies, laughed at us as we stalked the halls of Wiley Junior High acting out our mystery novel. We didn't even notice. That's how innocent we were.

The subject of our novel was the wicked Dr. Boris Schnauzer, who was, as Arlene called him, a marijuana fiend. The whites of his eyes were yellow, a dead giveaway, she said, to his true addiction. Dr. Boris Schnauzer had kidnapped a number of teenage girls and turned them into marijuana fiends, too. Our heroine, Christine (a name we both thought was impossibly cosmopolitan) Longstocking (a tribute to one of our all-time favorites), was also kidnapped by the evil Dr. Schnauzer. Christine freed the other girls, whom Dr. Schnauzer held captive in an abandoned tree house, and she destroyed the supply of marijuana that he fed them to maintain their addiction. Christine, in my mind, had the resourcefulness of Nancy Drew, the unshakable morality of Jo March, and looked like Barbie.

Arlene, the youngest of four sisters, seemed to have a ready supply of knowledge about the evil weed, marijuana. I wasn't exactly sure what it was, but I didn't feel comfortable admitting this to Arlene, since it was a large part of our novel. I suspected it was a yellow fluid you drank. As you drank it, the whites of your eyes would turn yellow, like the water level rising in the bathtub.

When we wrote together, Arlene would lie on her bed in odd positions and dictate while I typed.

"Okay, Donna, type this: 'Christine's eyes lifted over the tree-house floor—'"

"That sounds like her eyes are all by themselves, you know, floating over the floor of this tree house."

"Okay, 'Christine lifted her eyes over the tree-house floor—'"

"Doesn't that sound like she's weight lifting, like her eyes are really heavy?"

This struck us as funny, so we rolled around for a few minutes pretending to weight-lift a several-hundred-pound pair of eyes.

"'. . . and what should she see but five teenage girls, their hair matted and their faces streaked from crying.'"

"That's good. Wait, question: Why can't the girls climb down and escape?"

"Let's see."

Arlene and I wandered her cramped, jumbled room, pondering this. Arlene threw herself spread-eagle on her bed, took off her glasses and cleaned them on her T-shirt. I twirled a favorite lock of hair, then stuck it in my mouth.

"I've got it!" Arlene leapt to her feet. "Dobermans guarding the foot of the tree!"

"Great! 'Snarling and showing their gleaming teeth, snapping at Christine's heels, were six ferocious Dobermans.'" I typed furiously.

"Wait, Donna, say they're foaming at the mouth."

"They have rabies?"

"Yeah."

"Perfect." I hammered the keys. Of course I barely noticed that Arlene came up with all the ideas and I just did the typing. I was in heaven.

I don't remember when I noticed that people laughed at us. I don't remember when I began walking with Arlene only in side corridors of Wiley Junior High, and avoiding being seen with her in the main corridor, where the "popular" girls gathered. My locker was close to where some girls who wore saddle shoes and tailored Villager dresses gathered, chatting and tossing their hair and embroidering the air with their hands. I liked to eavesdrop on their conversations, often about topics I didn't understand, while collecting books for my next class.

The "popular" girls made fun of everyone. They made fun of

Arlene, imitating her gawky walk. They made fun of Marsha Watlington, who had a thick torso and thin legs, thus earning her the nickname "Humpty Dumpty." Humpty Dumpty's grades were bad because she was always in a dreamworld, scribbling poems in crabbed letters so small that only Humpty Dumpty herself could read them.

The "popular" girls even made fun of each other. I once stood by my open locker and listened in awed horror as they verbally vivisected a girl who happened to be absent that day. Each time they attacked someone, I listened with dread, wondering if the next person they lampooned would be me. But they never said anything about me, which was in a way even worse. I was a total nonentity.

The "popular" girls listened to the radio. One day I overheard one of them say that the night before, one of the deejays had locked himself in the control room and played "Shake a Tail Feather" twenty-five times in a row. How boring, I thought, but then realized, listening to the others talk, how foolish I was to think so. It was, rather, incredibly *cool* to listen to "Shake a Tail Feather" twenty-five times in a row, mainly because the song had been banned from most Southern radio stations due to its suggestive lyrics. I realized this was an open act of rebellion by the deejay, and felt excited by my new level of understanding about the world. I became obsessed with this mysterious song that was so filthy it had been *banned.*

That weekend, ensconced in Arlene's bedroom with root beers and Cheetos, I pounded the typewriter keys with orange fingers. Arlene's mother let you eat anywhere in the house. Mine made me eat in the kitchen.

"Arlene, how about this. How about if Dr. Boris Schnauzer discovers the teenage girls secretly listening to 'Shake a Tail Feather' on the radio?"

"Hunh?" said Arlene. She was lying on her bed, looking at the ceiling, slowly allowing herself to slide over the side toward the floor. "What's that?"

"It's a really great song," I explained.

"Who sings it?"

"The Beatles." This was a wild guess.

"What does it sound like?"

"I don't know," I had to admit. By now I had glued my ear to the radio for hours but no one, at least in Winston-Salem, ever heard that song again. "It's *banned.*"

"Well, I don't think we should put something in our novel that we're not familiar with," said Arlene.

I hesitated, my fingers tense in the asdf-jklsemi position on the typewriter. How come we were writing pages and pages about marijuana fiends, which I personally knew nothing about, but couldn't write about "Shake a Tail Feather," which I coincidentally also knew nothing about? And the seed of the thought that we were going with Arlene's Ideas and not My Ideas began to grow.

That night in my bedroom, I turned on the radio and heard the disc jockey announce that the Beatles were coming to Memorial Coliseum, one mile from my house. The station was sponsoring an essay contest: one hundred words or less on "Why I Want to Meet the Beatles." The winner would receive two free tickets to the Beatles' concert and get to meet the Fab Four in person backstage after the show.

I did not plan to enter the contest at first. After all, to me, in comparison to concocting dialogue with Arlene in her turretlike third-floor bedroom, most events in the world were vague and shadowy, hardly worth noticing. I entered the contest only after the following weekend, when Arlene and I had a major fight.

I remember Arlene was lying on her bed with her gangly legs in the air, pointing and flexing her toes. Arlene's mother had sent her to dance class for many years as an antidote for her natural clumsiness, but to no avail. I was, of course, sitting at the typewriter, with one leg underneath me.

"Let's see," Arlene began. "'Christina untied one bedraggled teenager—'"

"Whose tresses had once been flowing blonde."

"Okay, fine. 'He forces us to smoke marijuana,' the girl cried breathlessly."

"How about if he also tortures them with Chinese water torture?" I suggested.

"Chinese water torture?" Arlene contemplated her feet.

"Yeah, you know, when they drip water on your forehead for hours until you scream for mercy."

"No, I've got it, he forces them to listen to chalk screeching on the chalkboard."

A few weeks earlier I might have thought the idea of squeaking-chalk torture was fabulous. But now I possessed increased sensitivity to which were My Ideas and which were Arlene's Ideas.

"I like Chinese water torture," I said. I removed my hands from the keyboard and glared at Arlene.

"But how would he get water up in the tree house?" she argued.

"He could set up a running-water system with a paddle wheel, like the Swiss Family Robinson."

"A chalkboard would be easier to get up in a tree. Besides, remember the cardinal rule: Write about stuff you know. I don't know anything about Chinese water torture and you don't either."

"How do you know what's in my brain?" I shouted.

"Hey, you don't have to get so mad about it."

"Well, I'm sick and tired of you rejecting my ideas."

"Well, Donna, why don't you just go write your own mystery novel?"

"Maybe I will!"

"Go ahead. All you're doing is typing, anyway." Our eyes locked and I could see that Arlene immediately regretted what she had said, and I was already regretting what I was about to do, but it seemed too late to do anything about it.

I yanked the paper out of the typewriter and threw it on the floor.

"Fine!" I picked up my bookbag and stomped two blocks home. I stormed through the kitchen, scowling at my family, went upstairs to my room, slammed the door, and turned on the radio full blast.

". . . over one thousand entries to our Meet the Beatles contest! Just think, you could be the one to meet John, Paul, George, and Ringo!"

Now, deafening sound effects of thousands of girls screaming at the tops of their lungs.

"The winning essay will be chosen at six o'clock Friday, one day before the Beatles' concert. Send us your entry today!"

So Arlene thought all I could do was type. Well, fine.

The deejay played "Please Please Me." I pulled my hair into a fierce ponytail, shoved up the sleeves of my sweatshirt, and started to type. I had never felt myself to be quite so eloquent. I wanted to meet the Beatles, I wrote, not because they were cute, but because those four lads had changed the face of music forever. Passion flowed from my fingertips to the typewriter keys, then onto the paper like claps of lightning. I wrote with conviction. I wrote about rebellion. I used the word *splendid* because it sounded good with an English accent. I wrote about the Beatle song that symbolized the future force of rock 'n' roll: "Shake a Tail Feather."

The idea that I was sure to win comforted me over the course of the next week, since Arlene and I weren't speaking. I imagined calling Arlene and saying, in a magnanimous voice, that I had an extra ticket to the Beatles concert, would she be interested?

On Monday and Tuesday we both ate lunch in opposite ends of the cafeteria, alone. On Wednesday I saw Arlene having lunch with Humpty Dumpty Watlington, which sent blood throbbing through my temples. In confusion, I accidentally sat across from the new boy who had just moved from New Jersey. I became even more confused when he fixed his eyes on me with what seemed to be relief and joy and started to ask me questions about the South. He had very long eyelashes, for a boy. He told me he ran track. I inadvertently looked at his thighs.

That night I washed my hair, leaned close to the mirror, took my glasses off, and examined my face in extreme close-up, every pore, with dissatisfaction.

Six o'clock Friday found me sitting on the floor in the hall outside my room to hear the phone ring, since I was probably the only seventh grader in the entire universe without her own phone. I dug my fingers into Mom's plush new wall-to-wall carpet. I hated the sound of my voice on tape. What would it sound like on the radio?

"The next voice you hear will be the winner of the essay contest," announced the deejay. I heard the sound of dialing. Then one ring. And another.

The phone at my house wasn't ringing.

"Hello?" came over the radio.

"Hello, Marsha Watlington?"

"This is she." Puzzled.

"This is Ronnie Rocker from WTOB Radio, and you are our winner in the Meet the Beatles contest. What do you think about that?"

Marsha Watlington? Humpty Dumpty Watlington?

"Gosh," she said.

"The judges loved your poem, Marsha, which was entitled, 'To Paul, with Love.' Which means you get two free tickets to the Beatles concert here in Winston-Salem tomorrow night, and you also get to go backstage and—" here Ronnie Rocker paused for effect, and continued in a stentorian voice , *"—meet the Beatles!"*

There was gasping and sniffling on the other end of the line.

"Oh, my gosh, I can't believe it!" I couldn't believe it either. Humpty Dumpty Watlington, not me, was going to meet the Beatles.

Arlene didn't call me that weekend, and I didn't call her. I tried to reread *The Hobbit* but my heart wasn't in it. On Saturday night my parents called me down from self-imposed isolation in my room to see Humpty Dumpty on the news. I slumped sullenly on the couch and watched Humpty Dumpty in living color as she read her poem, "To Paul, with Love." Then they showed clips from the Beatles concert. The Fab Four clowned about on the stage in their tight black pants and Nehru jackets and Paul said Winston-Salem girls were really "gear." The screaming teenage girls in the audience, with their matted hair and streaked faces, looked exactly the way I had always imagined Dr. Boris Schnauzer's tree-house captives might look in Arlene's and my novel.

A year later, after I got contact lenses and used my spare time for sunbathing and attending track meets rather than writing, I learned "Shake a Tail Feather" was not, in fact, a Beatles song. By that time Arlene and Marsha were best friends and were working on a novel which, Arlene told me, might include some poems. Once they actually asked me to join them, and I said okay, but then the boy from New Jersey, whose name was Rob, called and invited me to a party. I was so excited I forgot to call Arlene to say I'd changed my plans.

I learned the truth about the song in Rob's basement, while listening to music and burning incense by the light of a lava lamp. I found an album called *Rock On* by the Five Du-Tones, featuring their hit "Bend Over Let Me See You Shake a Tail Feather."

I could feel my ears begin to burn with embarrassment, and I thought about how hard those judges must have laughed when they read my essay. Then I put the album on the turntable. After all, I had never actually heard the song, since it had been *banned* all over the South. I guess they weren't so strict about things like that in New Jersey.

Rob gave me a handmade, sweet-smelling cigarette. I took a long, deep drag, and held the smoke in my lungs as long as I could. Maybe it was the pot, but both of us thought the song was exceedingly silly, certainly nothing for the entire Southern seaboard to get all hot and bothered about.

Today, thirty years later, the mother and I look at the poster together. I am suddenly aware of being middle-aged and needing to lose some weight and rinse the gray out of my hair.

" So," says the mother. "Who was your favorite?"

"Oh, John," I say, without hesitation. "Because I wanted to be a writer. What about you?"

"George," she says. "He was the shy one. Besides, everybody else liked Paul. I wanted to be different."

"Me, too."

I touch her arm, and we laugh and become closer. I think about

Humpty Dumpty Watlington meeting the Beatles, about Arlene and the novel we never finished. Those weekends we spent writing our mystery novel seem now, across the hazy span of years, to be as close to perfect as any I have ever experienced. I wish we had freed those captive girls.

The Last Beatlemaniac

Ed Davis

"All Rusty does all day is sit listening to his old Beatles records, stoned out of his mind." Bruce was locking and unlocking his thick, sandpapery fingers, his eyes engaging mine and then flitting to a corner of the diner as if I were judging him guilty of his brother's ruination.

"CDs, you mean," I suggested.

"Nah. He still has a turntable."

"Well," I said after awhile, "the Beatles always were his favorite band. But he liked the Stones and Doors a lot, too."

Unlacing his fingers, he grasped the edge of the Formica-topped table, lowering his voice so the other diners wouldn't hear.

"I mean *all* day, Terry. He don't work, he don't sleep, he don't much eat—just pizza. Mary and the kids left him six months ago. I don't think Rusty's hardly noticed. And he never leaves the apartment."

"Does someone support him?"

Bruce eased back into the crimson vinyl cushions. "Oh, Ma gives him every dime she can afford, and I do, too, but I feel guilty as hell supporting his habit."

"Drugs?"

Bruce nodded, lips compressed and eyes lowered in misery. He had probably never smoked a joint, though he swilled draft beer and shots of Jack, I knew, from having run into him in bars. He had been twenty-one in 1969 when our band, Strawberry Fields, peaked, mainly due to lead guitarist and vocalist Rusty Martin. Bruce had always embarrassed Rusty, requesting Hank Williams and Bill Monroe, scratching his balls and telling filthy jokes while we practiced.

Now he was clenching his hands so tightly the veins bulged like steel cord beneath oil-and-grease-splotched skin. His iron-gray eyes suppressed any urge in me to smile. I doubted seriously that my old buddy Rusty was doing anything worse than a little marijuana.

He suddenly leaned forward. "I'm at the end of my rope. I was walking by and saw you sitting here, so I says, 'Terry MacKenzie was Rusty's best friend in high school. Maybe *he* could talk sense to 'im.'"

I became aware of his coveralls, only a little dirty, and my Brooks Brothers suit.

"Terry, I always admired you, even when you was in the band with Rusty. Those other assholes my brother hung out with didn't amount to shit. But you—you went all the way. The wife listens to you all the time, 'Rock Voice of the Queen City.'" He grinned. "I would, too, if you could work in a little Merle or Willie."

I confess I was pleased, though embarrassed. Reaching across the table, I mock-punched his arm self-consciously.

"What's his address?" I said.

His shit-eating grin would've lit up Riverfront Coliseum.

Standing before the paint-chipped, fist-marked door to Rusty's apartment, I heard *Sgt. Pepper's Lonely Hearts Club Band* filtering through the wood. After leaving the station at four, I'd come within a gnat's ass of going on home. But I couldn't get Bruce's dismal face out of my mind. I knocked gently at first, then harder, realizing Rusty would have a hard time hearing it over the music. Just when I had decided to give up, having at least made an attempt, the door moved inward a foot or so, and Rusty's face slowly materialized, half-enshadowed, half-illuminated by the single, naked low-watt bulb burning behind me in the filthy hallway.

"Hey, buddy, how are you?"

My voice rang too loudly in the hollowness of the hallway. There was no perceptible change in his face, eerily bisected by the door-shadow. As if he hadn't slept in days, his brown eyes gazed from cavernous sockets. His mouth hung open enough to let his lips grip his cigarette, and sunken, gray-bearded cheeks made his face look collapsed. Although a baby screamed in the next apartment, I heard his lungs whistle.

The thought teased my brain that, since he didn't appear to recognize me, I could simply apologize for knocking on the wrong door and split, having done my duty to Bruce, humanity, and myself. But something kept me rooted. Maybe it was the way his still-black eyebrows arched upward, reminding me of twenty-year-old Paul McCartney. Seeing him plunged me into the past, but at the same time that I was drawn backward, I found myself tempted to move forward, into the darkness behind him.

Suddenly I saw my chance: Ringo had arrived at the first chorus of "A Little Help from My Friends," and I joined him, singing the harmony I'd sung with Rusty in the band, putting him off his guard just enough for me to gently slide past him. Once inside, my eyes quickly adjusted to the dimness and I saw a candle gleaming ahead in the living room, dark and smoky as a wizard's lair.

"Rusty, it's Terry MacKenzie. Remember?"

"Ter-ry." My name took a couple of seconds to form on his lips, then issue creakily from his parched throat. He raised a skeletal hand a few inches, closed the door with the other one. "Come on in."

In the living room he collapsed onto an old mattress, his head rolling forward onto his emaciated chest. Mary seemed to have taken all of the furniture. Seated atop an orange crate containing albums, I wondered if he'd already forgotten I was there. But he was floating upstream:

> Picture yourself on a boat on a river
> With tangerine trees and marmalade skies . . .

I finally unglued my eyes from Rusty's face to gaze around the room. His Rickenbacker twelve-string lay in a small pool of sunlight slipping in from a crack between smoke-yellowed curtains. His old Gibson flat-top stood in the corner, dust coating its red face and three greenish-black strings. Splattered by sickness, burnt by cigarettes, and littered with garbage, the hardwood floor looked as black as earth where it showed beneath carryout pizza wrappers and soda cans. The smell sealed out fresh air like a wool blanket.

I grew increasingly depressed, sitting in silence through the next two songs. At first I thought it was revulsion at the way Rusty was living—I'd heard that all he'd done since high school was play in bands, many of them awful—so I tried to work up a good head of self-righteous steam about what my friend had let time do to him. But the more I listened to these tunes I hadn't heard in at least a decade—my head full of Whitney Houston and Michael Bolton—I began to feel a gnawing in the pit of my stomach. Hunger? Couldn't be—I'd had a steak sandwich for lunch a couple hours ago. No, this *music* seemed to be doing something to me, forcing me to think about Lennon's bones moldering in his grave, McCartney's double chins, Ringo's alcoholism, and Harrison's disappearing act. I was feeling more than just old and out of it, but I couldn't quite pin it down yet.

When Rusty held the joint out to me, my first impulse was to crush it out in the middle of his forehead. But its bittersweet bouquet time-machined me backward to rock concerts, peace rallies, and Monday night band practice in Steve Wade's freezing garage. I saw us—young gods, brash, arrogant, immortal—and felt the orgasmic thrill of playing music in a great band. Rusty's band.

I took the joint carefully and, ignoring the fifteen or so years since I'd last smoked, sucked the sweet scent deep, holding it, then holding it some more before releasing a thin stream. When I passed it back to Rusty, a hint of a smile played on his lips. I didn't feel any effect of the drug as I waited, while Lennon and McCartney sang:

She (What did we do that was wrong?)
Is having (We didn't know it was wrong)
Fun (Fun is the one thing that money can't buy)

Incredibly beautiful, I thought, my formerly grim mood as dead as the crushed cockroaches I'd noticed near Rusty's mattress. As the circusy tones of "For the Benefit of Mr. Kite" blasted, I began to *feel* more than hear the music, white stars sailing at the edge of my vision. Too late—I'd had a half-dozen tokes by then—I realized Rusty smoked the best. He stared from his mattress, grinning, his teeth huge and yellow. For some reason that look enraged me, and the music, booming from two huge speakers behind us, shrank me, made me feel impotent, though I'd always prided myself on my ability to handle anything.

Suddenly my entire adult life seemed ridiculous, and all my anger—at critics who pan my show, callers who curse me, and managers who demand sixty-hour work weeks—seemed as important as a bucketful of piss. Also, there was the growing conviction in my benumbed brain that Rusty, derailed somewhere in 1967, had beaten me. But at what? I couldn't begin to even say what the game was. Finally centering my frustration on the music, I decided I could at least control *it*. Springing to the turntable, I clicked it off, not even bothering to retract the record or remove the arm. The music ground to a halt.

"Hey!" Rusty roared. As he struggled to rise—the pot had clobbered him, too—my anger peaked, dissolving the fog inside my head.

"Don't yell at me, you son-of-a-bitch," I yelled. "Look at you, living in a fucking dreamworld." I gestured wildly. "You're listening to music that's dead. Here, man. Here's your fucking Beatles."

I plucked the album from the turntable and flung it hard against the wall. My fury died the instant the record shattered.

"Jesus . . . I'm sorry."

He wouldn't look at me, his head turned away, a child refusing to be comforted by an adult whose idea of punishment has gone too far.

I stumbled out of the apartment, amazed, once I was back in late September sunlight, to find I didn't understand a single thing that had happened to me inside that apartment. And I wasn't at all sure I was still the same guy that went in. It was almost five o'clock, and people were rushing by me to get home. It felt pleasant to be dissolved inside the herd of humanity, until the pot really caught up with me and I was suddenly as full of paranoid dread as the first time I ever smoked. Grinning like an ax murderer in training, I slunk down the sidewalk.

By the time I found myself behind the wheel of my Lexus, the worst of my paranoia seemed gone, though the pot was fueling some terrific flashbacks. I slouched down, squeezed my eyes shut, and roller-coasted back to February 1964, where a voice announced over a drumroll: "Live from New York, it's *The Ed Sullivan Show*!" There I sat watching our black-and-white Motorola with rabbit ears after the long wait through *My Favorite Martian*. The girls in the audience were going nuts, Dad was wagging his head and criticizing their hair, my sister Emily was kneeling inches from the tube, as if waiting at the rail to receive the Host, and my stomach was filling with helium. Then: "Close your eyes . . ." and every hair on my scalp saluted.

Merciful God. Before the first song was over, they'd pried open my skull, yanked out comic books, the Lord's Prayer, John Wayne, and Annette Funicello, and rewired me with a whole new neural interstate. The rules of the universe had changed in a three-song set. Anybody could play a guitar, write a song, an epic poem, a novel. The Beatles had proved it: Youth made truth.

As the last harmonic note of "She Loves You" soared away on a jet stream of applause, I hunkered further down into the leather seat. How could I have forgotten that Sunday night over thirty years ago, when I became a Beatlemaniac along with every other kid in America over the age of ten? Smelling the incense of hemp laced with pizza, dust, and piss, I started the engine. I knew exactly what I had to do.

By the time I got back to Rusty's place, it was dark. Good. The candle-glow would probably make a gentle pot buzz last even longer. It hadn't taken me long, once I recalled that Second-Hand Books on

Vine bought and sold LPs. Sure enough, I found a copy of *Sgt. Pepper,* still in its plastic wrapper. Some joker had decided not to change his life at the last minute after all.

This time the door immediately opened wide, and he scowled before trying to close it. But I blocked the door with my foot, shoving my gift into the darkening space. After a heartbeat, he let the door bang open and plodded into the bowels of the apartment. Grinning, I followed. Back in the living room, he flopped back onto the mattress.

"I'm sorry I lost my temper," I said quietly. The candle was out, and an overhead bulb cast a dirty yellow pall onto the room's contents. I refused to look too closely.

"Forget it."

"No. There was no excuse. But this one ought to be less scratchy; it's practically brand-new."

I propped the record against the wall, all the Beatles' heroes staring at me from beneath the plastic. For the first time it struck me that the cover looked like a funeral, complete with sprays of red and yellow flowers (and marijuana plants and palms).

"What do you want, Terry?"

The words chilled me. I tried hard to regain the born-again feeling I'd had in the car, but I couldn't do it. The speakers inside my head were now piping "If I Fell," I was seeing John singing sweetly to Ringo in *A Hard Day's Night,* and suddenly what had happened to us back at the end of our childhood seemed not initiation at all, but innocence.

"Bruce sent you, didn't he?"

The raspy voice came from the mat. Something told me he wouldn't be offering me any more pot. In another couple of seconds I was freezing, the lovely dream slipping away. How could I tell him that, yes, I'd come because of Bruce, but I'd come *back* because of September sun making the leather seats of the Lexus gleam like fire, because workers rushing past me on the street below had filled me with love, because the long-gone odor of pot still made my knees go weak, because two boys had been in a band together and thought they'd never die?

"You're right about the Beatles, Terry."

"Huh? How so?" My hands were ice.

"They *are* dead."

It took a few seconds to register. Then, with horror, I realized what I'd done. I shakily rose and crossed the distance between us, knelt beside him, touching his shoulder as if it might shatter.

"No, no, man," I whispered. "As long as one person still enjoys those tunes, they're as alive as me and you."

He looked straight ahead. "Maybe you're alive, but I ain't."

I could hardly breathe, realizing with the part of my brain still working that it was probably the mattress, reeking like a sulfurous sewer, that was making me dizzy. Then he whispered, "But for a while they were something to believe in, weren't they?"

His voice was growing smaller, and his body, too. If I didn't connect soon, he'd slip away and it would all be gone forever, would never even have *been.*

"They still are," I said, though the walls ate my words, spat them back at me. I considered crawling onto the mattress and clasping him to me, but I knew it was the pot talking and I'd be left holding a corpse. I stood up, patted his shoulder again.

"Listen, Rusty, I'll be back."

"Sure."

At least we were gentle enough to let that lie endure.

"Take the record," he murmured, eyes closed.

"All right."

But I left it on the kitchen table. If I could've stood the smell of his death for a few more moments, I might've made him believe the world *had* been changed by four guys with guitars and drums. I might've even made myself believe it—at least for an album's length longer.

Following the Genius with Four Heads; or, Why I Became a Composer

James Russell Smith

I am a musician. A composer of classical music and a concert percussionist, to be exact. However, I began my life in music purely as a drummer, nothing more, nothing less. In Memphis, Tennessee, where I grew up, down in the delta land of the Mississippi, music of every kind settled in the air as thick as the muddy smell of the great river itself. The blues music that poured in on the radio at night was full of rhythms and longing, enticing yet unattainable to a middle-class white kid. More often I listened to my parents' music, which was okay, though similarly I felt somehow disconnected from it. But from the moment I saw one of my neighbors playing a set of beautiful black pearl Rogers drums in a high school production of *Bye Bye Birdie*, I knew: that was something I had to do.

By April of 1963 I had become a teen, and I begged for a used Ludwig snare drum for my birthday, which cost my fireman dad about three days salary from his moonlighting job. Thus doubly inspired by desire and obligation, I began studying diligently in lessons at a local music store, and I was able to enter the junior high band that fall. For the time being, my first great passion had been met and was working its way into my life. My dream kept me busy as I plowed through the rudiments and the mysteries of rhythmic notation and sight-reading. Learning any instrument is hard work, but it was all I wanted to do: that is, until February 9, 1964.

Watching *The Ed Sullivan Show* that night, I saw my future. And, from the Beatles first solo pickup notes in "All My Loving," I was hooked. But what I couldn't yet recognize beyond that common, ecstatic response experienced by so many of my generation was a far-reaching consequence that would completely determine the course of my life. The Beatles brought something more to me and certain others of my generation that night than just their hair, clothes, looks, and voices. It was something from which many of us would never recover, something mysterious and even disturbing; and that "something," for me, was the urge to create.

Past centuries have all had their creative idols. Bach, Haydn, Mozart, and Beethoven all had to produce constantly to keep pace with their royal patrons' lust for new and original music. The nineteenth century's Romanticism brought in popular idolization, and even found a near equivalent to a rock star in Franz Liszt. However, the change in art in our century has been as drastic as all of the other advances and catastrophes of science, technology, and ideology. If a new idea creates a better toaster, we welcome it; if it challenges our concept of pleasure, we often recoil. One of the great musical creations by Igor Stravinsky, *The Rite of Spring,* was greeted with a riot at its premier in 1913 due in part to its revolutionary assault of rhythm and harmony. Today, due to time and exposure, it is a much beloved concert piece . . . by a very dead composer. And that is part of the rub. Our modern orchestras are now mostly living museums. Our century prefers to turn to the composers of antiquity for its appreciation of classical musical, to the extent that the art of the past has usurped the rightful place of the art of the present.

Yet this situation has allowed a counterculture of popular music to flourish in our time like never before. Aided by scientific breakthroughs in recording, radio, film, and television, creators have been able to reach an incredible audience that cuts across all social barriers. But until the Beatles hit the scene, the popular and classical listening public had inherited the long-held Romantic attitude of awed detachment toward an artist's creative fruits. Genius was seen as special, separate, and unattainable. By the fifties and sixties even the pop music of the growing younger generation was more concerned with personality than with content. Certainly the song "Hound Dog" had a base charm of its own, but it was the style, looks, and voice of the singer that really sold the song. No one yearned for "Hound Dog," they yearned for the King.

But the fans of 1964, who certainly yearned for the Beatles as persons, were also struck with a surprising new longing. We wanted the songs themselves. The songs were king. Our generation now had its creative genius, its composer, which, simply put, had four heads. Thus we began to participate in that ancient lust for every new creation by our "geniuses" in a way that royalty and the aristocracy have done in the past for their top composers. And some of us began to think that maybe, just maybe, we too could strike a spark from the once-forbidden fires of genius.

A veritable songwriting renaissance exploded as a response to the Beatles' work. They had short-circuited a system whereby singers were the front men, and songs were quietly written behind closed doors by invisible professionals. The attitude was, "Don't try this at home kids," and creation was left to the pros. But we saw the result of the Beatles incredible audacity in convincing George Martin to allow them to try out their own compositions. And the profession soon demanded an original mind for songwriting, supported secondarily by playing and singing ability. Almost every group that followed the Beatles was characterized by its own brand of songwriting. The industry quickly caught on, for better or worse, and responded with a golden era of experimentation where practically anything that came along got a chance. Certainly not all of it was good, but surprisingly, quite a lot was. Suddenly we were surrounded by this creative outburst, and the Beatles were our undisputed masters.

All of this is to say that, in spite of the enormous hero worship the Beatles inspired, they made the act of creating seem human. I saw creativity brought down to earth, and it was only reasonable to believe that even a drummer like myself could also aspire to write. I knew that writing from a drum set was unthinkable; you couldn't write songs with all rhythm and no melody. I had, however, begun to learn the basic chords on a $15 Sears guitar that my younger brother had gotten for his previous birthday.

I had a Beatle buddy at school, and every day in the lunch line we would talk up our favorite songs. Soon we were driving our friends crazy as we quickly moved from talk to singing the sweet harmonies from the latest hits. We were Beatle nerds: goofy, uncool, and completely unashamed. My friend took up the bass guitar and came to school claiming to have figured out the chords for certain songs. On one such occasion he claimed to have found the "changes" to "Eight Days a Week." By this time I finally had enough chord knowledge, and I couldn't wait to get home and try them out. To my surprise, they were wrong! In frustrated haste I searched my inner ear (and mostly the guitar neck) until I had found the correct chords. In those moments I began to discover that I too had a musical ear like my friend. I could do this! It wasn't long before I went from figuring out the structure of Beatle songs to the magic of conjuring up my first original composition.

I would venture to guess, in those days, every group of kids had its resident troubadour. In my group that role quickly fell to me. At almost any gathering it was natural for me to tote the guitar along for the inevitable sing-along. And, of course, we would sing mostly Beatle songs. What seductive power those songs possessed! By extension, I felt like the carrier of the flame. Empowered. Soon the long-awaited occasion presented itself, and someone finally asked to hear one of my own songs. Trite as they were, they impressed my friends. Even better, the young lady of my unrequited affections was quite taken by them, especially since it took little insight to realize that they were about her. I never got the girl, in spite of those songs, but it no longer mattered. I was immediately hooked by this strange new power to move people, and to a certain extent I have never given up trying to relive it.

I saw the Beatles "live" in August of 1966 during their concerts in Memphis. This was just after Lennon's infamous Jesus statement.

The southern religious "cracker" element was running hot and high with outrage that week. There was a great deal of talk about a possible cancellation of the two shows that had been scheduled. I remember being mad at John Lennon for his untimely statement—not for its content, but because it jeopardized my chance to finally see them. In the end, cooler heads prevailed. After days of intense angst I went to see both performances in a victorious daze.

During the evening concert someone lit a cherry bomb in the seat right in front of me and my brother. At that moment I happened to be watching McCartney through some borrowed binoculars. In front of my eyes he turned in horror and would have dropped that lovely Hoffner bass had it not had a neck strap. Then he looked quickly to John. The police came and yanked the kid and his compatriot. They asked up and down our row if anyone had witnessed the event. The lady next to me said that she had, and they took her and her young daughter away too. When the police looked my way, I shook my head and quickly threatened my brother with his life if he opened his mouth. The whole show lasted only thirty minutes, and I wasn't about to miss a beat.

Years later, after Lennon's death, I read a sadly prophetic interview in which McCartney admitted that they had all been on edge in Memphis. He was sure that John had been shot when that firecracker rang out. I will never forget his panicked look over at John, and then his nervous relief. But, beyond the cherry bomb adventure, those two concerts marked the high point of another realization about my life. That day brought into clear relief a knowledge that had been slowly growing within me for the past two years. I knew I was in love with music and everything about it. I knew that I was part of this world. I was a creator. I was a musician.

I am a "classical" composer now. During my undergraduate work in music, the Beatles split up. Like many, I was devastated. I didn't want to believe in the last magnificent cut on *Abbey Road*. How could they so coolly declare their own end? What would I do for inspiration? Being vulnerable at that moment, I discovered Beethoven and Brahms and Bach, and quickly joined the "adult" world of musical taste. But the Beatles have never left me.

I've taught classical composition for over twenty years now in various colleges and universities around the country, the last ten of those at the Berklee College of Music in Boston, known as the world's premiere jazz/rock college. I've watched generation after generation discover the Beatles' music. I even watched my own children go through their Beatle phase quickly one summer after seeing the video of *Help!* They still like the songs, but the passion has passed for them. Not so for me. I look at where the Beatles have led me, and at what a composite of elements my musical life has turned out to be. Here I am, a classical musician teaching in a jazz/rock college; a classically trained composer who listens to and writes music in every style; a percussionist who plays the spectrum from rock drum-set, to jazz vibes, to orchestral timpani, to the most mind-bending contemporary chamber music multipercussion. But to me this odd mixture of abilities and tastes doesn't seem at all strange. In fact I'm not alone in this. I've encountered many other concert composers of my generation with similarly eclectic musical skills and tastes—composers who are also unabashed Beatle freaks. And I'm convinced there's a connection.

It's sometimes a chore to convince my young Berklee students of the need to learn the rudiments of classical voice leading, chord progression, melodic structure, and counterpoint, when what they *really* want to do is write jazz and rock tunes. But that wasn't the case for the young composers of my generation. As our role models, the Beatles introduced us to the essence of great choral writing in "This Boy" and "Yes It Is." Vocal counterpoint was in plentiful supply in "Help!" and "You're Going to Lose That Girl." Instrumental counterpoint thrived in "Lucy in the Sky with Diamonds" and "In My Life." We got sophisticated mixed meters in "Good Day Sunshine" and "Martha My Dear"; jazz-band elements in "Got to Get You into My Life" and "Good Morning Good Morning"; strings in "Yesterday," "Eleanor Rigby," and "She's Leaving Home"; baroque trumpet and French horn in "Penny Lane" and "For No One"; and the whole orchestra in "I Am the Walrus" and "A Day in the Life." And of course there were the exotic sounds of sitars and tablas, as well as harpsichords and circus organs, and a multitude of electronic gimmicks. We even got a John Cage–cum–Andy Warhol collage in "Revolution 9." All of this was served up unfailingly with beautiful and graceful melodies supported by strong and charming chord progressions and balanced by a perfectly clear sense of form. The Beatles gave us a seven-year lesson in the art of composition, along with a minicourse in the development of music history. How could we help but to want to master all elements of the art with idols like this?

I recall trying hard during one class years ago to make an analogy that would get a point across to my students. Quite naturally for me, I referred to the Beatles when we were discussing the relative merits of inspired creation versus mere technical production, and I'll never forget one student's response. With matter-of-fact innocence he said, "Well, the Beatles just wrote good songs," and went on to say that, to his generation, songwriting was a secondary consideration because the ability to write well was just a lucky fluke. Production was everything. This was a stunning revelation to me. Obviously, from the respect in his tone, he admired the Beatles' music, but it was also obvious that to him such good songwriting was not only unnecessary, it was mostly unattainable. And so I've had to face this fact: The renaissance days of my youth are past. My sense of the attainability of compositional art is no longer in the air. The Beatles have long since come full circle to join the past masters of music. This doesn't affect me personally—I still feel like a kid when I hear them—but I hope that my students, and those yet to come, can experience that power we felt. I hope they can find teachers as capable and inspiring as the Beatles.

I have never met any of them. Perhaps that's best. But I did once have the good fortune to meet George Martin, who was the honored speaker for Berklee's 1991 graduating class. That year, as usual, I played timpani in the faculty band that marches the students in and out for this grand occasion. The ceremonies had ended. Mr. Martin gave an excellent speech, and I decided to hunt him down and shamelessly try to get his autograph. When I looked up, there he was, walking toward me down a hallway of the Hynes Convention Center. I introduced myself as a Berklee faculty member, told him I much admired his work, and added with great pride that I was an old Beatle fan. Without missing a beat, he smiled at me and said, "So am I." I suppose that, in the end, my eclectic musical personality has come more to resemble his than theirs. I can easily live with that, and envy his gargantuan good fortune: he observed the miracle of their development firsthand.

Nevertheless, I have my memories. That day in 1966 at the Memphis Coliseum. I'm looking through those binoculars as the Beatles leave the stage. From where I'm sitting I can see a bit of the backstage area, which has now been lit for their exit. The Beatles hastily toss their guitars to the roadies standing nearby. Then, in the best *Hard Day's Night* fashion, they tear out around a corner in the backstage corridor. Gone in a blink, but that parting vision, those sounds, that joy, will burn in me forever.

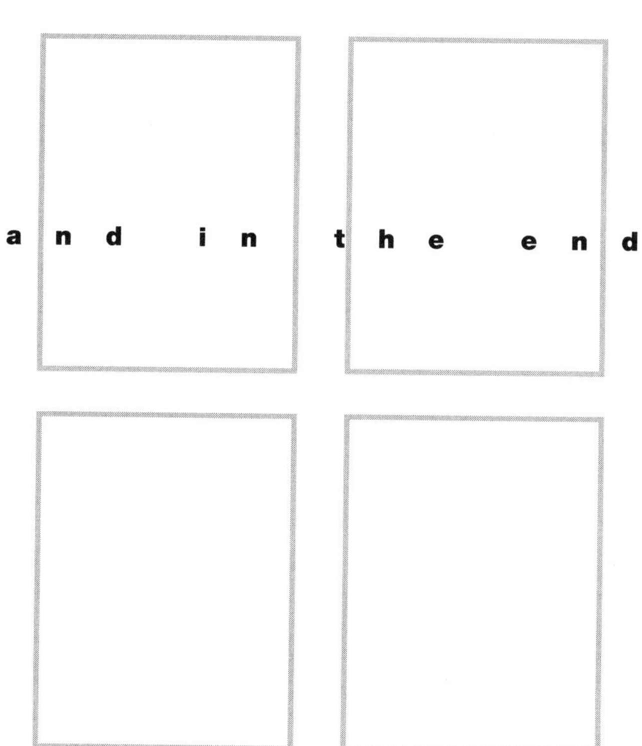
a n d i n t h e e n d

Introduction to *The Beatles*

Leonard Bernstein

I fell in love with the Beatles' music (and simultaneously, of course, with their four faces-cum-personae) along with my children, two girls and a boy, in whom I discovered the frabjous falsetto shriek-cum-croon, the ineluctable beat, the flawless intonation, the utterly fresh lyrics, the Schubert-like flow of musical invention, and the fuck-you coolness of these Four Horsemen of Our Apocalypse, on *The Ed Sullivan Show* in 1964. Jamie was then twelve, Alexander nine, and Nina two. Together we saw it, the Vision, in our inevitably different ways (I was forty-six!), but we saw the same Vision, and heard the same Dawn-Bird, Elephant-Trump, Fanfare of the Future. What future? Here we are, fifteen years later, and it's all gone. But for a decade or so, or even less, it remained the same Vision-Clarion, yet increasingly cogent, clear, bitter—and better.

Perhaps the clearest, bitterest (and maybe best) was an album called *Revolver* (pace *Sgt. Pepper, Abbey Road,* et al.). Of this album, perhaps the very best was a little-known ditty called "She Said She Said," the very thought and memory of which recalls all the beauty of those Vietnamese varicose veins. The notes healed, the words teased; or perhaps it was vice versa. But *something* teased, and something healed, year after year, Rigby after Rigby, Paperback after Norwegian, perhaps ultimately signified in the gleaming, dreary truth of "She's Leaving Home."

Meanwhile, there was a slim volume of pure verbal genius by a new author called *John Lennon: In His Own Write*. If this weren't enough to rhapsodize upon, there were the notes (and the sylph-siren voice) of one McCartney. These two made a pair embodying a creativity mostly unmatched during that fateful decade. Ringo—

a lovely performer. George—a mystical unrealized talent. But John and Paul, Saints John and Paul, were, and made, and aureoled and beatified and eternalized the concept that shall always be known, remembered, and deeply loved as the Beatles.

And yet the two were merely something—the four were It. The interdependence was astonishing and in some ways appalling; do we really need all this to sustain us when we're sixty-four? Well, today I am almost sixty-four, and three bars of "A Day in the Life" still sustain me, rejuvenate me, inflame my senses and sensibilities.

Nina, who was two way back then in '64, is now seventeen; and only last week we took out that thick, wretched Beatles volume of ill-printed sheet music and reminisced at the piano. We wept, we jumped with the joy of recognition ("She's a Woman")—just the two of us, for hours ("Ticket to Ride," "A Hard Day's Night," "I Saw Her Standing There").

That was last week. The Beatles are no more. But this week I am still jumping, weeping, remembering a good epoch, a golden decade, a fine time, a fine time . . .

October 9, 1979

I Wanna Be Your Man

Robert Sullivan

My son recently passed a developmental milestone that is not mentioned in any parenting magazine I know of and yet is, I believe, one of the major choices he will make in the course of his life. He has chosen his favorite Beatle.

I'm speaking of the British pop foursome, of course—any bug is a good bug to a four-and-a-half-year-old—and my anxiousness over his Beatle choice peaked as the latest round of Beatlemania came and went, because the Beatle you pick can say as much about you as your DNA does. In fact, it wouldn't surprise me if geneticists one day discovered somewhere along the alphabet-soup-like tangle of the human genome the letters *J, P, G,* and *R*. Such a discovery could lead to a new kind of genetic fingerprinting—something that could be administered by the state during the marriage-license process, or entered as evidence in court cases. ("I submit to you, ladies and gentlemen of the jury, that a Ringo could never have masterminded such a sophisticated crime.") I have a special interest in my son's Beatle decision, because if I could go back in time and choose my favorite Beatle all over again I'd choose differently.

As it was I chose Paul. In admitting this I am presenting a picture of myself as someone with a smile on his face all the time—someone who thinks happy, hummable thoughts and dots his *i*'s with little flowers. Unfortunately, this is not so far off: choosing Paul made me what I am today, which is not as edgy as I'd like to be; a little low on irony, a little too, well . . . Paul. As a result, my inner soundtrack tends toward cloying love songs, and I spend most weekends at home while perpetually wishing I could find the nerve to lie in a hotel bed naked with my wife in front of TV cameras where we might declare our love in a way that also protests war.

Naturally, the Beatle I wish I had chosen is John. As a John wannabe who considers himself a progressive parent, I found waiting for my son's decision particularly excruciating. I wanted him to make up his own mind but feared I might force John on him in some way—or, worse, subliminally suggest Paul. Ringo never seemed to be a candidate. This is the case with my son's friends as well, most of whom are leaning toward John. One might expect Ringo to have made inroads in the favorite-Beatle category—given his role as the voice of Thomas the Tank Engine and his locomotive friends on *Shining Time Station,* the children's television show, for example—but children somehow know instinctively that Ringo is a nonchoice, a wasted vote.

It was with great pride, then, that I learned my son had chosen George, a choice that is so clearly his. And yet when I speak of this milestone with my friends they congratulate me hesitantly. Are they thinking my son voted for the somber, cult-oriented man who lost a wife to Eric Clapton and sued his manager for allegedly bilking him out of millions of dollars? Or do they think he's sided with a level-headed individualist, a stylish and spiritual virtuoso, who is attuned to matters of social justice and rarely susceptible to temptation by peers? To me, my son's choice is perfect: in the very act of choosing George, he has proven his Georgeness.

Of course, four and a half is young, and at some point on the long and winding road of adolescence he may switch Beatles. (This could be problematic—I know a guy who grew up thinking of John's face when he heard Paul's voice, and in some ways he's still dealing with that.) And then, after any Beatle realignment, my son will face other popular-music life choices: the Beatles or the Stones, the Grateful Dead or the Sex Pistols, Björk or Hole. Someday, he may even feel that he, too, should have chosen John, but I wouldn't wish that upon him for the world.

I doubt that he will ever choose Paul. Last week, over cereal, I asked him about Paul, and he nearly spit out his Kix. "Paul sings all those lovin' songs," he said disdainfully. He then broke into a very Georgesque rendition of "Roll Over Beethoven." It hurt, but he was right. Now I can't help worrying over the next Beatles-related development issue: What does a guy who chose George do when he discovers he was raised by a guy who chose Paul?

Imagine

Laura Gamache

"It's called punk yellow."

My thirteen-year-old daughter, Julia, swishes her hair side to side. I think of Big Bird, of yellow crayon, of the lumpy braided lanyard key fob I made at camp. I decide to nod admiringly rather than speak, in case I might accidentally mention one of these things.

"First," she says, "I bought a pair of Felix the Cat socks and a box of dark chocolates for Dad for Father's Day. Then I saw the special at Hair Masters. Dad said it was okay when I called."

We've nixed a nose ring, a belly button ring, and a tattoo featuring a snake, its open mouth dripping blood, entwining the thorny stem of a black rose. Hair grows out.

"Also"—she pauses theatrically so I know this is the most exciting purchase—"I bought this really great poster of John Lennon, from the *Imagine* sessions. He has the thumb of the hand with the cigarette in it sort of dug into his cheek and he is looking off into the distance. It is really cool. His hair is kind of weird, but it is a great poster."

Julia knows all the words to every Beatle song, and especially loves John, who wasn't so accessible, so easy to love, but then neither, I guess, is she. He was martyred in 1980, two years before she was born, but I hear John Lennon music wafting through the heat duct from her room nearly every day. She most likes the solo recordings he made after leaving the Beatles.

When I was thirteen, my mother said, "Kids, we're moving to a foreign country," and then we drove from Seattle to New Orleans. I decorated the walls of my new room in this faraway land by thumbtacking the jackets of my favorite Beatles' 45's up on the wall like posters. I loved all four Beatles as a group, and vehemently opposed the continued radio play of solo recording artists, who were a genre as embarrassingly passé as Elvis.

I started seventh grade in Louisiana, at the all-girl T. H. Harris Jr. High, where I, lonely and undermatured, wandered crowded halls bursting with Amazonian big-haired drawling girls wearing penny loafers and aggressive makeup. Eventually I found my way into a group of girls more like myself. We got A's on our report cards, had talked our mothers into bras we didn't yet need, were forbidden by our mothers to wear excessive, i.e., visible amounts of makeup—and we loved the Beatles.

The four of us furtively passed notes we folded into an accretion of ever-tinier triangles after writing about our imaginary borderline-titillating adventures with our make-believe boyfriends, the Beatles. Cleverly, we renamed the Beatles to protect ourselves in the event our notes were confiscated by a teacher or one of our physically precocious classmates and read aloud. Having overheard a casual remark from one particular Barbara Winslow about a something dirty she called French kissing, we knew we were in way out of our depth with the women who sat in the desks around us. We would not be further humiliated by their discovering we pretended to make out with John, Paul, George, and Ringo.

We had a very serious get-together in my bedroom where we decided on the alternate names for our guys and, more important, paired ourselves off. Blonde, dimpled, and always sure of what she wanted, Dee Dee Myers got Paul. My thoughtful best friend of all, Glenna Griffin, chose quiet George. Anne Setz, who had a crooked smile and a zany cockeyed view of the adolescent success ladder we were hip enough to know about but not "developed" enough to climb, got John. When I complained that Ringo was the least attractive, the others assured me that he was the shortest and most lovable, like me. Dee Dee generously allowed that also, of course, Paul was my brother. We renamed them Wayne, Ron, Bobby, and Stuart.

We lived out our alternate world while "Evangeline," Spanish verbs, and manned space flight were being explained in front of us. Our math teacher, Mr. Bernard, declared that delta *y* over delta *x* yielded slope, and my eyes dropped to the note in front of me. My pencil flew, complaining to Glenna that Stuart seemed to be getting more moody, which was making me worry that he loved me less and less.

After school I would barricade myself in my Beatle-walled sanctuary at the end of the hallway, lie on my bed, and stare up at Ringo-Stuart, George-Bobby, John-Wayne (an intentional joke of Anne's), and Paul-Ron. I never spoke aloud to them, or concretely and definitely acknowledged to their photographs the fantasy connections my friends and I wrote about during the day. I adored them: their songs, the pictures and text in the fan magazines, the things my friends and I made up.

I studied the images on the 45 covers as if I could pick up clues to the sensual realities of the erotically charged older, teen world they sang about and which I yearned and feared to enter, memorizing the Beatle boots, the tight black slacks, the way a leg was raised upon a chair, the angle of a neck to head, the almost sneer of John Lennon's smile. I read their facial expressions as a language it was essential that I learn. My eyes traced hair curled over a collar line, the placement of a hand on a sleeve. I studied, I stared, I sought secrets in plain sight. Through the miracle of mass production I had the Beatles trapped there on my wall where I could examine their images like insect specimens. I idolized the Beatles, but my friends and I decided what they would say and do with us when we went out with them on dates. If anybody was difficult to control, it was Dee Dee, who kept writing outside the boundaries of good-girl date behavior and embarrassing the rest of us. Okay, me.

I identified with the way the Beatles lived under constant scrutiny. The fan magazines carried countless photographs and reported monthly their height, their weight, their favorite thises and thats, interviewed their girlfriends, and asked their neighbors what they had to say about them. I felt that every time I left the security of my room my parents, my teachers, my buxom classmates, all were watching me, taking notes, making judgments—all eyes were on my missteps and my physical backwardness.

One sunny weekend my family walked around Jackson Square, in New Orleans' French Quarter, where the portrait painters set up shop on the sidewalk. Samples of their work hung, with price tags, along the decorative iron grillwork fence that also served to contain the lush plant life behind. The painters and their easels, paints, and cafe folding chairs were ready to receive new portrait subjects. TV tray tables were open beside them, cigar boxes set on top for the putting in of money and the giving out of change. I imagined myself minutely observed by these artists, who could surely see beyond the storky knock-knees, the stringy hair and scowl, the lurching gait. One of them would certainly burst from his station, or want to, and offer to paint my portrait for the sheer passionate necessity of doing so.

In the last few months before we moved back to Seattle, Glenna and I joined a square dance club where we allemande lefted away muggy evenings touching the hands of real boys. During breaks we'd grab juice and cookies from the side room and spill down the stairs to the relative coolness of the fecund-smelling night, where the boys and girls milled about, chewing. I stood beside some living, breathing boy, studied the line of his jaw, the little stubble there, while he and I struggled awkwardly to produce a halting but excitingly actual conversation.

And now Julia, my daughter, is thirteen and listens to Beatle songs over and over, knows all the words to every Beatle song, and especially loves John Lennon.

"When you saw the Beatles in concert, did you touch Paul McCartney?" she asks me. "My friend Britt asked me to ask you. She's obsessed with Paul McCartney."

I tell her how at the matinee concert in 1966 the Seattle Coliseum got quiet when Paul came out with his guitar and stool and sang "Yesterday" all alone, and how somebody a row back from me loaned me their binoculars so I could see Paul's lips move.

We both go quiet a moment. She walks down to her room and closes the door. "Imagine" wafts up the stairs, and I imagine she's on the phone relaying this new information to Britt, her eyes reading the way John Lennon's thumb indents his cheek.

1996

Ellen Kahaner

On the third play of the Beatles' *Anthology 2,* my fourth graders at P.S. 50 in East Harlem plead, "Play 'Strawberry Fields Forever' again!" This is my first real full-time job with benefits and a pension, a far cry from my years as an adjunct college instructor with free-lance writing gigs precariously balancing my checkbook. I rewind the tape and press play. Normally at lunchtime the kids listen to LL Cool J and Mr. Boombastic. So it surprises me that they like the Beatles. They sing along on the chorus. Miguel stands and sways his arms over his head, then bangs his pencil in time to the music hard enough for the point to break. Erin drags his pen over the spirals of his notebook. Yazmine, Jennifer, Frieda, and Sharnay, who come into class singing Jodeci's "I Love You for Life," play air guitars, clarinets, desk piano, and violins. Joanna wobbles around the room, half bent over. "Let me take you downnnn!" she sings.

"Use your pencils as *writing* instruments," I say.

"This music makes me feel like screaming," Joanna writes.

"Somebody likes strawberries," Jennifer writes.

"It's a dancing moment that brings people together," says Miguel.

"A big tough man in his mind," Erin writes.

"A night at the prom and he has nobody to dance with. He looks at someone dancing with her boyfriend and feels sad," Yazmine records.

"Draw what you hear in the music," I say.

They show me giant strawberries growing next to an apartment building, the sun's rays as streams of musical notes, the word *music* in big colorful letters, a strawberry tree identified with the phonetic spelling *swter breey fealds.*

We crowd around the computer and look up the Beatles in the on-line *Golden Book Encyclopedia*. The children take turns reading aloud: ". . . 1964 marked the beginning of 'Beatlemania' in the United States."

"Is that like when someone's crazy?" Frieda asks.

I explain Beatlemania, the screaming girls rushing to touch the ground the Beatles walked on. "For example, I went to a Beatles concert at Shea Stadium for my birthday in the summer of 1965. We waited on the field for the Beatles to arrive. Their van drove by. I saw Paul McCartney in the window. Everyone was screaming at the top of their lungs."

"Even you?" Miguel asks.

"Even me. Then when the van passed, we all dove on the grass and pulled it up, to save it. I had a little grass in my wallet for a long time."

"Wow, Ms. Kahaner. You were crazy," Joanna said.

Then we click and a picture of the Beatles comes up slowly on the screen. "This is when the Beatles first started performing. They were very young," I tell the students.

"The young Beatles," screams Miguel. "Look, it's the young Beatles!" I identify who's who, and Jennifer says that Erin looks like Paul and we all laugh.

"So were you a Beatlemaniac?" Yazmine asks.

"Oh, sure, of course," I answer in all seriousness. "I always will be."

from *The Old Life*

Donald Hall

        Fifteen years ago his heart
infarcted and he stopped smoking.
        At eighty he trembled
like a birch but remained vigorous
        and acute.

                                When they married
fifty years ago, I was twelve.
        I observed the white lace
veil, the mumbling preacher, and the flowers
        of parlor silence
and ordinary absurdity; but
        I thought I stood outside
the parlor.

                        For two years she dwindled
        by small strokes
into a mannequin—speechless almost, almost
        unmoving, eyes open
and blinking, fitful in perception—
        but a mannequin that suffered
shame when it stained the bedsheet.
        Slowly, shaking with purpose,
he carried her to the bathroom,
        undressed and washed her,
dressed her in clean clothes, and carried her back
        to CNN and bed. "All
you need is love," sang John and Paul:
        He touched her shoulder; her eyes
caressed him like a bride's bold eyes.

Family Reunion

E. J. Miller Laino

We picnic on the roof
of my sister's houseboat in Key West.
Norman cooks hamburgers
and hot dogs. Sara makes potato salad.
Grace slips the Beatles into the tape player
and Budd begins to dance.
Three stories high
in the Florida sky we all dance
Give me money
that's what I want. No
railings to keep us from falling
and still we dance, moon
slung like a cradle,
above it, the North Star waiting
to be tucked in. We wish on it
the way our mother taught us to.
She would wish this night
for us, though we all agree
she'd be screaming
Don't you dare go near the edge
and we'd tease her, of course,
dangling our legs over the side,
Beatles blasting into the still pink
sky. *It's what I want, yeah,*
what I want. It's what I wa-a-a-nt.
It's what I want.

My Mother Met John Lennon

Robert Wallace

My mother's house contains hundreds of clocks. Their sounds are perpetual, varied: not all tick-tocks are the same. Thank God all the chime mechanisms have been disconnected. I don't tell her this, of course; my sensitivity to sounds is known only by my wife, someone who knows me very well.

My mother left my father and three children for her current husband in 1965. I was nine. She wasn't hard to find: my father and grandmother had criticized the name of Earle for years. It became indelibly printed in my memory. I simply called information, got her phone number, and after thirty years spoke to my mother as if she had been away only for the weekend.

"My family will be on vacation in July," I said. "I'd like to see you."

"Yes," she said, as if she had been expecting my call.

I gave her the details of our arrival, and after hanging up the phone I immediately wondered if I had made a mistake. After all this time, what was I wanting, a normal mother-and-son relationship?

It is four o'clock and we sit at the kitchen table. My mother pours me a cup of hot tea. She tells me she works at a rest home for the elderly. "I'm the laundress," she says.

I smile. Her English accent seems less prominent than what I remember as a child. I tell her how much I adored her voice while growing up.

"You did? You can't imagine how much nagging I took for it. Oh, your Uncle Wayne was merciless."

"Really? I don't remember."

"Of course you don't."

I sip my tea, cross my leg, look around the kitchen. I notice a cuckoo bird sticking out of an antique wall clock above the refrigerator. Because it's quiet, it looks as if it's in suspended animation.

"So, Bob, what made you decide to see me?"

The question surprises me. It has a confrontational tone. My mother leans forward, her chin resting on her open palm. It occurs to me that she is afraid, just like me. She has no idea why I decided to see her, what my motives are.

I tell her that I felt it was time. That I have no expectations.

She nods her head.

I'm not sure she believes me. "I really don't know why I'm here," I say. "I guess I just wanted to see you."

"I'm glad you did," she says. "I wish you would have brought your family, though."

"I thought it was best to come alone first."

"Maybe so."

She gets up and walks over to the kitchen counter. In the few pictures I have of my mother she is wearing tight nylon pants, short at the ankle, with white socks and tiny white tennis shoes. She looks like she hasn't gained a pound, though there is a slight roundness in the middle; her green slacks fit snug.

She turns on the radio and music fills the kitchen.

"Want some cookies?" she asks.

She places a plate filled with chocolate-chip cookies in front of me.

I look up at her standing at the table. She's taller than I remember. Probably about five feet, five inches tall. She wears glasses and her neck skin is beginning to sag, but there is still a youthful look about her. Her forehead is unwrinkled. I know she is nearing sixty-years-old.

"How's your mom?" I ask.

"She's fine. She's eighty-two. I'm going back next summer."

"Back?"

"For a visit. It's been ten years since my last trip."

I take a cookie. "I remember England."

"You do?"

"I remember the parks, fish-and-chips, buying frozen ice-on-a-stick for a penny. I remember watching cricket matches and the players wearing all white."

"I'm surprised you remember so much."

"Why?"

"I don't know. You only visited twice, and it seems like such a long time ago."

She returns to the counter and refills the kettle with tap water. She puts the kettle on a burner and turns on the stove.

"I'll be right back," she says.

Her black pumps click against the linoleum floor then become silent on the living room carpet. I take a sip of tea and notice my hand is shaking. I get up and walk into the living room. On a round table in the corner, pictures of my mother's children lean against some potted plants. I try to imagine my picture among them, or my brother's or sister's, but none of them seem to fit. We are of different families. I know she was pregnant when she left. Rick Earle, the father. Her daughter must be about thirty now; her son a few years younger. Somehow my mother has gone on with her life. She has made a home in Tipton, Indiana, worked in the same community, mothered two children, and now is a grandmother to her daughter's two children. Because she had left, I had envisioned her life full of regret, turmoil, and attrition as recompense for her flight. Only a folded note left on the dining room table, found after school, and she had vanished. My father had crumpled up the paper and put it in his pants pocket, never sharing with his children what the note said.

The last time I had seen her was the day of my father's funeral, five years after she left. Rick had driven her up to Michigan. She stood on my grandparent's driveway, an apparition, her diminutive figure hidden by my Aunt Pauline's six-foot frame. I was walking into the house while they talked. Like a yo-yo, my mother's head kept popping above my aunt's shoulder. She resembled a child standing on tiptoe trying to see over a fence.

I hear the toilet flush and walk back into the kitchen. The kettle whistles, and I remove it from the burner.

"I'll get that," my mother says.

"I don't want any more."

"No?"

"The cookies are great, though."

"I have to admit, I drink too much tea," my mother says. "Up to ten cups each day. I've been doing that since I was a little girl in Leicester."

As I sit down at the table, I begin to feel trapped, that we are too close. I don't know this woman. What am I doing here? In the living room would be better; my mother sitting in a chair, perhaps her favorite, and me on the sofa, some distance between us. I look at the clock above the table. It's a small clock, all wood, even the face and the moving hands. It has a loud sound for a little clock, as if wood is knocking against wood, and suddenly I feel I can hear all the clocks: their tick-tocks and all the workings inside. The sounds fill my head, reverberating against my skull.

"Are you okay?" my mother says. "You look flushed."

"I am hot. I guess it's the tea."

I get up and fan myself with my hand.

"I could turn on the air-conditioner. Rick doesn't like to run it, but it really cools the air fast."

"No, no, I feel myself getting cooler already."

"You sure?"

"Yes. I could use a glass of water, that's all."

"The cupboard right above you. Glasses are in there."

I open the cupboard and remove a glass. I turn on the faucet and run the water for a few seconds, fill a glass full, and drink. The water feels cool going down my throat. As I'm drinking I see my mother sitting at the table. I see her through the water and the glass first, then when the water is gone through the glass alone. I want to keep the glass tipped for a while. She looks wavy, unclear, but somehow closer, as if magnified. Because I'm looking through the glass I feel disguised, as if I can stare without being seen, like a stranger peering through dark sunglasses.

“Why don’t we go in the living room,” my mother says. “I’ll turn on the fan.”

“That would be good.” I fill another glass full of water and follow her.

My mother chooses a small rocker. It has embroidery on the seat and back. She turns on the fan. I take a seat on the sofa. The fan showers me with air. My mother’s house is small but very neat, in a cluttered way. She has lots of antiques besides the clocks. Beyond the living room, in a small adjoining room, I can see quilts and numerous stuffed bears. In that room and the living room baskets filled with small and large knickknacks consume the tables and floor. It is all very country looking, orderly, but dark with the stained wood paneling. There’s a cozy feeling about the place. My mother seems at home here, comfortable. She rocks in her chair, smiles at me, and we gaze at one another, both, it seems, surprised at this moment in time. *Here we are. Who would have ever thought?*

“So, what do you do, Bob?”

I tell her that I work in nursing homes and rest homes, too. I tell her that I go from place to place to make sure that the staff treats the residents right.

“Really, sounds like an important job. I bet you’re good at it.”

“Thank you. It’s a serious job, but I like it.”

“Of you three kids I thought you would be the one to make something of yourself.”

I don’t say anything. I believe my mother is trying to be complimentary, but how could she say that? She doesn’t even know Gary and Andrea. They were only six and seven when she left. But she is right. Andrea is struggling on a blueberry farm in Michigan with a husband that abuses her, and Gary has been in Las Vegas for the past six years, gambling his life away. *Maybe things would have been different if you hadn’t run away* is what I feel like saying but don’t.

“Gary and Andrea are doing the best they can,” I say.

“I’m sure they are. Maybe they will contact me someday, too.”

I shift in the sofa. Turn my head. My mother has no pets; there are no longer small children to mess up her house except when her grandchildren come over.

I try to recall the nature of my childhood home. What kind of housekeeper was my mother? Did she become frustrated when the house was a mess? I don't know when she became angry, when she smiled or laughed. I only remember my father and her fighting once. It happened late at night, and I got out of bed when I heard loud voices. My parents were in the dining room. My father sat at the table wearing only his boxer shorts. My mother stood over him, a robe pulled tight about her, arms crossed at the waist. My father was rubbing his leg. A red mark showed near his right knee. He was crying.

"What's wrong?" I asked.

"Your mother doesn't love me anymore," he said.

"Oh, Bob," Mom said. My father has the same name as me.

I started rubbing my father's leg.

"You love him, don't you Mom?"

My mother was quiet. She said nothing more. As a child I had always thought my father was more hurt because he had been smacked by my mother. I never associated words or lack of them with any problems they might have had. What I remember was that my mother was quiet by nature, reserved.

My mother must have so many more memories.

"Rick not only collects them, he works on them too," my mother says.

"What?"

"The clocks. You seemed to be looking at the clocks."

"Oh. Yes."

"He's retired. Now he works on clocks. It keeps him busy. He's out in the workshop now. I'm expecting him to come in and say hello."

What I feel like telling my mother is that I don't want to see him. I'm glad he had the sense to not be here when I came. But I don't say anything. I hear John Lennon's "Mind Games" coming from the kitchen. I sing a verse silently, *Love is the answer,* but I know nothing can convince me to extend any civility to the man who took my mother away.

"I met him," my mother says.

Here it comes, I think. She's going to tell me what happened. Why she left. How she met Rick.

"Yes."

"He was probably about twelve, I guess."

"Twelve?"

"Yes, I'm sure it was him. Of course I don't know why he was in Leicester. He was coming out of the store. With his parents, I guess. You know that corner store where you and Andrea and Gary bought Popsicles?"

"Yes."

"That's where I saw him. Of course he wasn't with Paul or George or Ringo."

I realize my mother is talking about John Lennon. It surprises me that she recognizes the song, even though it is being mutilated into Muzak.

"You met John Lennon?"

"Actually I kind of bumped into him. That's why I'm sure it was him. He was running out of the store in a hurry to eat a chocolate bar. Mother had sent me to the store to buy some tea and honey. He dropped his chocolate after we knocked into each other."

"What happened?"

"I thought he was going to cry, but he picked the chocolate off the sidewalk. It was broken in several pieces but it was still wrapped. He sat on the bench and ate it."

"How old were you?"

"Fifteen."

"I didn't know you knew his music."

"I know some. There's a lot you don't know about me."

It's hard for me to believe my mother could know John Lennon's music. Then, of course, she's only nineteen years older than me. She left England in 1956 after marrying my father, who was stationed there in the army.

But bumping into John Lennon?

"How could you be sure it was him?"

"I can't. It just looked like him. And some woman shouted 'Johnny, don't eat it all at once,' as he was running out the store."

I don't know why, but I believe her. What I remember about my mother is largely a sense of comfort, that she cared for me and my brother and sister. I also remember a sense of distance, as if she were a spectator to our growing up, watching closely but not in the middle of things. She was young and, I know now, afraid.

"You must miss England," I say.

"I do. Even after all this time. I was terribly homesick at first. I missed my mom so much."

"I know you look forward to going back next summer."

"I do. Your father came with us once when we visited. Do you remember?"

"Yes."

"That's something Rick has never done."

"Oh."

"Bob, I don't know how to explain to you what happened between your dad and me. All I can say is that he was kind to me. I think he loved me. And we had some good times as a family.

I nod my head but don't say anything. I don't know what to say.

"But Rick has been good to me too. Why don't you come out and meet him? He's out in the workshop fixing his precious clocks."

"No, I don't think I'm ready for that," I say.

My mother grins.

"I can understand that," she says.

As if we are both ready for me to go, we stand up, together. We have said enough for now. My mother walks me to the door. I turn and give her a hug, and I feel her small arms around me and smell the hair spray in her auburn-red hair.

Outside, under the patio roof, I stand and wave while she leans out the open door. She waves back. It's hot outside, and I immediately begin to perspire. I wipe my brow and wave some more. As I wave I think of another of John Lennon's songs, "Imagine," and I try to bring to mind what my life would have been like with my mother these past thirty years. What have I missed? What other secrets does she hold? I know that her leaving isn't as simple as writing a note on a crumpled piece of lined notebook paper while I'm at school. That things happened between her and my father that even as an adult I'll never understand.

And this is my understanding of what it means to be a *son:* it's about coming home, acceptance, taking chances. A lone phone call in the night. Forgiveness.

What's ahead for me? For us? At this time there is today, me walking to my car, hearing the noise of my mother's husband inside as I move by the workshop. I fight the urge to explode through the door and take some blunt instrument and break every clock I see. Instead I think about my wife and daughter back at the hotel. I think how my wife is worrying about me, wondering how things are going. I think how the air-conditioner in the car will feel cool and that I will call my mother when I get back to my room: I will listen to her words, and to the sound of her voice.

from *The Duplex Planet*

David B. Greenberger

In interviews conducted at the Duplex Nursing Home, Jamaica Plain, Massachusetts, by David Greenberger, from 1981–1990, residents were asked what they knew about the Beatles.

GEORGE VROOMAN: They're singers, they come from England, and the women were screamin' over 'em. I couldn't see nothin' in it—they didn't do anything for me.

LEO GERMINO: Do they talk? *(Sure they talk—they sing, too.)* They sing, huh? Then put that down: "The Beatles sing."

ERNIE BROOKINGS: Is it a fraternal organization?

ED ROGERS: They're a whaddayacallit, a music, a whaddayacallit—they're in the music business. That's what you call rock and roll. They're on the, ah, music—show business—they were on the radio.

LARRY GREEN: The Beatles were good singers. They're a good quartet. Apple Blossom Time, God Bless America—Kate Smith sang that, she sang it way down yonder in New Orleans. I'll be seeing you in apple blossom time. You are my sunshine, my only sunshine. God bless America, land of the free, stand beside us and guide us—I forget all the words—I used to know them. Apple Blossom Time, God Bless America. *(What did the Beatles look like?)* Oh, geez, they was elderly. I don't know, it's been a long time since I've seen 'em. They make good records. I'll be seeing you in apple blossom time. Ain't misbehavin', savin' my love for you. Molly and me, baby makes three. *(What were the Beatles' names?)* Larry, Moe, and Joe—the Beatles! One got shot, didn't he? *(Yes.)* Killed him outright? *(Yes.)* Oh, Jesus, that's tough. Was it a fight over a girl? *(No.)* What was it, gamblin'? Crap game? Card game? Poker? *(No, it was just someone crazy.)* Ohhh, that's too bad. They were good. . . . Did you ever hear the Mills Brothers?

BILL NIEMI: They were a musical organization. They're still playin', aren't they? They were in Hollywood for a while, making pictures. It was on television that one of them was murdered in New York, that John Lennon. They'll probably have to reorganize the whole dance band.

FRANK HOOKER: I don't know too much about the Beatles now. There were four of 'em, weren't there? They were pretty good English singers. That's where they're from actually, England. They made some good hits. They started off on the show that's on there Saturday nights . . . uh . . . *Lawrence Welk Show,* that's what started them off! Just gettin' on that program got the ball rolling. They're still floatin' around now, exceptin' two of 'em is deceased.

WILLIAM "FERGIE" FERGUSON: Sweet beetles, oh, they're the sweetest little animal you ever saw. They come right up to you and chew up the ice cream for you. And they hand the pecans to you. And those pecans aren't celluloid either, they're the real thing.

BETTY WEILS: I remember them a little bit, but not too much. I remember that I didn't like them, I just didn't like their way of singin'.

ROY ELLIOTT: You mean the men? I used to hear 'em once in a while on TV. They're good. Look at the crowds they've drawn all over. I haven't heard 'em in quite a while—are they still on?

GIL GREENE: I don't know anything about the Beatles, except John Lennon died. "I Want to Hold Your Hand" is one of their numbers. I didn't think too much of them when they came out—I didn't think they'd ever amount to anything. I was surprised at their overwhelming acceptance.

FRANCIS MCELROY: Oh, them. They're a nice animal.

JEANNE MALONE: I saw their show at SPAC, that was a couple of years ago.
D.B.G.: The Beatles?!
JEANNE: Oh, no, that wasn't them, it was the other ones, they do the song "Barbara Ann"—what's their name?
D.B.G.: The Beach Boys.
JEANNE: Oh, yes, the Beach Boys.
DAPHNE MATTHEWS: Oh, they're good!
JEANNE: I don't know anything about the Beatles really except that as far as I was concerned they brought in a new era of music. There was some nice music from the Beatles—you remember?
GEORGE VROOMAN: Yeah, I remember I never liked 'em.
JEANNE: Well, maybe that's because you're older.

CHARLES SHEA: They're good. My nephew's got records of 'em.

PASQUALE TROIANO *(sings):* I wanna hold your hand! I wanna hold your hand! I like the Beatles, Rolling Stones. *(Sings:)* Roll out the barrel, we'll have a barrel of fun!

JOE CIARCIAGLINO: I don't know who they are—that's before my time. You mean the real beetles, like the Japanese beetles? *(No.)* Oh, you mean the singers from England. I don't know about them. Are they still in business? *(No.)* They say when a person is born he is given the gift of life and he should live to the fullest because someday it'll be taken back. That's when you're dead.

Jack Mudurian: I don't care for them. They're alright, but I don't care for their kind of entertainment.

Andy Legrice: They're good singers. They're good Americans.

Walter McGeorge: I can tell you what I like about 'em and what I don't. They seemed to stay original—I like that. There's so much I don't like about 'em though—like harmony, I don't like that harmony. I don't give a damn about their looks—that thing don't bother me—I'm just talking about their sound. I like the fact that they're original, but I don't like the songwriting.

Edna Hemion: Oh, I can't remember that far back! I used to go to musicals in New York. There's no place like New York—my father said that and his daughter says it now.

John Lowthers: I can't tell you about the Beatles—I don't know a thing about them. I never worked for them and they never worked for me.

Bill Hughes: Don't know about 'em, actually. That's not a good question to ask me. Except that they were young men from Liverpool, England, and unemployed at the time. They were poor young boys—fifteen, sixteen—kicking bricks in Liverpool, England, and they either found, stole, or were given some cheap instruments.

I think I explained to you once why that should be pronounced L*i*verpool. *(Why is it pronounced* L*i*verpool*?)* Oh, I didn't explain it to you. Well, it's named after a lake which is a fairly large lake to the northeast of the city and it's inhabited by birds which are called l*i*vers—not livers, which is an organ of the body. They're l*i*verbirds—you underline the *i* to emphasize it, pronounced like *lie.* It's kind of a fish-eating water bird, something like a cormorant.

VILJO LEHTO: I heard 'em singin' back in the forties and thirties. They were singin' about band music. Times Square, Radio City—I used to live in New York City. Radio City—thirty-five dollars a night. Everybody can't get in there. I even stopped goin' in one time 'cause I didn't have no luggage.

WALLY BAKER: They started in England and toured the United States and one got bumped off. Anything else you want to know? *(Tell me about their music.) (Puts his hand up:)* That's as far as I go.

FRANK WISNEWSKI: Yeah, yeah, yeah, yeah, yeah, yeah! I was one of their fans. Ringo! They're all dead, I think. What, was there five of them? They're all gone.

BILL LAGASSE: They were pretty good—the greatest team goin'—a quartet. I guess they made their money and went home. They had long hair and looked pretty good—the girls liked 'em. They had a guitar and another electric guitar, and of course you couldn't tell the names of the songs—I was sleepin' most of the time when he said 'em.
One of the Beatles got shot. And he died. He was syndicated—turned to ashes. That was the end of him. A gunman shot him. Thirty-fourth Street. Gunman shot him because he spit on his shoe and he said it wasn't him, it was his brother and he made a mistake. That's all I know. The rest of them are still around, playin' on the stage. They went to the funeral I guess, when he died. He was syndicated.

GEORGE STINGEL: I never seen them. They're the English ones, ain't they? I heard one song of them, but I don't know what one it was, someone said it was the Beatles. I never saw them on television. I just woke up a few minutes ago.

HERBIE CALDWELL: I don't know much about the Beatles. They chirp and play around. I'm supposed to have coffee but I don't know where it is.

Ken Eglin's Reviews of Records

"Two of Us"—Nice endin', very nice endin'. That's new, nice endin' to it. Now who's that? Some young kid. *(The Beatles.)* That was the Beatles? It didn't sound like them, not to me it didn't. It was very good.

"Don't Let Me Down"—Man, that's lovely—I was gonna say that, you know that. Beautiful. That's the Beatles—there's nobody else like 'em—where you gonna find 'em? It's beautiful. "Don't Let Me Down," it's a lovely song.

"I'm Only Sleeping"—It's fabulous, oh, man, it's great! Hey, now who is this? *(The Beatles.)* Was that Paul McCartey (*sic*) singin' that?" *(John Lennon sang it.)* John Lennon, he did all the writin', he was a good man. It's too bad they had to do that. Why do they do things like that? *(Cries.)* Oh, man, why, when you start likin' musicians, they go. He was just startin'.

Beatles 4ever

Chris Bruton

Todd Blowe lived in what was an anomaly for Moultree Shoals, a subdivision. The neighborhood of thickly shrouded split-level homes stood at the edge of a cotton field. It was an odd mixture, the suburban flavor given off by the smooth cement driveways and basketball goals, the hedges, and the shrubbery, and the sunbaked rows of crops lying just beyond the clotheslines.

We got to Todd's at dusk. The locusts were cranking up and lights were starting to flicker on in the neighborhood. Walking to the rear of the house past flowerbeds neatly trimmed with little bunch grasses, we caught a glimpse of Todd's mother bustling with the dishes at the kitchen window upstairs. Todd lived in the basement.

From inside we heard the sound of the television. Jamie rapped on the sliding glass door and Todd pulled the curtain back and let us in. "Just in time," he said distractedly. "I was just getting ready to start it."

"You gonna tell me what it is now?" Jamie said, going straight to the nicked dresser where the liquor sat. "You made such a mystery out of it on the phone."

"It's this Beatles video I ordered for the store, a documentary."

"More of that old shit."

"It's supposed to show some old footage from the Hamburg days, take them all the way up to *Abbey Road*. This is rare, man."

"Okay, Mr. Nostalgia."

The dank basement with its cinderblock walls smelled of pot and mildew. Courtney Fuchs lay on the bed, Lee Bachelor sat at its foot. I didn't know any of them very well. These were people Jamie had taken up with after I left Moultree Shoals to go to college. We were all about the same age, in our mid-thirties.

I sat in a busted wicker chair next to Courtney and said hello.

He must not have heard me. He was looking up at the ceiling, grinning. His long, effeminate body, his pale face with the mournful mustache, seemed as relaxed and weightless as a man made of straw. Courtney had a long history of mental illnesses, for which he received ample medication. He was said to have been permanently fucked up by a psychologist who had fallen in love with him when he was a teen. He lived with his parents.

Suddenly Courtney cackled. "*Rare!* Did you hear that? Only a Beatles *nut* would say a thing like that. Goddamn, Todd, you can go to fucking *Wal-Mart* and buy *Let It Be*."

Todd shook his head as he fiddled with the VCR. He was a stubby, combative little guy with springy hair and a chalky, sculpted face that was beginning to look haggard. "I don't believe this," he said. "Didn't you hear what I said? The Hamburg days, man! Some kraut with a Super-8 filmed them at the Star Club. This shit's never been seen!"

"You're a *fanatic*, Todd. Admit it. Just like with all these books of yours on the Kennedy assassination, all these videos—"

"Kennedy was killed by a conspiracy."

"No shit."

"Don't get the bastard started on that," Jamie said, handing me a drink and flopping down on a lizard green beanbag.

Lee Batchelor sucked at a joint with a quick, sidehand motion. He was a handsome, slow-spoken man with the kind of barrel chest and reddish, stiff hair and mustache that put you in mind of a genteel Southern planter. Lee had never, according to Jamie, held a job. His father had gotten rich by selling a key piece of land J. P. Stevens needed to build a co-generation plant on. The trust fund must have been adequate for Lee's needs. They were simple enough. He spent his days hunting and fishing and lived alone in a tenant house on the family farm, with his baying assortment of dogs.

Suddenly Todd shushed us.

"It's starting," he said.

The famous image of Lucy from *Yellow Submarine* flared across the screen, soundlessly. Then, in *Rubber Soul*–era script, appeared the title BEATLES 4EVER, followed by the opening beats to "Sgt. Pepper's Lonely Hearts Club Band." At first I felt a keen embarrassment. It was like seeing a picture of yourself as some bemused adolescent in bell-bottoms broadcast before a roomful of strangers. But then as the song played on, another emotion began sweeping over me, disquieting and contradictory, more like what an old veteran of the Confederacy must have felt when hearing "Dixie": *It was twenty years ago today . . .*

"I thought that was really well done," Todd said as the credits ran. "Really. What'd you guys think?"

"Light another joint, Beatlemaniac," Courtney, who had raised himself slightly, demanded.

A drab waterfront of cranes and rusted freighters in grainy black and white appeared on the screen, followed by the legend HAMBURG, 1960. There was no voice-over. It gave the film a strange patchwork quality, which could have been an intentional effect or simply the mark of a clumsy amateur.

STAR CLUB. A sea of blurry heads facing a distant, squat stage upon which stood several vague figures in black. The camera, as in a pornographic film, zoomed in on the figures, ballooning them until they filled the screen like gigantic shadows. A monkeyish George crouched over his guitar with concentration. A figure that was probably Stu Sutcliffe stood with his back to the camera. The drummer remained in darkness.

"That's Pete Best," Todd stated.

"How do you know that? You can't see him."

"Had to be. Ringo hadn't joined the band yet."

"Know-it-all."

We saw John and Paul, their scrawny white necks and hick faces paired over a microphone. A coarse, scratchy song was aired. Todd identified it as the German version of "I Want to Hold Your Hand," available on bootleg.

The vaunted Hamburg footage lasted only a few minutes. There followed a series of still photos accompanied by the early tunes. The derelict facade of the Kaiserkeller. A hooker on the Reeperbahn. The Beatles as thuggish greasers, in leather jackets. John, bangs plastered over a clammy face, swilling beer from a liter mug. George with his arm around a plump barmaid, smirking and displaying his bad teeth, his hand cupped over her breast as if he were about to nick it. The photo montage ended with Paul, a bottle of beer in one hand, his dick in the other, poised like a gunslinger as he pissed into the gutter.

"Look at that asshole."

"He was an asshole even then."

"They should've got rid of *him*, instead of Pete Best."

"Wait a minute," Lee interrupted. "Didn't none of y'all like Wings?"

There was a silence.

"He did a few good things with Wings," Todd conceded. "I always liked 'Another Day.'"

"And let's not forget the classic 'Live and Let Die,'" Jamie added.

Courtney giggled. "I used to know this dude, a studio wiz, who figured out some way to isolate Linda's singing on all their records. It was cruel, man, cruel."

The film had leapfrogged to 1964. The Beatles wore suits; they had been sanitized, made fit for consumption. We saw them at a news conference fencing with reporters, befuddling them with Liverpoolisms and jaded one-liners. Then we were helicoptering over Manhattan, a vast grid of steel gray hulks and rooftop air-conditioning systems. What were they thinking? None of them was yet twenty-five. How is the ego disturbed, what grain of sand implanted in its membrane to know at that age that a city like New York waits at your feet?

And then there was the Ed Sullivan segment—the icy glare, the blue-gray thickness in the television image that the mind would forever link with the Texas School Book Depository, Parkland Memorial, Oswald.

A memory possessed me. It had visited me many times before, I don't know why. I was a small boy, walking with my sister at the edge of a suburban street on a hot summer day. The suburb seemed limitless, the dips in the road made valleys, the rises staggering hills. I remembered we had to stay off the black asphalt because it was sticky from the heat and would cling to our bare feet, and there on the white curb I stumbled upon a pocket diary. My first thought was, *Somebody's lost this, I better not keep it.* It was bound in navy blue, "1963" emblazoned in gold on the cover. It was a valuable find to me. I remembered looking at the numbers as we toiled up the street under the obliterating sun and thinking, *1963, that year is over.* Up until then I had had no notion of time, but now I seemed to see it; it seemed endless, stretching away before me like the Milky Way into the vast, diaphanous reaches of the future. How restless it made me! I could hardly bear to think that I was only seven years old.

Todd was holding the joint end out to me. I waved it away, and grinning modestly he took another toke and passed it on to Courtney. Todd grew his own smoke under fluorescent lights in the attic.

Beatlemania had turned to Beatle Hate. There were scenes of teens stamping up and down on Beatles albums, tossing them onto bonfires. An earnest, neatly groomed young man proclaimed that he and his fellow church youth had passed a resolution to never again buy another Beatles record, since they had put themselves on the same footing with Our Lord Jesus Christ. John Lennon appeared, head sunk low, elbows on the table at a news conference. He had the look of an adolescent dragged by the scruff of his neck to justice. He was sorry if what he'd said offended anyone, he claimed. All he'd said was they were more popular than Christ. He didn't mean they were better, or more important, or anything. He wasn't comparing the Beatles to Jesus at all. But his voice said something different from that. In his voice there was the fury of a caged animal. It was a glimpse of the heretic in embryo.

Interspersed among snippets of songs from *Rubber Soul* and *Revolver* we saw images of marches, sit-ins, soldiers fanning out across rice fields, a crowd slammed to the ground by a sniper's bullets. A clip of Walter Cronkite reporting the rising use of pot among the nation's youth. "Good Day Sunshine" and a shot of a schoolbus being pelted with rocks. "Norwegian Wood" and a photo of a beautiful long-haired blonde on a stoop looking dolefully out at the camera. I remembered going around with a tom-tom hanging from my neck I'd fashioned out of a Quaker Oats box, with the slogan "Make Love Not War" printed in pencil across the bottom. I remembered that with every sonic boom I'd hold my breath for a few seconds, waiting to see if the world was going to end. At night we ate watching the six o'clock news, and a little of that grayness—the casualties in Vietnam, the latest occurrence of campus unrest—would seep into our suppers. I remembered on the way to school hearing "Ticket to Ride" and my dad unaccountably letting the song play, and for the space of those minutes I was taken out of that car: I felt awe, I felt beauty, the crushing pathos of life.

"Strawberry Fields Forever." From the very first bars as with a snap of the fingers, one passed into another dimension. The song would forever recapture a specific time and place—it was a world in ferment over closed strictures. The old verities of a generation that watched itself nightly recover the shores of Normandy and raise the flag over Guadalcanal were being shoved aside. We wanted to try something new. Young men publicly opined that maybe it wasn't always right to fight for your country. Vietnam veterans, incongruously bearded and long-haired in their olive fatigues, their wheelchairs, their missing limbs lending them an undismissible authority, clamored at the head of the antiwar marches. And how was it that in Mexico City, on the medals stand, the spectacle of black fists defiantly clenched before the flag, spoke more eloquently of America than any teary-eyed mouthing of the National Anthem? Wedded to that voice with its inimitable mixture of anomie and yearning, Lennon's babble attained a prophetic urgency; it was one of those points at which you can mark a clean break with the past. Who could listen to the phrase *That is, you can't, you know, tune in* and not believe that all the pettiness and meanness, the ignoble hates and philistine loves of people's lives would soon cease to be?

There was a video to the song, the Beatles as wispy, ethereal beings popping in and out from behind trees in a misty landscape. Afterward, a scene from *American Bandstand,* Dick Clark sticking a phallic microphone at a blonde in a beehive: "What did you think of the song?" She didn't like it, it was so weird, and their look—yuck!—all that facial hair. Clark then turned to the boy beside her: "What did you think?" The boy grinned and swayed, his bangs dipping into his eyes. "Far-out," he answered. "Far-out!"

The period of psychedelia and eastern mysticism arrived. Clips were shown from *Yellow Submarine* and *Magical Mystery Tour*. The movies had not aged well.

"Look at that," Courtney said, indicating a scene in which multiple images of George, seated gurulike as he sang "Within You Without You," whirled about the screen. "That's pathetic, man."

"Hey, man," Todd objected.

"Oh, come on, Todd," Jamie said. "George looks stupid as hell there."

"Self-indulgent bullshit," Courtney added.

"You have to look at when it was made," Todd countered.

"No you don't," Jamie said. "Just look at it: the fat lady wolfing down a mountain of spaghetti, the Beatles in white tuxes dancing a two-step, and all these cosmic 'special effects'—where's the great meaning? It's just stupid, man. It was stupid then, it's stupid now."

Todd was silent. On a stage in a meadow the Beatles, costumed as mythical shaggy beasts, pretended to play "I Am the Walrus."

"I mean even you, Todd," Jamie went on, "would admit that they weren't perfect."

"They were the greatest band of all time. No one's ever equaled them."

"I agree with you. They did some great stuff. But that doesn't mean they didn't do some crap, too."

"I don't know of any."

"You don't know of any? What about 'Octopus's Garden'?"

"It's not so bad, for Ringo."

"What about 'Ob-La-Di, Ob-La-Da'?"

"That's a reggae song! When they recorded that, nobody even knew what reggae was!"

"Come off it, Todd. It sucks. John didn't even want to play on it."

"Look, man, I'm not even gonna talk to you, Jamie," Todd said, standing and shoving a cigarette in his mouth. "You're on some kind of weird persecution trip and I'm not gonna play that. I know what it is, though. You're bitter. The dream is over. A lot of people have been misled by those words."

"How've we been misled? The fucker's dead. What does that tell you about the dream?"

"I'm not believing this," Todd said, striding back and forth with his head bent down, his fists involuntarily clenched. I remembered that he was supposed to have been something of a bad-ass in school before his parents pulled him out and enrolled him in a military academy. "You think the sixties died with Jimi Hendrix? With Janis Joplin? That's what John was saying, that it didn't have anything to do with personalities. The Beatles are gone. The dream is over. Now you've got to carry on. Just listen to the song."

"I remember the song, Todd. He said: *I just believe in me, Yoko and me.*"

Courtney guffawed.

"Go ahead and laugh. It just shows how empty your life is. I think it took strength to say that."

"I'm not laughing, Todd. That was Courtney. But how can you stand there and defend that line? It's phony, man."

"Not to me. To me it's the same old message. You know, *If you go carrying pictures of Chairman Mao, you ain't gonna make it with anyone anyhow*. Don't follow leaders. Don't follow anyone. Straighten yourself out, not the world. Listen to the song."

"And you've straightened yourself out."

"I'm doing all right."

"Todd Blowe, Beatles disciple, living his life according to the gospel of the sixties."

"Why don't you just shut the fuck up."

"I bet they really love you at the Dixie Mart. What do you do, try to raise your customers' consciousness while you're making change?"

There were no recriminations, no shufflings of discomfort, not even a sigh. None of them would ever have registered emotion in any such obvious way. Only the silence intimated that something uncalled-for might have been said.

"I can see right through you, Jamie," Todd said, sitting back down in front of the TV. "You look at the world around you and think the sixties were a sham, the Beatles were a bunch of fakes. Well, that's your hang-up, not mine. And as for working in a convenience store, yeah, I know that's no great achievement, but I also know it doesn't define me, it doesn't limit me."

"Forget it, " Jamie said. "My job's nothing to boast about either."

"Fuck you. I don't need you to put yourself on my level."

"I'm already on your level, Todd. I think you know that."

They exchanged a look, a look almost of intimacy; whatever it was, I knew I had nothing to do with it.

"Hey. Y'all look," Lee said.

LONDON, 1969. The Beatles were giving their last performance, from the rooftop of Apple. Businessmen stopped and stared disconcertedly on the sidewalks below. Slender young women in miniskirts craned their heads upward. The wind was blowing and the Beatles' long manes were thrown back as they played, giving them the heroic aspect of young martyrs. I noted that as John sang "Don't Let Me Down," a boy knelt at his feet, eagerly holding up the words of the song.

Splice

E. J. Miller Laino

Cocaine, methedrine, heroin,
percodan. Fat Elvis,
dead. Sam Cooke mysteriously dead. Joplin
drunk and dead. Lennon.
Hendrix. Morrison, Cobain. Whatever
the price, they were willing to pay. Yeah,
yeah but I say rock and roll
is a church meeting, a gathering
around tribal drums. Boys
and girls sing to mothers and fathers.
Gods sleep like kittens
in the hollows of guitars.
The Beatles reunite
and here's the proof: In *Real Love,* McCartney
wraps his voice around the voice of his dead
partner. Don't we all wish for one more chance
to get it right, lights shining on a photograph
of four new leather jackets or the snapshot
where we circle around a Formica kitchen table,
Scrabble game in progress.
Behind our seven letters we wonder
how to connect one word to another.

When the Last Beatle Dies

Francine Witte

It'll be Maine, and the snow melted down
to a paragraph. My son, Jim, blows in
stamping the cold through his shoes.

The newspaper, George Harrison, dead at 84.
Well, no one lives forever, Jim says,
flattens his face into the stew. I pinch
my baby grandson, whisper, Bill, you don't know

this, but my generation has just been stubbed out:
a thousand spins of *She Loves You,* a yeah, yeah,
yeah that salved me past my first Kennedy.

Bill starts to fuss and I croon him down
like my father on a Perry Como night. He's crying,
he wants answers, how can you live this long

and never learn a thing? I say, Jim, you got yourself
a fighter here. He smiles, eats his stew.

But as for now, I have no kids and only a postcard
from Maine. More likely I'll be ducking clouds
that roll off a pot of "Soup for One." My sister phones,

quick, get the paper, page 24, Real Life Section,
past the things to float in a Jello mold, past the ads,
Jack's Valu Days, year-end blitz of ballpeen hammers,
socket wrenches, all the tools you'd ever need
to build a better world.

Biographies of the Contributors

Pam Bernard, a Boston poet and painter, has been awarded an NEA Fellowship in Creative Writing, Nimrod's Pablo Neruda Prize, and the Grolier Prize. Her first book, *My Own Hundred Doors* (1996), won the Bright Hills Press Poetry Competition. She has an MFA from Warren Wilson College.

Leonard Bernstein was perhaps the most renowned American composer and conductor of his generation. His openness to all forms and styles of music, his composition of such popular works as *West Side Story,* and his televised concerts for young audiences in the 1960s earned him a place in the American consciousness that few composers have enjoyed.

Janna Bialek grew up in Cincinnati and currently resides in Washington, D.C., with her husband, her dog, and two children who listen to music she doesn't understand.

Rosalind Brackenbury was born in London and moved to the United States in 1992, where she now resides in Florida. She has published three poetry collections—two with Stride Press in England and one with Fithian Press in Santa Barbara, California—and eight novels, all in the United Kingdom. Her latest novel appears this year.

Chris Bruton, a resident of North Carolina and graduate of Duke University, writes fiction that has appeared in such publications as *Viet Nam Generation.* He works in the area of environmentally sensitive pest control.

Lisa Clark is a book artist and graphic designer from Cambridge, Massachusetts. "She Loves You" was her first 45, John was her first love, and this is her first published piece.

Robert Cording is the author of three collections of poetry: *Life-List, What Binds Us to This World,* and, most recently, *Heavy Grace* (Alice James Books, 1996). His work has appeared in such journals as *Poetry, The Nation, Orion,* and *The New Yorker.* Cording lives with his family in Woodstock, Connecticut and teaches at Holy Cross College in Massachusetts.

Cortney Davis, a Connecticut nurse practitioner in women's health, is author of two poetry collections, *Details of Flesh* (Calyx Press, 1997) and *The Body Flute,* and coeditor of *Between the Heartbeats: Poetry and Prose by Nurses*. She has received an NEA Fellowship and the Anna Rosenberg Award.

Ed Davis is a writing teacher at Sinclair Community College in Dayton, Ohio. His fiction has appeared in such publications as *Vignette, Riverwind,* and *The New River Free Press*. Sometimes Davis's Hofner bass guitar comes out of the closet for artistic inspiration.

Carol Ann Duffy attended university at Liverpool before moving to London. She is author of five books of poetry and has edited an anthology for teens, *I Wouldn't Thank You for a Valentine*. Her awards include the Somerset Maugham and Whitbread Awards.

Richard Foerster is the author of *Sudden Harbor* and *Patterns of Descent* (both from Orchises Press), and Trillium (forthcoming from BOA Editions). He is a recipient of the "Discovery"/*The Nation* prize, *Poetry*'s Bess Hokin Prize, and an NEA grant. He lives in York Beach, Maine, and is editor of *Chelsea*.

Nancy Fox, author of a children's book, *Clarence When You Are Sleeping,* and *The Writer's Notebook,* currently runs an on-line writing school called Folios: The Electronic Writing Shop, and is writing another book. She lives in Virginia.

Laura Gamache runs the Writers-in-the-Schools Program for the University of Washington and teaches creative writing in the Seattle area. Her work has been heard on NPR's KUOW radio and has appeared in journals, including *The North Atlantic Review* and *Bellowing Ark*.

Eric Gamalinda was born in Manila, where he published three novels, a collection of stories, and a collection of poems. He won several national awards in the Philippines, including the National Book Award, as well as publishing extensively in the United States and England. He now resides in New York.

Allen Ginsberg was born in 1926 in New Jersey. After the publication of *Howl* in 1957, he became a pivotal figure in American poetry as well as in the Beat generation counterculture of the 1950s and 1960s. Other major works include *Kaddish, Reality Sandwiches,* and *Planet News.*

David B. Greenberger has been recording the funny and philosophical remarks of residents of the Duplex Nursing Home in Jamaica Plain, Massachusetts, as well as a variety of nursing homes in New York, for nearly twenty years. Greenberger, a conceptual artist, is a graduate of the Mass College of Art.

Euron Griffith was born in Bangor, North Wales. He earned an M.A. in creative writing at the University of Glamorgan, has published work in many British magazines, and was awarded the 1997 New Writers Bursary by the Arts Council of Wales. He lives in Cardiff and is a freelance broadcaster.

Donald Hall, one of America's most venerated poets, lives on his family's ancestral New Hampshire farm and has served as that state's poet laureate. He is a member of the American Academy of Arts and Letters. His many books include *The Museum of Clear Ideas, Old and New Poems,* and *The Old Life.*

Mark Halliday has published two volumes of poetry. *Little Star* won the National Poetry Series, and *Tasker Street* was the winner of the 1991 Juniper Prize. He teaches at Ohio University.

Robert Hemenway lives in Arizona. Two volumes of his fiction have been published, *The Girl Who Sang with the Beatles and Other Stories* (Knopf, 1970) and *At the Border* (Atheneum, 1984).

Norman Paul Hyett is a psychologist and writer who lives in Brookline, Massachusetts. Much of his work is about his experience growing up in pre-casino Atlantic City, New Jersey, with its remarkable backdrop of amusement piers, elephant-shaped hotels, and high-diving horses.

Shelli Jankowski-Smith's poems, essays, and reviews have appeared in such publications as *Agni, The Boston Globe, CrossCurrents, The Literary Review,* and *Harvard Review.* She earned an M.A. in creative writing at Boston University and works as director of B.U.'s Office of the University Chaplain. She lives with her family in the seaside Massachusetts town of Swampscott.

Ellen Kahaner teaches reading at an elementary and middle school in

Long Island, New York, and has also taught in public schools in East Harlem and Queens. She has published five children's books and numerous articles and is researching the transition of immigrant families into U.S. public schools.

Lisa Williams Kline writes stories for children and adults. Her work has appeared in *Plum Review, Spider, Echoes,* and the anthology *An Intricate Weave: Women Write About Girls and Girlhood*. She and her husband live in North Carolina with two young daughters.

Philip Larkin is the author of seven books of poems, including his *Collected Poems,* and is editor of the *Oxford Book of Twentieth Century Verse*. Larkin was perhaps England's most celebrated poet for the last forty years.

Timothy Leary, once a lecturer at Harvard, went on to found the League for Spiritual Discovery and became a pivotal figure in the drug and expanded-consciousness movements of the 1960s, championing the use of LSD. He was the author of many books, including *The Politics of Ecstasy*.

Timothy McCall, a Boston-area physician, has published work both in *The Exquisite Corpse* and *The New England Journal of Medicine*. He is author of *Examining Your Doctor: A Patient's Guide to Avoiding Harmful Medical Care* (Citadel), and is a regular commentator on public radio's *Marketplace*.

Greil Marcus is a well-known rock and roll essayist and critic whose work appears in such publications as *The Rolling Stone Illustrated History of Rock and Roll* and *Mystery Train*.

E. J. Miller Laino's first book, *Girl Hurt* (Alice James Books, 1995), won a 1996 American Book Award. Her poetry has appeared in such journals as *American Poetry Review, Prairie Schooner, The Southern Review* and *The Boston Phoenix*. She resides with her family in Key West Florida, where she teaches writing at Florida Keys Community College.

Larry Neal, poet, essayist, and critic, had works appear throughout the 1960s in such publications as *Negro Digest, The Journal of Black Poetry,* and *The Tulane Drama Review*. He coedited, with LeRoi Jones (Amiri Baraka), a pivotal anthology of poetry entitled *Black Fire*.

Philip Norman is the author of *Shout! The Beatles in Their Generation, Slip on a Fat Lady, Plumridge, Wild Thing,* and *The Skaters' Waltz.*

Joyce E. Peseroff's two books of poems are *The Hardness Scale* (Alice James Books) and *A Dog in the Lifeboat* (Carnegie Mellon). She is an editor of the literary journal *Ploughshares.* Her favorite Beatle was John.

Stefany Reich-Silber grew up in London, where she studied art and languages. She came to the United States in 1971, settled in Berkeley, California, and began to pursue dance and writing. She lives with her teenage son and her cat.

Hillary Rollins is a New York writer for TV, film, theater, and print. Her scripts have been produced on USA Network, ABC Daytime, Nick at Night, Nickelodeon, and the Disney Channel, and she has won a Gold Medal International Film & TV Award. She has also been published in *Cosmopolitan.*

Larry Schug's collection of poems, *Obsessed with Mud,* won the 1997 Poetry Harbor chapbook competition. He currently works to make our planet a better place, as a recycling coordinator at the College of St. Benedict in St. Joseph, Minnesota.

Kay Sloan is author of a novel, *Worry Beads* (1991), and two books on U.S. cultural history. She is also coeditor of *Elvis Rising,* a collection of short stories. Her fiction and poetry have appeared in numerous publications. She teaches creative writing at Miami University of Ohio.

Dave Smith is author of over a dozen books of poetry, including two *Selected Poems* (1985, 1992) and, most recently, *Civil Rites* (Black Scholar Press, 1997). He is a professor of English at Louisiana State University and coeditor of *The Southern Review.*

James Russell Smith is a composer whose work has been performed by such groups as London's BBC Symphony Orchestra; a freelance percussionist who has played with rock bands, the U.S. Marine Band, and major New England orchestras; and a conductor. He teaches at Boston's Berklee College of Music.

Gary Soto is the author of a number of books, including *New and Selected Poems.* His work has regularly appeared in numerous literary magazines, including *The Colorado Review, The Michigan Quarterly, The Nation, Ploughshares, Poetry, Prairie Schooner,* and *The Threepenny Review.*

Susan Stemont is a writer and visual artist with a special interest in book-as-object and collage. She is completing a poetic journal/book/object-in-progress entitled *In Strawberry Fields.* Stemont lives in Bloomsburg, Pennsylvania.

Henry W. Sullivan wrote *The Beatles with Lacan: Rock 'n' Roll as Requiem for the Modern Age* as a psychoanalytic and sociological study related to the theories of Jacques Lacan.

Robert Sullivan wrote the essay "I Wanna Be Your Man" for the Shouts and Murmurs column of the January 29, 1996, *New Yorker.*

Stuart Sutcliffe was a talented painter from Liverpool who met John Lennon in art college and became a member of the original Beatles. His aesthetic influence on the early Beatles, until his death in 1962, was immeasurable.

Tobi Taylor lives in Arizona and is doing graduate work in anthropology at Arizona State University. Her writing has appeared in *Archeology, Rockford Review,* and *Oregon Review,* and she was awarded an Arizona Governor's Award. She is the editor of *Kiva,* an international anthropology journal.

Susan Terris lives in San Francisco. Her newest book, *Curved Space,* is forthcoming from La Jolla Poets Press. She is author of *Killing in the Comfort Zone, Author! Author!* and *Nell's Quilt,* and her work has appeared in numerous journals, including *Antioch Review* and *Beloit Poetry Journal.*

Jacques Wakefield, poet, playwright, and actor, lives in New York with his family, Lisa and Jessica. His literary career was founded by publication in the classic anthology *Black Fire* (eds. Immamu Baraka and Larry Neal, 1968). His recent work appears in *Urbanus Magazine, 12 Gauge Review,* and *Urban Desires.*

Robert Wallace's work has been published in *The Spectator* and *The Independent,* and he has received a Durham Arts Council Emerging Artist grant. He lives in Durham, North Carolina.

Terry Watada, playwright, poet, fiction and nonfiction writer, and musician, lives in Toronto, Canada. His books include *A Thousand Homes, Daruma Days,* and *Bukkyo Tozen: A History of the Buddhist Church in Canada.* His play *Vincent* recently toured Ontario and Manitoba, Canada.

Priscilla Webster-Williams grew up on rock 'n' roll in Chicago and later migrated to New England, where she thrived on the Byrds and Aretha Franklin. Her work appears in many publications, including the anthology *Ad Hoc Monadnock* and the magazines *Yankee* and *Soundings East.*

Francine Witte teaches creative writing in New York City. She has published a chap book, *The Magic in the Streets* (Owl Creek Press, 1994). A number of her one-act plays have also been produced on New York's Theater Row.

David Wojahn is the author of five collections of poetry, most recently *Mystery Train, Late Empire,* and *The Falling Hour,* all published by the University of Pittsburgh Press. He lives in Chicago and teaches at Indiana University, and in the MFA writing program of Vermont College.

Tom Wolfe grew up in Richmond, Virginia, and received a doctorate in American studies from Yale. His books include *The Right Stuff, The Bonfire of the Vanities, The Electric Kool-Aid Acid Test,* and *The Kandy-Kolored Tangerine-Flake Streamline Baby.*

Joseph Wollenweber lives in Los Gatos, California.

Ellen Zabaly, a writer of fiction and nonfiction, is also an Academy Award–winning filmmaker and is currently at work on a novel. She inhabits a parallel universe by maintaining residences both in the upper Midwest and in southern California.

Acknowledgments

"Fab Four Tour Deutschland—Hamburg, 1961" from *Mystery Train* by David Wojahn. Copyright © 1990. Reprinted by permission of the University of Pittsburgh Press.

Excerpt from a letter to Ken Horton by Stuart Sutcliffe from *Backbeat* by Pauline Sutcliffe and Alan Clayson. Reprinted by permission of Macmillan Publishers Limited.

Introduction from *The Beatles with Lacan: Rock 'n' Roll as Requiem for the Modern Age*. Copyright © 1995 by Henry W. Sullivan. Reprinted by permission of Peter Lang Publishing, Inc.

"Hello, Goodbye" first appeared in the *San Francisco Chronicle*. Copyright © 1996 by Stefany Reich-Silber. Reprinted by permission of the author.

Excerpts from "Another Version of the Chair," by Greil Marcus. From *The Rolling Stone Illustrated History of Rock & Roll* by Anthony DeCurtis and James Henke, with Holly George-Warren. Copyright © 1976, 1980 by Rolling Stone Press. Copyright © 1992 by Straight Arrow Publishers, Inc. Reprinted by permission of Random House, Inc.

"Portland Coliseum" from *Collected Poems 1947–1980* by Allen Ginsberg. Copyright © 1984 by Allen Ginsberg. Reprinted by permission of HarperCollins Publishers, Inc.

"Annus Mirabilis" from *Collected Poems* by Philip Larkin. Copyright © 1988, 1989 by the Estate of Philip Larkin. Reprinted by permission of Farrar, Straus & Giroux, Inc.

"Sod Manila!" by Eric Gamalinda is excerpted from the novel *Empire of Memory* (Manila: Anvil Publishing, Inc., 1992). Copyright © 1992 by Eric Gamalinda. Reprinted by permission of the author.

"Playland" by Richard Foerster first appeared in *Poetry* and subsequently in *Sudden Harbor* (Orchises Press, 1992). Copyright © 1992 by Richard Foerster. Reprinted by permission of the author.

“Thank God for the Beatles” by Timothy Leary. Copyright © 1968 by the League for Spiritual Discovery, Inc. Reprinted by permission of Futigue Trust.

“First Party at Ken Kesey’s with Hell’s Angels” from *Collected Poems 1947–1980* by Allen Ginsberg. Copyright © 1965 by Allen Ginsberg. Reprinted by permission of HarperCollins Publishers, Inc.

“Cloud” from *The Electric Kool-Aid Acid Test* by Tom Wolfe. Copyright © 1968 and copyright renewed © 1996 by Tom Wolfe. Reprinted by permission of Farrar, Straus & Giroux, Inc.

“The Moment of Truth” by Terry Watada first appeared in a longer version in the short-story collection *Daruma Days* (Ronsdale Press, Vancouver, British Columbia, 1997). Copyright © 1997 by Terry Watada. Reprinted by permission of the author.

“Roots” by Mark Halliday from *Tasker Street*, copyright © 1992, University of Massachusetts Press. Reprinted by permission of the author.

“A Different Bag” by Larry Neal first appeared in *The Beatles Book*, ed. Edward Davis (Cowles Educational Corporation, New York, 1968). Reprinted by permission of Mrs. Evelyn Neal.

“Dizzy Girls in the Sixties” from *New & Selected Poems* by Gary Soto, copyright © 1995, published by Chronicle Books, San Francisco. Reprinted by permission of Chronicle Books.

“The Endless Days of Sixties Sunshine” from *Fate’s Kite: Poems 1991–1995* by Dave Smith. Copyright © 1991, 1994, 1995 by Dave Smith. Reprinted by permission of Louisiana State University Press.

“The Girl Who Sang with the Beatles” by Robert Hemenway first appeared in *The New Yorker*. Copyright © 1969 by Robert Hemenway. Reprinted by permission of Harold Ober Associates, Incorporated.

“The Assassination of John Lennon as Depicted by the Madame Toussaud Wax Museum, Niagara Falls, Ontario, 1987” from *Mystery Train* by David Wojahn, copyright © 1990. Reprinted by permission of the University of Pittsburgh Press.

“Liverpool Echo” is taken from *Standing Female Nude* by Carol Ann Duffy, Published by Anvil Press Poetry in 1985. Reprinted by permission of Anvil Press Poetry.

“Prologue—December 1980” from *Shout! The Beatles in Their Generation* by Philip Norman. Copyright © 1996 by Philip Norman. Reprinted by permission of Sterling Lord Literistic, Inc.

Introduction by Leonard Bernstein, copyright © 1980, Leonard Bernstein. Reprinted by permission of the estate of Leonard Bernstein. Originally appeared in *The Beatles* by Geoffery Stokes, Rolling Stone Press, 1980.

“I Wanna Be Your Man” by Robert Sullivan first appeared in *The New Yorker*. Copyright © by Robert Sullivan. Reprinted by permission of the author.

Excerpt from “The Old Life,” *The Old Life*. Copyright © 1996 by Donald Hall. Reprinted by permission of Houghton Mifflin Company. All rights reserved.

Excerpts from *The Duplex Planet*, ed. David B. Greenberger. Copyright © 1981, 1986, and 1990 by David B. Greenberger. Reprinted by permission of the author.

“When the Last Beatle Dies” by Francine Witte first appeared in *The Greensboro Review* and subsequently in *The Magic in the Streets* (Owl Creek Press, 1994). Copyright © 1994 by Francine Witte. Reprinted by permission of the author.